Progress! Progress! What Progress?

William J Hatten

 A catalogue record for this book is available from the National Library of Australia

Copyright © 2020 William J Hatten

All rights reserved. No part of this book may be reproduced or transmitted in any form or by any means, electronic or mechanical, including photocopying, recording, or by any information storage and retrieval system, without permission in writing from the copyright owner.

Publisher:
ASPG (Australian Self Publishing Group)
P.O. Box 159, Calwell, ACT Australia 2905
Email: publishaspg@gmail.com
http://www.inspiringpublishers.com

National Library of Australia Cataloguing-in-Publication entry

Author: Hatten, William J

Title: **Progress! Progress! What Progress?**/*William J Hatten*

ISBN: 978-1-925908-45-9 (print)
      978-1-925908-46-6 (ebook)

Genre: Self-help spiritual...not religious.

Note from the Author

The inclusion of the author's fictional characters of Alf and his adopted son Stephen, both as narrators and a reference in his books, is not due to multiple personality disorder, as has been suggested by his good wife. They are fictional creations of the author, to make the content of his writing more varied, family orientated and to bring humour, to a complex and difficult subject in order to explain namely, the spiritual workings of Nature and its Laws. The knowledge of which does not exist in our current education system, since it is a yet to be acquired, spiritual understanding and knowledge of the world. The author's books are an attempt to address that spiritual deficiency, starting in the family home.

Miscellaneous.

OTHER BOOKS BY THE AUTHOR:

- Absolute and Relative in Verse and Rhyme.
- Questions and Answers for the Verses Absolute and Relative.
- With Families in Mind.
- The Articles of Alf - A Crossroads of Information.
- Prisons - Internal and External.

Dedication

In sincere appreciation of the lives and knowledge of Guru Dev and Maharishi Mahesh Yogi to create a unified world. Their unique legacy lives on in the lives of many. The author did not know them but owes them so much.

WJH

The Progress Plot

The Enlightenment of Past Trashing
The Enlightenment of War Trashing
The Enlightenment of World Trashing
The Enlightenment of Political Trashing
The Enlightenment of Science Trashing
The Enlightenment of Techno Trashing
The Enlightenment of Space Trashing
The Enlightenment of Commercial Television Trashing
The Enlightenment of Advertising and Promo Trashing
The Enlightenment of Commercial Product Trashing
The Enlightenment of Saturated 24/7 Media Trashing
The Enlightenment of Anything goes Entertainment Trashing
The Enlightenment of Global Corporate Business Trashing.

Conclusion: We are excellent at trashing progress as a species.

Translation of *tongue in cheek* history tablets by Stephen son-of-Alf.
Narration from Alf. CEO of Spiritual Boot Camp.
Licence Number A.D. 1999 – 2000. Issued from Upstairs.

Introduction from a Spiritually Acquired Perspective

Q: *How not to win friends and influence those in high places in the coveted driving seat of progress.*
A: Question the validity and truth of democracy, science, technology, big corporate business and politics not forgetting, the commercial media product, promo and entertainment empire in the A.D. spiritless progress mix.

About Democracy, the New Holy Crusade to the Middle East and other Pagan Lands.

The opening salvo from the ancient past:
It is a Law of Nature, common to all mankind which time shall neither annul nor destroy, that those that have greater strength and power shall rule over those who have less.

The above long ago observation from Dionysius, a pragmatic B.C. Roman/Greek historian. Reflecting on inevitable perpetual wars and the also inevitable rule of the most powerful over the less powerful and cynically inferring, that democracy has and always will be mere rhetoric.

So, what do you think?

8 | Progress! Progress! What Progress?

Is it a divine Law of Nature, that the born gifted, entrepreneurial and powerful, through the circumstance of gifted genes, birth and high IQ automatically inherit the right to rule the world and dictate its direction and progress? According to their human-created education/university/political/cultural/social/business/corporate/science/technological and religious indoctrinated realities. Otherwise known as human-created dissolvable ideologies and realities in Nature's non-dissolvable spiritual dictionary.

What does Alf think?

No, he does not think it is a divine Law of Nature one little bit. Neither does Upstairs, who created the Laws of Nature and everything else for that matter. Therefore, it must be a perpetuated law created by the born gifted, ambition consumed, entrepreneurial, innovative, power and ego driven/conquer the world/dominant alpha human beings, that fill our blood-soaked history books past and present.

It is time for our civilisation, to understand what has always been followed and worshipped on the pages, i.e., ancestral karma inherited pathological/psychological dominant alpha disorder, that is called power, control, conquering, acquisition and winning also called progress. Its primordial origin in humanity, has its roots in the instinctive self-preservation function of the ego, for acquiring a chemically activated brain high called self-esteem. That re-enforces our created individual persona, identity and reality, but has gone way past the use-by-date in the evolution of the human species.

Clarification from a spiritual perspective.

1. When ego-driven ambition becomes all-consuming in physical structured consciousness, then megalomania, delusion and other human disorders are never far away.
2. We are not civilised, we only THINK we are, because all material and ego driven progress, has nothing to do with acquiring

spiritual consciousness and its non-dissolvable spiritual progress, but primordial governed physical consciousness and its human created dissolvable progress.

Q: *What does the fictitious Gleek translation section of the British Museum think?*

A: The following translation by Stephen son of Alf, of a fictional Gleek tablet to Dionysius from Plato. Found recently on the Island of Boggos, located south of the Bay of Figs not far from Zork.

My dear learned Dionysius, how goes the grape and olive harvest this year?

Unfortunately, we have a shortage of pickers on the mainland. It is owing to everyone taking off for hacking and whacking duties overseas, to spread Athenian democracy around again. It was the same back in Socrate's day, no one left to pick them you see, that is why he had to resort to Hemlock. So, if you could clear it with your esteemed faculty, to send me a few of your students for picking duties here, it would be most appreciated this end. Like you, I can't do without my wine tipple when I'm marking illegible student papers and that hemlock, merely further aggravates my student acquired ulcers.

I have also read your recent article in the Athens/Rome Gazette. It is explaining that democracy is a load of codswallop and should be sent to the Island of Knossos for the bull to snort at and trample on.

However, dear good friend Dionysius, it was not the idea of democracy that was at fault, but those waffling Athenian politicians and city merchants on the innovative fiddle. All living the good money-making life and stoned out on café latte that was running it.

If it helps, I have always impressed on my students, to acquire a simple, age-old technique to read between the lines where business, power, politics, and democracy is concerned. Where anything human is concerned. Because as dear pungent Socrates would often shout in the deaf ear of the market place, ever since Adam and Eve was expelled out of the faculty gardens for playing doctors and nurses instead of studiously swatting, mankind has been doing their own primordial ego self-esteem thing and not the Laws of Nature thing. So, I would most respectfully suggest, it is not democracy or the Gods at fault. However, those power, money and economic obsessed human beings in the Parthenon running the whole show.

Incidentally, I believe there is now a new updated American version out, called Corporate Globalisation Commercial Product Democracy. It appears to be very popular with merchants, traders, bankers, lawyers, senators, politicians, and travelling magicians called commercial spin doctors. As a result, just like a money-making religion, it is spreading very fast around the Holy Trading Empire. Keep a watchful eye out for it as it is very contagious. Then please do let me have your learned opinion when it eventually reaches Boggos.

In the meantime, let us pray that the fickle undemocratic Gods, have not got planetary indigestion and that you have a bumper harvest. As a word of caution from much experience, do not let your students get stuck into the grapes before they have picked and trampled on them. Adam and Eve had this problem with the apples and look at what happened to them?

Your good friend Plato on the product
saturated democratised mainland.

Section One

The Enlightenment of Past Trashing.
Featuring King Sargon and the Iron Battering Ram

A historical tongue in cheek tablet deciphering, of the B.C. trashing progress of Sumer and Akkad. The Mesopotamian hotspot of trashing approx, 800 to 600 B.C. in present-day Iraq. It is subtitled: The Big Business Bovver Boys of Ancient Assyria.

Now, you may think the Macedonians under Philip and Alexander in our history books were tough nuts in the trashing and dismemberment department. Alternatively, perhaps, the first Emperor of China and his weasel PM, (*the Mr. Fix-it and Unfix-it of anything and everything in the political power department?*) would be slightly ahead on points, in the premature redistribution of human resources to the heavenly bodies. Because of their great skills in birth control and building walls, they never had to worry about a population explosion occurring in that nation one little bit.

Compared to the Assyrian moguls at the dawn of the Iron Age in Mesopotamia, the others were just average at trade, mere learners. When compared to Sargon the battering ram, Sennacherib who was no cherub. Esarhaddon - the Badden and Assurbanipal - the Pineapple. The latter, having tapered off the birth control method of other nation's, to concentrate on reading their history tablets instead. Nevertheless, would have been no slouch with the tools of trade if you accidentally trod on his foot when bowing and scraping.

Alternatively, perhaps even worse, found interfering with his collection of historical clay tablets in the palace library. No! They were not nice dudes to visit for a pleasant chat over tea and biscuits or after dinner mints at all. If there were a "Guinness" tablet book of trashing around in those days, then from 750 to 650 B.C, there would not have been any room left in its pages for other claimants.

Now when, "Sargon the Second of Assyria," took off on his trashing expo around the Middle East circuit or global expansion, creating democracy and affluent techno-progress as we call it nowadays, the B.C. technical trashing tools of the trade, had stepped up a notch in the human hacking, whacking and dissection business. Progression from softcore copper and bronze weapons, to hardcore iron weapons, became the order of the day. That was a huge leap in the cost savings to the economy of a nation. They lasted twice as long on the job which, unlike now, was very labour intensive indeed.

Interlude

The unemployment then unlike now, was not a disguised politically manipulated all-time low, but really at an all-time low. A great achievement made possible, through the very clever solution of seconding all males to the Army for global conquering trashing business. Along with the manual removal of other nation's borders and the unofficial acquisition of their treasuries. However, as we shall find out in due course, putting all your eggs in one basket is not always the clever thing to do. As some opportunistic politicians and greedy big corporate businesses know well?

Thus, spreading your options around the corporate and shareholder owned globe has become survival procedure in the political kingship and big business corporate stakes and as a further comment, when in damage control from previous boardroom boo-boos, is initially always the best way to go. At least, until a few product phone calls have been organised and its conversation put into motion by outside P.R. contacts and as a double surety? A personal appearance on a commercial radio station for political and product double speak and prompted pats on the back from the host, who also belong to the same mutual admiration winning elite in the top end of town.

Alternatively, perhaps from big business, a lucrative advertising contract and then let the local commercial shock jock, who, being a self-made millionaire out of a make make-it-up-as-you-go-along intellectual articulating product oiled motor mouth and authority on everything and anything in society, obviously knows all the answers to societies problems. Thus, will subtly alter the thought flow of the waters of public perception, in the right direction and at the right price, of course.

The above accomplished through spin doctor acquired expertise and vast experience in whipping up and directing public opinion at the drop of a mesmerising vocal cord. A human skill that of late, has become highly sort after in the top end of town and their very enterprising manipulative P.R. image making subsidiaries (marketing geniuses incorporated) in the next office block. Waving their magic wand (verbal diarrhea and images) and creating silk purses out of sow's ears for public consumption. Which as we know, is impossible unless you are God. However, that information is top secret, available only to big business, piggy banks, commercial radio, television and party-minded opportunistic politicians. So, do not tell anyone else, otherwise, everyone would be doing it in society.

Thus, King Sargon of Assyria, was to add to his growing list of personal firsts. By equipping his army with bigger, better, and harder dissection tools, for anatomical dismemberment and the repositioning of the body parts of his neighbours. A progress step that could be compared to equipping a modern army with tungsten armour … and then pitting it against another equipped in ordinary steel. Thus, in a shoot-out, the outcome would be very one-sided indeed. Now during King Sargon's early apprenticeship years of trashing, a great deal of his spare time was spent in dreaming up bigger and better tools for mass destruction.

Note, in fact, not unlike some of our military hardware scientists and their big business free-lance equivalents. Who, likewise, are unable to help themselves in the positive department of logic and creativity?

Simply because as you sow, then so do you reap in this world or the next world sooner or later. However, spending so much time in a science fixated, ambition-driven emotionless world, in spiritual deficit minds and divorced from Nature synthetic experimental laboratories, have lost the spiritual plot of life. Especially the desensitised cloning and life rearranging Frankenstein version. Who has lost touch with the real world of the living and of life and its spiritual purpose? That of course, has nothing whatsoever to do with blindly experimenting on it, changing it, dissecting it, re-arranging it, creating new versions of it, selling it, placing a global patent on it, destroying it, pickling it and storing it in freezers and warehouses. All in the name of glorious scientific progress, but not spiritual progress.

The Secret of All Time in Respect of Human Trashing

The only way to avoid self-destruction is not to create the physical means for it in the first place. Because once we create *anything* in this physical world, then its created influence (karma) always returns to its point of origin, both individually and collectively. Negative to negative and positive to positive, bigger and better, sooner or later. The karmic influence that is returned to individuals, to families, to tribes, to nations, to this physical world. From within a no-time spiritual continuum, that underlies this physical Universe. A returning process, linked to the karma created out of thoughts, deeds, and actions of human beings.

Explanation, AS WE SOW, SO DO WE REAP with our human-created progress in nature's primordial archetypal intelligence. A physical and spiritual interactive process that is governed by laws above mankind. That simple spiritual fact of *as we sow, so do we reap*, is what all those past deceased civilisations were never told before they went on their all-conquering trashing expeditions for global supremacy, expansion, power, wealth and self-esteem. A pathological megalomania ancestral inherited disorder that is not normal at all, but very abnormal in a human beings. It arises in human beings, through becoming lost from the *order out of chaos* function of the spiritual self-referral Laws of Nature in the mind. Its inherited ancestral nemesis is sourced to all-consuming ambition for power, control and fame, that culminates in megalomania and a mind divorced from the Spiritual Laws of Nature. As a dead-end result, that negative accentuated mind becomes a law unto itself and therefore, a dysfunctional spiritless human being. Sociopathic and psychopathic tendencies become the norm when trapped in its megalomania nemesis. This ancestral dominant alpha negative affliction is most noticeable in those that acquire power through corrupt, manipulative, exploitative, clandestine and violent, brutal means.

The positive suggestion to all nations is to use that spiritual information and stop repeating the megalomania mistakes of past all-conquering self-destructive civilisations. Therefore, stop perpetuating the self-destructive karmic influence and its corresponding entity, created out of conquering, greed, and a lust for power and control of the world's direction in any field of human endeavour. A spiritless ego driven direction, that has become the driving force behind capitalism, and it's out of control global trading. Out of control global greed activity, it is sanctioned under the big corporate business flag of free enterprise and corporate law. Also called, entrepreneurial free trade and democracy functioning on a level playing field. That spiritually translates as manipulation and exploitation of the people born less fortunate by the people born more fortunate. Also called creating glorious economic progress, by governments and big corporate businesses that have obviously come to think alike in the winning but spiritless top end of town.

Returning to King Sargon and his Offspring and their Natural gifts and Talents

Because their natural gifts and talents were not all destructive, King Sargon's dynasty has been credited with creating the first large scale aqueduct, long before the Romans in Europe did. The only problem being that the family did not use their genius for the public welfare, a common kingly trait in B.C times, but to bring the water down from the local mountains to their palaces for personal ablutions. Plus, supplied nourishment to their extensive gardens and private hunting grounds. In which it is claimed, that a regular family custom at afternoon smoko, was to spend time admiring and conducting one-way conversations with the severed heads of recent protagonists. Which, under artistic instruction from their Lordships, had been strung up and left dangling on the fruit trees in the orchard. This for decoration and the teaching of family history and its trashing accomplishments.

Now, you may think that the above is taking education and trashing to the extremes of poor taste, however, for those B.C days, it was average trashing. Because that nation had spent so much time in the human dissection business, that it had become second nature to them. Even their laws were based on body part removal if you transgressed them, e.g, A finger cut off for rude hand gestures. An eye out for looking at the King's wife the wrong way. A hand removed if you had been caught with it in the tax till. A leg off if you did not bow and scrape properly. A nose off for sneezing in the presence of royalty, while serving up the soup. An ear off if you kept saying pardon after receiving the King's instructions, hence, there were a lot of human spare parts floating around the system, that hanging heads in the treetops and talking to them was not bizarre at all, just normal behaviour.

On a philosophical note, you can see that once it becomes fashionable in the top end of society/civilisation to do what you like in it, then it becomes acceptable behaviour for everyone and not abnormal at all. Because once an example of behaviour is set in the ruling classes, i.e., those that are directing a nation with their gifted intelligence and creativity, then for good or for bad, the rest of the population copy its expression and created reality. Along with also reaping the returning karmic influence out of its activity sooner or later. So if narcissism, corruption, deceit, greed, hypocrisy, exploitation, manipulation, doublespeak, self-admiration, self-aggrandisement, celebrity worship, bigotry, racial and religious intolerance, the indiscriminate experimentation on life, the degradation of sexuality and human dignity, are the prevailing expression in powerful elements creating and directing reality for the masses. Then through its saturation from the top end of town, the bottom end of town accepts it as being a normal activity and behaviour. To then become the normal expression and behaviour of that society/nation/civilisation.

To make above matters worse, there exists a pathological sourced quirk of sociopathic behaviour, in power and ambition consumed, negative-accentuated, dominant alpha human beings ... those that lead? Not life-supportive expression and behaviour that emanates from the sub-conscious located child in the ego deluded adult and, it manifests as misplaced reasoning out of negative structured logic. It is simply that any action can be justified to oneself as being legitimate on the path to acquiring success, fame, status, glory, wealth, power and clout to get what you want in society. Therefore, the *got it wrong* human idea, that all is fair in love, war, business dealings, politics, and interaction with other human beings, who become cannon fodder, to be used along the way to its winning worshipped successful attainment? As-long-as-I-win is its habitually intoned ego mantra. Vibrating under a very thin veneer of social, business and political correctness, from out of very clever, ambition consumed, opportunistic, charismatic, powerful intelligent minds. Minds with no spiritual connection to the intuitive self-referral Laws of Nature, that are responsible for *order out of chaos* in life and Creation.

Note, divorced from the Laws of Nature minds, that consciously or unconsciously, seek to control and subjugate everything they interact with. Called success and winning, in our private enterprise, corporate and shareholder owned, big business run consumer civilisation. Whether the adult's activity to achieve its coveted crown is right or wrong, becomes immaterial and of no consequence, from within an ego manufactured delusion of self-importance amalgamated to conceit, or self-confidence as it is called. When also possessing the charm/magnetic power of alpha charisma, articulate speech and a position of influence in society, then it is not difficult to sway others, with a promise of big bucks, the good life and a similar affluent lifestyle if they follow them. Especially in politics and big business. Because it is a natural primordial driven survival instinct, to follow the worshipped winner/leader in any field of human achievement. As the 24/7 media know well, as the exclusive reporter of all the winners in society called news. To then also create yet another no, no, to our human spiritual evolution, called celebrity worshipping neurosis - ugh!

How to solve the above human created contagious delusion:
The silent product acquired out of transcendent meditation accelerates our spiritual evolution. Along with enlivening the, *order out of chaos*, function of the Spiritual Laws of Nature in our consciousness. In that invisible process, to then also dissolve not life-supportive delusional behaviour in a human being. Behaviour that does not complement our spiritual evolution but retards ... it as above.

Returning to the storyline.

About Prince Sargon and the Tablets of Accreditation to the Family Kingship Business.

Plus, the translation by Stephen, of tablet correspondence between Sargon's father the King, who was always away from his kingdom on trashing duties in other nations, another family custom? While Prince Sargon was left behind doing renovations and extensions to the palaces. Along with keeping law and order and dismemberment policies active in the nation. This activity, a necessary duty during his early apprenticeship years, to acquire a firm understanding of the fundamentals and science of human trashing.

Prince Sargon had reached his eighteenth year and, like all exuberant, boisterous young alpha males and females, was itching to claim a piece of the adult action. Instead, there he was stuck at the palace and bored to tears with menial state duties of dismemberment. Along with having to accompany his mother on all the picnics in the palace grounds and the replacement of decorations in the fruit trees. This to maintain the family records, as they did not have photo albums in those days. Along with conducting a special head removal ceremony, that also acted as a deterrent to the palace servants to keep them on their toes, those who had not had theirs chopped off that is. As well as a daily reminder to never forget to bow and scrape before speaking ... those that had tongues left that is, and most importantly, to comb their hair before serving meals ... those who had hair left that is, along with the blowing of noses before entering a royal chamber ... those who had noses left that is. That was how mundane and ordinary young Prince Sargon's palace duties were. No wonder that he was itching to move on to bigger and better trashing. It came to be, that late one morning in a fit of frustration out of boredom and after a right noisy argument with his mother over sleeping in late, that he summoned one of the royal scribes to the tablet room, who still had all his fingers intact that is, to dictate a communication tablet to his father the king. So, under very strict dictation rules, the scribe duly scribbled in the cuneiform script the following message for his uptight very frustrated master.

Tablet Translation by Stephen Son of Alf

Dear father, you do not love me, why else would you not let me join you? I've really had enough of minor trashing here ... and I'm old enough to go trashing big time, like you. It's not fair that you see all the global trashing action and I don't see any. How come I'm stuck in the palace twiddling my fingers and everyone else's, getting under mother's feet and continuously counting shekels in the treasury, to make sure that none are missing?

   Also, I'm really getting cheesed off with continuously polishing the wheels of the ceremonial chariot for my promised inauguration into big-time trashing, only minor trashing of the people and servants when they annoy mother. Also, mother says to hurry up and enter the city gates of Samaria and send some replacement servants and to make sure they arrive here without parts missing off them this time. Not like the last lot you sent. They take too long to do the palace duties with parts missing.

20 | Progress! Progress! What Progress?

Plus, mother also says not to forget to wear the sweater she sent you for chilly morning trashing in your chariot without windows. You will be pleased to know also that I've been using the tools in your shed and made up an extra trashing device for attaching to the wheels of our army's chariots. I've tried it out on the servants ... and it works smashing. That is why you must send replacement servants for mother urgently.

In closing this tablet, please write a note to mother and get me off the hook here. She's really mad at me for staying out late and waking everyone up. 'Cos, I lost the palace keys last week ... and you know what mother is like when she goes on the warpath big trouble? So please send for me soon.

Signed - Your dear son, Sargon.

P.s. I've also dug up the palace grounds for a new orchard and planted some more fruit trees in its west wing, as there is not enough room on the trees for any more decorations in the old orchard.

End of tablet translation.

About Sargon's Law and Order -
the Family Motto and their Marketing Genius

Well, the scribed tablet was duly given to a palace runner in good condition ... the runner that is, in which it must be said, was a very rare occurrence indeed. Owing to dissection mania being a prolific past time of the ruling classes and obviously, requiring many subjects to practice on. However, tablets, unlike human beings, were much more venerated and valuable within the aristocracy than mere subjects. They did not suffer the same fate as dissection. That is why we have so many tablets in the museums but not the humans who wrote them, or those who did delivered them.

As indicated, a complete runner was dispatched to the battlefront with strict instructions not to dally along the way, under the threat that he would not be a complete runner for much longer. A standard marketing threat but a very effective one, and a most necessary one of course. This to extract maximum productivity from one's employees, who were likely to disappear on the job and end up in the nearest tavern, if not instructed properly first. Thus, after many gruelling weeks trekking through the desert, the palace runner duly arrived at the city gates of Samaria, still in one piece and clutching his tablets.

Sargon's father, the king, had been away from his nation for nearly two years, and spent most of that time camped outside of the city gates of Samaria. With the daily practice of making rude gestures and yelling expletives at the besieged occupants demanding entry. However, the Hebrews inside were certainly not naive or lacking in business acumen, for they had slapped a 50-shekel entry fee on any Assyrian's entering the gates, which had not gone down well with Sargon's father. Thus, in an apoplectic fit, had cause to berate and remind them, that he was there to collect their shekels and relieve them of their possessions ... which most certainly did not entail him having to pay an entry fee to do so.

Thus, it was stand-off time between the two warring factions, and it was at this point in the proceedings, that the tablet messenger from the city of Assur turned up at the king's tent. That of course, had been pitched outside of the city gates of Samaria without permission of its residents. However, it must be said, that with all due thoughtfulness and political correctness of the era, that it had been erected with its entrance facing away from the gaze of the city inhabitants. Who also lay claim to being civilised, despite their shekel orientated disposition and unfriendliness towards visitors.

Well, the tablet messenger duly presented his tablets to the king, observing due bowing and scraping procedure in the process to maintain his status as a complete runner ... as opposed to an incomplete runner. Subsequently, he was then told to go and have a cup of tea in the officers mess, as it was tidier than the sergeant's mess ... and most definitely tidier than the soldiers mess, who were always getting into trouble for all sorts of mess, that they got the blame for whether they had made it or not. Because like all good organisations, you do not blame the top when there is a mess. No! You blame the bottom, it is called political logic or big business survival procedure and its doctrine has not changed throughout history. So, it must be a very effective damage control mode indeed and well worth writing down in one's pocket business/political tablet organiser.

Note, because you must always have a scapegoat that's lower in the ranks, to take the back lash for one's mistakes. For surely, you do not make any, after all, only human beings make mistakes, not kings and gods. That is called high echelon logic within power gamesmanship. Alternatively, kick butt clout status, in the ranks of Machiavellian high achievers that have made it to the throne of absolute power in kingly and queenly places. The lesson to be learned from this perpetuated dominant alpha intrigue is not to become it, the scapegoat that is.

The King Encounters Murphy's Law - no Respecter of Royalty

The King was highly delighted to receive a tablet from his son to brighten his day, because up to that point, it had been an horrible one. Everything that could go wrong had gone wrong. Firstly, the royal tent had sprung a water leak in the early hours of the morning, from late night reveller's mistaking it for the ablution tent. Then the royal valet, awakened by the roar of the royal vocal cords rushed into the royal quarters, tripped on the royal persian rug ... that turned into a royal flying carpet. That aerodynamically bowled the royal presence for a metaphorically speaking royal six. As a result, the king was most displeased, and the royal valet became an incomplete valet, as opposed to a complete valet. Thus, was the royal status removed from the said valet, along with a few other parts for the royal measure, as was the royal practice for incurring royal displeasure.

Now, as if the above happenings were not bad enough, the royal kitchen staff then made matters decidedly worse. Because as every wise royal chef knows you do not serve the king scraped burnt toast and cold tea at breakfast, least of all when he had suffered a horrible night. Thus, it came to be, that a few more of the royal household were relieved of the royal status and suffered the bodily fate of Greek statues in the process.

Now you might think that nothing else could go wrong that Monday morning ... but, Murphy's Law is no respecter of royalty and once you start the day off wrong, you can bet your boots that Murphy will tag along all day to enforce his law. This truth became evident, on the king's daily early morning, constitutional chariot trip around the city walls of Samaria. Where it was the royal custom to go charioteering around its perimeter shouting rude obscenities appertaining to excessive entry fee charges. This balanced precariously on one foot, with the other dangling out the side for braking on tight turns. Along with one hand on the reigns and the other, outside of the chariot making inverted rude gestures at the dwellers inside the city walls.

About Pride and Prejudice.
Plus, the King Replies to his Son and Heir

From the above shenanigans, you can see that kings in those days had to be multi-skilled in all the arts. Tough royal cookies indeed. All was proceeding by the royal schedule for the day's opening activity, until the preverbal camel dung hit the fan so to speak, for on the third sharp turn on the west wall, a most undignified event took place. One of the king's chariot wheels took off on its own flight path and overtook the chariot. Which of course is not allowed especially on a royal chariot that had a daily inspection by the royal mechanics, but you guessed it, not for much longer would they retain the royal prefix. They, were shortly to be separated from more than their tools, they were, to join the numerous ranks of the incomplete, as opposed to the unemployed.

Now among the aristocracy and the elite, there is absolutely nothing worse than suffering embarrassment, which means being compromised, by an undignified occurrence during one's official duties. Historical wars have erupted from out of that ego immaturity of false pride and subliminal conceit. That is called, "loss of face" in some cultures. Wars that started from out of delusions of self-importance, from very bad manners and loss of self-esteem. Anyway, the king was no exception to the rule and true to form, in a right foul uncompromising mood by the time he limped back to the royal first aid tent for the royal treatment. This after suffering the jeers and leers along with catcalls and encores and more, that poured down from the battlements of the city walls of Samaria.

No! it was not a good day at all and by kingly nature, the boss was about to make sure that no one else had one either, a good day that is. It was at this point in the horrible proceedings that the tablet runner had arrived with news from home. Otherwise, the inventory in the spare parts department of the army would have become very inflated indeed. Thus, did Murphy's Law depart with the arrival of the royal tablet messenger, to everyone's great relief and obvious concern for their spare parts, which meant that the king's attention became diverted from bruised pride, self-esteem, and bodily anatomy, to become attracted to more pleasant happenings in his nation. Thus, the King, having absorbed the contents of the tablet over a hot cup of tea ... of course, *because it is always handy to learn from the mistakes of others?* Then summoned the royal scribe to make a prompt reply. A tablet translation of the king's reply to his son, and his indignant harangue follows.

Tablet Translation by Stephen

My dear boy, thank you for your cuneiform tablet explaining your dilemma. Now firstly, do not be so impatient, you have a lifetime of trashing ahead of you in the family kingship business. It has been predicted in your stars by the soothsayers, so, you must learn to be patient. Trashing, like all great human achievements in life, takes time to perfect and administer with skill. I say again, be patient and just like me, you will acquire much in the world that belongs to our family of course.

Now, it is time to assist me with these delinquent Hebrews in the city of Samaria and instruct them, that what is theirs is ours, and what is ours is not theirs. For they are very uncivilised barbarians indeed and of all things, want me to pay first before trashing them. Thus, read this tablet very carefully, for I can only write it once as I am now down to my last royal scribe. The others have displeased me by wanting a five-shekel pay rise and better working conditions. As a result, I have had to send them for thought rehabilitation and new trade training skills using their feet. So, if your mother approves, take the next chariot to Samaria, for I have need of your irritating ways, unlike mother, whom you must placate and not annoy.

Now before you leave the palace, you are to spend time modifying grandfather's battering ram. That is to be found in the back of the tool shed. Make sure the family motto inscribed, "Headus will Rollus" is enlarged and repainted. Use subtle Assyrian pink and not, grandfather's gory red. We do not want to give those on the receiving end the wrong impression. It is called being politically correct. Thus, you must always remember to only tell the truth to camels, not to mere subjects, it would be most improper and out of character to do otherwise within kingship. It just upsets the nations tablet scribes recording it all for public consumption.

Also, enlarge grandfather's wheels so that better traction is achieved when running over people. It becomes very congested at the gates of city via those windbag protesters lying in front of them. Complaining about their rights, not enough shekels, the environment, tax on chariots, not enough freedom, too much camel dung and goodness knows what else. When will they learn that they are only people and not tablets and understand the words progress, innovation and expansion? Let me tell you; it was the same story in grandfathers' day. Nothing but constant complaints and ungratefulness from these conquered nations.

I sometimes wonder if it is worth all the glorious trashing. You get nothing but abuse afterward and often, only new words to put into our nation's tablet dictionary. I did say to these ungrateful people, that words do not put grain into my nation's granaries, bread and wine on my table, jewels and trinkets in the queen's boudoir, pay for the gold wheels of the ceremonial chariot, finance the new palaces or produce shekels in the Assur treasury. You are not trashed and conquered to complain about it, and I have enough problems in my nation. Why should I listen to your bleating if I don't listen to them?

No! you are just selfish, bone idle and measly minded. You are sons and daughters of squint-eyed camels and mules. May your ears drop off, your noses block up with sand, your teeth fall out, your bottom have pimples, your fingers poke you in the eye, your toenails grow backward, your hair turn purple, your tongue becomes mute, and your in-laws move in with you. What is the point of me dedicating my life to helping other nations at great expense to our treasury and long years away from my palaces and dear wife? Plus, having to pay a standing army of half the nation to keep the peace and putting up with incompetent scribes on the fiddle to record it all for posterity.

No, my boy, let this be a lesson to you. You must be firm with placard-waving protesters, not panda to them and give them anything. Next thing you know they will want their freedom and sick pay and holidays abroad and free chariots. If you give them one grain of sand, they will want the desert. Let them drink at the oasis, and they will scoff all the dates and spit all the stones in the well. Upon my grandfather's head that is in the upper orchard, leave not one rock unturned in your camp, lest it arbour the scorpion that crawls in your bed and bites your posterior. Leave not your sandals outside of the tent, lest they disappear into the desert night on the back of a camel's hump. All these things you must learn my boy if you wish to prosper in the world.

Thus, do not give a scarab's hair to the people. They will only want more and more and then you will have nothing. No wine to sip, no shekels to count by the light of your candle, no harem for rainy days, no chariot to polish, no orchard trees to decorate, no summer palace to sip mint tea on barmy nights and reflect on past conquests, no servants to admonish and re-arrange. Truly I say, the world would be as black as a bat dropping without our family's gift of trashing the people in it. Bear witness my boy, and soon, you will follow your father's steps into trashing immortality. It is but a short time we are given to accomplish our kingly purpose in this world, so always trash it well for posterity.

In due course, heed not the protests and banners of the city rabble when we rearrange the city's foundations. You are to put four extra wheels on grandfather's battering ram, then it will be the biggest and the best in all the lands with its superior protestor traction, and an iron tipped people pounder, we shall make quick our conquest and victory. Then we will return with many slaves and decorations for the orchard, and both be in mother's good books.

Now be of good cheer and polite to your mother and do not forget your manners amongst the servants which is called kingship correctness. Always remember to conduct yourself in a manner befitting your status in life. that is called political correctness. Think not what you can do for others, however, think about how best they can do for you. Always trash first and expect everything. Give nothing unless you know there are shekels in it, for that is the Assyrian way since time immemorial and how we have aspired to become a great nation. Remember, winning is everything, and taking is the way to success in the world my boy. For how else would you aspire to greatness like your father? Have trashing power like your father? Bowed down to like your father, acclaimed as a genius like your father, crowned king like your father, become a celebrity like your father? Verily I say, it would be a poor world indeed if we could not trash it and those in it.

Your Loving Father - The King.
Royal afterthought:

When you have finished these battering ram modifications then for goodness sake, do not try it out on the servants. You are in enough trouble with your mother as it is. So, go down to the village and make sure it works properly down there, not in the palace or on the palace - right?

End of tablet translation.

About the King's Tablet, the King's Advice, and Sargon's Epitaph

Well, as the history books reveal, the city of Samaria did indeed fall under the battering ram of "Sargon the Second." As well as the mixed fate of its in-dwellers, which, as the custom of the day demanded, were separated into those that were useful and those that would not be useful. The latter constituting the majority were assisted into chariots that ferried them to the heavenly crossroads, where further division took place under the supervision of St Peter this time and not Sargon.

As to the destiny of others?

The artisans and scribes and non-combatants were granted assisted passage to the city of Assur ... and from there, issued free work permits to construct the new palace of Dur Sharrukin, or Sargonbug; as it was affectionately known by those who did build it and of course, by those who did slave in it for the love of the king and progress, which, as we all know, must have been dearly constructed indeed. Because all that is left for us to see and speculate on is a heap of rubble a lot of tablets and two miles of broken alabaster murals. It is depicting Sargon's great contribution to civilisation, the Assyrian way, with a lot of human trashing and of course, glorious human progress through being a worshipped winner.

King Sennacherib - The Next Generation

The Nation of Assyria was prospering. Alternatively, rather the new king and the aristocracy and the big business elite were prospering. King Sargon, the second, had carried out his father's instructions to the letter; thus, was a good son indeed. Making many conquests in many lands, re-arranging their cities and issuing free travel passes to their inhabitants well, certain inhabitants. After all, what is the point of paying out good shekels in transport costs for the rabble and unskilled? No, they are just a burden on the economy and contribute nothing to progress. Better they stay in their nation and enrich the land permanently.

It was but the way of doing things in those days of high population turnover and intercity disputes. It was not personal only practical, because like now, economic rationalisation was a highly prized tablet profession and the cause of many economy altercations and punch-ups within nations. King Sargon, after a short reign of empire building, winning and achieving, suddenly departed to the afterlife. To then join the rest of the family clan in the wrong end of creation. As in, stoking the boilers in the basement for you-know-who permanently, of course. Along with chatting to old friends and other big business and political trashing acquaintances and generally, having a hot time while waiting to be re-employed once more in human progress affairs downstairs.

It came to be, that Sennacherib, the king-in-waiting who was no cherub, took up the family kingship business to carry on where his father had left off. Therefore, keeping the economy trashing business in expansion mode. Reaching far into Greece, the Phoenician ports along the Mediterranean and deep into Asia Minor and along the way, becoming an ardent collector of collectibles, other people's that is. All duly catalogued, carefully packed and sent back in chariots built with extra-large wheels to negotiate physical obstacles, this, due to all the roads being packed with horizontal people, cobblestones, being far too expensive to use in those days of course. Eventually, all the goodies arriving none the worse for wear to fill and compliment the new palace at Nineveh and owing to the old palace of Sargonbug, busting at the seams with previous collectibles. That, of course, acquired in like manner by his illustrious father and grandfather.

It should also be said that rather like the pyramids in Egypt, bigger and better after ascension to the royal or political throne, was obligatory in those days. Thus, the new ruler must always outdo the last ruler in whatever, otherwise, you could not use the prefix 'great' in front of the word king on the tablet stationary. A modern equivalent understanding of this strange contagious perpetuated human behaviour, would be the expression, "keeping up with the Joneses". Alternatively, more correctly, outdoing the Joneses, which of course, would mean you were better than the Joneses. Therefore, they could rightly claim to be superior to the Joneses. You could also say you were more successful than the Joneses. You could rightly feel very accomplished in life and all that it had to offer, thus depart earthly matters peacefully.

Interlude.

About Expansion and Progress and its Scientific Trashing Formula

Now there was a correct economic formula for trashing expansion and building palaces, that was rigidly adhered to by B.C. past rulers. That states (6yp + 5xy) - (8nm + 3xc) +7te to the power of 10zz multiplied by (4rs-10py) +(15sd over 23bs) where (small x = p and p+ t = big X to the scientific power of whatever you like. That is a very powerful economic mathematical formula and should never be attempted with a morning hangover after a late-night binge.

If you could work the above equation out, then you could be said to be very successful indeed. You could rightly place the prefix, "great" in front of your name, as well as having lots of sculptures, murals and portraits made of your great personage expressing its humility and philanthropic nature. Plus, to remind others of your great accomplishments in life. Just like the ancient kings and big wigs were accorded in the B.C. progress of human things. Ditto in the boardrooms of the industrialists, arms manufacturer's, piggy bank dignitaries and entrepreneurial corporate mogul movers and shakers in the A.D. expansion and progress of human things. With, "God is great indeed" as a suitable caption. To then also compliment both sides of history and keep human innovation in perspective for posterity, such is progress.

Now it came to be, that King Sennacherib, while away on one of his many business trashing trips abroad, decided to take a brief trip home from its hectic trashing schedule. This for a bit of R and R, solve a few family domestic problems, and to make sure that the expansion formula was being strictly adhered to by those in charge of the palace extensions. Along with updating the alabaster history murals that adorned its many corridors, with painted picture stories of his recent conquests and most important of all, expand the inventory of the family orchards out of the captured royalty from other trashed nations.

Unfortunate ex-royal's indeed, who were first paraded through the city streets of Assur, minus their apparel and a few spare parts and dragged along via a bull ring through the nose, before ending up in the fruit trees in the orchard. A very strange activity indeed, but its occurrence was the cause for much celebration among the locals, who took it all in good heart with much cheering and rejoicing in the misfortunes of others and as the day closed, ended up in the city taverns for a celebratory ale or two, in which to toast the king's royal health and for bigger and better economic progress next visit. Just like in 21st century big corporate business and right-wing political ideologies that have merged into one economic winning team for themselves and the top end of the town of course.

Now to us civilised human beings in this modern day and age with our deep concern for the humanities and its born IQ underprivileged, its dispossessed, its helpless and homeless. Not forgetting to mention the starving, the maimed, the oppressed, and the downtrodden. Along with the parentless children, the drug and disease afflicted children and the work conscripted children in developing nations, working for the rich nations. Not forgetting the abused and exploited masses in war-torn, religion torn, and politically torn nations whose people are living in tents, etc. The above celebrations would seem very strange behaviour indeed to adopt towards another human being's misfortune. However, in those far off days, they knew no better because life for the masses was very hard indeed and they had no say in their nation's progress. Only the guidance from those who were born privileged with high IQs in charge of the nation to give them direction ... to give them morals ... to give them ethics ... to give them life-supportive example ... to give them all-important economic progress.

So, unlike nowadays, where affluence, education and kind thoughts saturate the world, the citizens of those days, had an excuse for their strange celebratory behaviour at another people's misfortune. Consequently, they should not be judged too harshly for their actions. They were but pawns, to be manipulated by a few privileged families, who over many centuries, had accrued much wealth and power from either trade and commerce, or plundering, as it came to be called by the feudal lords and aristocracy. More commonly known in today's world, as the big corporate business elite and entrepreneurial successful in society ... otherwise known as the media saturated winners in life. However, of course, bear no resemblance to those mentioned above because we are civilised now, of course, we are.

Returning to King Sennacherib and the Royal Duties. Plus, a Tablet from Egypt

Now it came to be, that King Sennacherib, after a hectic day, attending royal business breakfasts, royal re-arranging ceremonies, toasts and doings, business lunches, cocktail parties, business teas, coming out balls that had backlogged in his absence, visits to the family orchards and late night business suppers. Then finally turned in for the night, and with a final check of the palace security systems and the placement of an early morning call, finally rolled into bed and fell into a peaceful, blissful, business sleep — knowing that all was well in the world and that much progress had been achieved on his first day back from organising other nation's internal problems. For such is the duty of powerful men and women of course, on the international circuit of big international business economic and political affairs.

However, as all very busy statesman and stateswomen know well, the bed is no guarantee of peace, because it was but a few minutes later, that King Sennacherib, was sorely awakened by the clatter of chariots in the palace courtyard. Along with a medley of high-pitched voices clamouring to see the king most urgently, the king, gave a royal sigh of resignation, grumpily kicked the bed and donning his tools of the trade, switched off the valet that forgot to cough before entering the royal chamber. Ditto the high-pitched voices that had received attention from the king for this problem before. Then, over a cup of tea, sat down to read the urgent tablet that had arrived from Egypt — sent post-haste by the king's chief collector of other people's collectibles. Namely, el Akbad Grovel.

A Stephen Translation of el Akbad Grovel's Tablet Follows

My King, Lord of the four lands. Lord of all the water holes, (very valuable in those days, rather like oil wells today), Lord of the blistering deserts. Lord of all the red lands. Lord of all the green lands. Lord of all the black lands. Benefactor of all nations. Giver of innovative progress and thought bubbles to other nations. King of all the other trashers. King of all the collectibles. King of the mathematical formula for all palace extensions. Greetings from your dutiful, humble, worthless, miserable, unimportant servant.

Great king, much unrest has occurred of late amongst the learned scholars in your faithful employ. They did find in the land of the sandals and pyramids much evidence of righteous doings. Very sinful doings occurred by those who did rule that nation of pyramid dwellers many orchards in the past. In fact, long before our great trashing civilisation conquered the other minor trashers.

I bring to your attention my king' nay I most humbly bring to your attention my lord king, their economic blasphemy and thought bubbles. Such terrible hieroglyphic words inscribed on the walls of their tombs. Words that did all but blind my collectors, nay my lord your collectors. For I am but your eyes and ears and of no great importance, of worthless lineage, of miserable existence, of no consequence, blab blab ... but I beseech thee, my lord, to post haste deal with this grave problem. Lest it infects our nation infects the world destroys our very existence, should we not immediately trash those who would say and do such unspeakable things to others.

Be it known my lord, the following hieroglyphic tablet translation by your most humble servant el Akbad Grovel of no consequence, is done under great duress and the torture of my mind and thought bubbles and my blasted Egyptian sandals.

el Akbad Grovel Goes Over the Top and Down the Sides and Makes "Uriah Heep" Seem Pedestrian

May I be clothed in ignominy and cast into poverty and relieved of my shekels should I neglect to bring his to your attention O' great king of trashers. May my worthless spirit be banished forever to the land of bad business dealings and unscrupulous collectors, should I be found to write them for another. May I forever walk the corridors of ill repute and be banished from the halls of piggy bank solicitous fair dealings, should I be forced to utter them again. May I forgo all claim to my meagre possessions and position in life as the king's collector of other people's collectibles, should I ever speak of such diabolical doings of others again.

Thus, my magnanimous king, it is with the utmost reluctance from my miserable personage, that I bring this matter before your illustrious presence for immediate attention and would beg my glorious king's benevolent magnificent munificent presence, in its administration of justice and fair treatment for all subjects in the land. A light that does bedazzle all other incompetent kings of the lesser realms. Reducing them to mere mortals of insignificance and incompetence, as rulers of men in the lands of Akkad and Sumer and other nations of no consequence. I do beg to bring their tribute and present it at thy scented feet and would ask for your forgiveness in subjecting this tablet upon your illustrious dazzling personage ... phew!

In this connection, my bountiful king, I would ask of a posting to a less terrible commercial media plagued decadent land to serve you as a chief collector of other people's collectibles. For truly I say, what has been written, comes from the mind of the deluded surely possessed of evil demons addled by sour wine and fermented camels' milk.

Thus, I have post-scribed an extra tablet to place these abominable words upon. Least they are attributed as the authorship of this humble scribe on the fiddle in any way your glorious eminence. One in whose grace and employ as a chief collector of other people's collectibles I have served with scrupulous honesty in all dominions in the four lands. Who would never discriminate between rich and poor and take equally from both? Who would no more take that which did not belong to him, than taking from the public shekel box at the temple of Marduk, located in my humble residence at the city of Assur? Who would seek no more than the royal decreed 50% of all collectibles? As contracted on tablet K4893621, located on the third shelf up on the east wall at the Ministry of Acquisitions and countersigned on tablet, A7903762 located in depository, 96004571485534987 at the Akbad Grovel city bank and duplicated in the Akbad Grovel chamber of commerce dwellings next to the Akbad Grovel emporium of used goods for the royalty in mint condition. I remain your faithful, trusted, a loyal servant in all things my generous King and await your trashing instructions accordingly.

el Akbad Grovel - Royal Collector of
other people's collectibles and shekels.
Licence number A776051 B.C.

Additional Tablet.

Translation of an Epitaph from the Cliff Tomb of an Egyptian Nobleman

There was no citizen's daughter, whom I misused.
There was no widow whom I oppressed.
There was no peasant whom I evicted.
There was no shepherd whom I expelled.
There was none wretched in my community.
There was none hungry in my time.

When the years of famine came, I ploughed all the fields of the Oryx Barony - my estate, preserving its people alive and furnishing its food so that there were none hungry therein. I gave to the widow as to her who had a husband. I did not exalt the great above the humble in anything that I gave.

Egyptian Nobleman - deceased but not forgotten.

Spiritual Boot Camp Comment on the Epitaph from Alf

Progress! Progress! What Progress? Oh! That Progress. No, never heard of that progress.

Signed ... Big global greedy corporate business, the commercial media empire, the Akbad Grovel global piggy bank brigade, synthetic polluting science, and big business educated socially blind governments. Not forgetting, other past the use by date political ideologies in the divisive mix and for appearance money only, the two bob each way sit-on-the-fence and choose which way the public wind blows on controversial social issues. This for the preservation of their precarious held political seat at election time. Yep - that's real progress in the A.D. political survival stakes.

So now, we know the true origin and basis for that worthy title of a nobleman, originating over four thousand years ago. They are also called, being civilised in nature's non-dissolvable spiritual dictionary. So, a special posthumous thank you to James Henry Breasted, past director of the Oriental Institute at the University of Chicago. Whose acquired knowledge, and dedication to uncovering the history of civilisations and whose concise literate and teaching skills, the author is greatly indebted too. The author knew him not but respected him much. For his contribution as a scholar, teacher and meticulous recorder of past civilisations. A legacy and historical gift for others to learn from. They are evidenced in the pages of his informative work "Ancient Times."

Returning to the Assyrian Plot

King Sennacherib, muses on the tablet and its implications and upholds the ancient universal tribal edict of the elite and powerful.

"I've got, so what your pain my gain - so tough camel's udders."

King Sennacherib much irritated, pondered long upon the contents of this annoying tablet. This was bad news, indeed, that did bring a dissection mood upon the king. Nobles helping vassals the rabble treated like nobility. Was there no sense of trashing responsibility in those that ruled the land of the pyramids? How can business be conducted with such brain addled nincompoops that treat the common rabble as themselves? How can trashing progress be maintained in the land, if you do not use the fools in it? Why give to others, when it is they who should give to you? Have you not risen above those in the marketplace with the science of the business mind and the power of the shekel and claimed the right to trash others? Is it not written in the sands of time, that success comes from subjugating and exploiting others? What is the point of being born if not to covert everything, to own everything, to have everything? To hold the world and its lesser beings in your hand, at your feet, in your power.

Thus, Echoed the Big Business Words of the Father, in the Big Business Thoughts of the Son

Surely, King Sennacherib mused, this must be the Dark Age that the great business conquering minds of old had spoken about with much sorrow. A dark blight that had once covered the four lands long ago. A plague of do-gooders, the likes of that Babylonian usurper King Hammurabi. Whose black cursed tablet does grow dust in the palace archives. Who did defile the land with righteousness and business law and order? Who inscribed a code of good conduct towards the rabble from the elite and wealthy, one of equality and justice for the trodden on? With codes of right conduct for trade and commerce.

Bah! Such weakness doth churn the stomach, turn men into fools, destroy the will of the strong. Reduce a powerful man to a windbag of nothingness. How should a man live if not to rule over others? Is it not written that taking everything is the way of all progress in the world? How should a man survive and prosper, if not on the back of the weak? From out of the purse of others, from the sweat of others, through the toil of others, the weakness of others, the manipulation of others, the glorious domination of others. For how else, should success be measured than through the degree of power and control one has over lesser beings? How else is it possible to proclaim success other than squashing those who would frustrate the path to its summit … to its adulation to achieve its acclaim and worship from the public rabble? To be accorded subservience and admiration from fools, to be worshipped for ruthlessness and acquisition, to be held omnipotent, omniscient, omnivorous of others in the marketplace.

Verily I say, the shekel is the very breath of sweet success in all men of consequence. A man's life would be a desolate waste, but an inconsequential event, without the power that it brings. Truly, a man is not king, unless he be the holder of vast possessions and held in awe through them.

Such Were the Thoughts of Sennacherib Great King - King of Kings

Thus, did the King study well the tablet from el Akbad Grovel and its implications? Surely, another dysfunctional age of righteous doings could not descend like a dark blot upon the land. Was this dark event not in the primitive past, before man had become civilised and cultured? Well versed in the noble arts, big shekel business, and other glorious human sciences. Surely that past ignorance from fools could not travel forward in time and destroy such great accomplishment and glorious progress made now? Was not this age the pinnacle of mighty doings, of unparalleled trashing, of glorious acquisition, of material comforts, of much subjugation of lesser beings by those who have risen by right of born superior intelligence to control them, to educate them, to rule them with superior intellect in the fields of ownership, of one-upmanship, of commercial commerce, of new innovative science, of tall temples and worshiped wealth?

No, surely this could not be, this shall not be, wrote the king in his daily tablet of trashing business. So much vexed and deep in further thought, the king did pace the corridors of the palace consulting its alabaster murals for trashing inspiration, to resolve his dilemma. Finally, with no solution forthcoming, the king did don his night vision goggles and headed out into the orchard, where he sought solace from the stars and other fixed ornaments.

About the Path to Success and Prosperity - for One's Self

At the time of the king's dilemma, Assyria was at the height of its trashing power, which meant, much tribute was pouring into that nation's coffers or banking institutions, as they are now called. Mostly from one-way trade with other trashed nations. In that process, whole populations were being made redundant. Alternatively, superfluous to the needs of glorious progress and economic innovation in political correctness terms. Much turmoil and unrest abounded everywhere in nations, especially among the dispossessed and of course, in its necessary economic rationalisation, many people uprooted and stripped of more than their dignity. Those few that could be said to be useful were then transported to the land of Assyria for further trade training skills. Alternatively, for home duties, as it was then called, those that could be said not to be useful, owing to their verbal objections, were impaled on stakes and left dotted around their respective nations. Waving to all and sundry and extolling the virtues of glorious global progress and innovative expansion.

However, most of the disposable people without disposable incomes, were made into huge mounds in their trashed nations. To then create another first from the ingenuity of the Assyrian moguls. Human progress signposts along the busy one-way trade routes of the all-conquering Assyrian empire. That was a very practical innovative idea in terms of deterring other nations, employed in the same business of trashing and expansion, from muscling in and taking one-way trashing trade away from Assyria.

For as we know well in our present age, commerce, and big business is the golden egg of the world. It is not only the root cause but the continuing glorious economic path to all progress and prosperity in life. To all fulfilment, personal happiness, achievement, success, and acclaim in life. For if one is rich in life, how can one be poor in death? Thus, the golden big business egg must be protected by whatever means necessary, from those who would equally seek a piece of the egg for themselves. However, of course, in those B.C. trashing days, they had no private enterprise corporate power to exert in the right places, as in, gaining the king's ear. That was the secret of acquiring power then, or the government's ear, or lobbying, as it is called nowadays.

Thus, the fervent whisper of shekels and after dinner mints in the right ear, conquers all before it and believe it or not, it still works very well in these A.D. big business enlightened times. So, do not forget to enter that also in your new age high tech electronic pocket business organiser gizmo.

A tongue in Cheek Look at the System of Progress Past and Present

It came to be that Assyria becomes all-powerful in the four lands, and just as others had done unto Assyria in the past, then so did Assyria do unto others in the present, only bigger and better, as is the way of all human progress. Those who could trash well were accorded great honours in society. Especially the society of the privileged, wealthy and elite, that formed the powerful minority running the nation, that is the way of progress. Thus, were awarded iron statues, small ones of course. Only the king was allowed big ones, statues that is. This much-coveted award, for excellence in global business trashing and people trashing that go hand in hand nowadays. So too, accruing vast shekel accounts along the innovative way in the Akbad Grovel piggy bank. That had expanded as is the way of progress, to trade throughout vassal subservient conquered nations.

Indeed, chariot fly by tablets and shekel credit tablets became the status of high standing. They are becoming the signature of influence, status, and great affluence, of envied position in life, of great success in life, of much clout in life, in the marketplaces of society and great business doings. *Have shekel well shall we travel"* set to a five-string harp, was hummed throughout the many Akbad Grovel controlled emporiums, trading houses, tall pyramids, elite wine bars, high cuisine alacarte restaurants, entertainment tents, stretched chariot limo's, tablet exchanges and luxury holiday resorts, that thrived in the midst of all the excellent trashing going on. Thus 'trash first pay later,' became the coat of arms of success and opulence among those who could do it well. Yes! A powerful progressive, innovative nation indeed was Assyria in 700 B.C.

About Placing all your Eggs in One Basket - or Catch 22 of Progress

To achieve the above trashing success, had meant conscripting half the Assyrian nation into its armed forces, and as expansion and corporate take-over of other nations grew, this problem was compounded even more, by the need of the army to collar more and more conscripts from the working classes within Assyria, to replace its very high mortality rate. Because in those days, *unlike now and its global corporate takeover megalomania for progress and affluence for the few*, peaceful nations did not like being invaded, and their culture trashed. Their economics shattered, their currency disrupted, their established workforce made disorientated and insecure, its commerce and industries monopolised by multi transnationals and overseas shareholders. Alternatively, just as thoughtless, bought and sold by big players from other nations to make big bucks. Also, its resources then channelled out of the nation and the proceeds into the pockets of global entrepreneurs, other Nations, and corrupt officials. As well as its population brainwashed and seduced, by the commercial you know who brigade and told what to do, where to go, what to say, what to buy, what to wear, and how to wear it.

No, nations in those far off days were not happy one little bit at having to pay big brother Assyria heaps of shekels, for the privilege of all its glorious cultural and social trashing and global progress. Thus, there were many conflagrations and on-going punch-ups to the bitter end, as is the way of human progress. Thus, much Assyrian human resources required in conquered nations, to ensure that those that had not departed to the heavens, were made to tow the private enterprise corporate line, so to speak. So, as we speak of the "brain drain" nowadays to describe the exodus of skilled human resources to another nation, it was the, "peasant drain," that ultimately sealed the ignominious fate of Assyria.

It should be further explained that the land and its development of agriculture, were the lifeblood of a nation. Its produce fed the nation, the harvest of which, created business infrastructure and many trades in cities and communities alike. Barter and exchange were a Nation's currency, a way of social interaction, a way of doing things that had nothing to with today's big business predatory antics. So too, everything was performed manually. Full employment and economic security in life was a natural process among agricultural nations. A harmony, upheld by the maintenance of age-old codes of social conduct, that formed its customs and traditions.

Note: A natural *Laws of Nature* governed process, that celebrated and cemented that way of life. A spiritual process that developed a harmonious flow with human beings and their environment, tuned into the rhythm of the seasons and the primordial archetypal intelligence of nature. Self-referral Laws, that, at the spiritual level of life, process and evolve life and Creation, that compliment life and Creation. That upholds the evolution of Creation and life, through maintaining law and order in the archetypal spiritual intelligence of primordial nature and human beings. When *spiritual* based positive cultural traditions and customs are upheld, then so too are the people in touch with the spiritual base of physical Creation. However, when a nation's culture and unique traditions become lost, then so do the people become lost to their spiritual roots — lost to the spiritual foundation of life and its interactive communication with nature's laws.

Clarification: Ancient positive traditions and customs, are those that celebrate and rejoice life. That do not harm life. That do not exploit life. That do not degrade life. That do not inflict pain on life. That do not subjugate life. That do not destroy life. That do not trash the spiritual dignity of life for religious, political, scientific, sexual, or monetary reasons. Traditions and customs that do not comply with that positive life-supportive format are most certainly not the ancient traditions and customs. However, have been inserted into the culture of a nation to control its people to have power over them. Thought up by power and control negative accentuated creative minds, just like those perpetuating ancestral sourced life-degrading creativity in this present age?

Explanation: Positive cultural ceremony, means a life-supportive non-manipulative ceremony that supports life and its evolution. The ceremony that has nothing to do with the delusion of worshipping powerful human beings for their acquired status. However, as respect, acknowledgement and reverence for nature and life. Positive cultural traditions and ceremony, that did not degrade life, but celebrated life and upheld nature's spiritual laws. It also required a mature age, extensive life experience, and spiritual maturity, to become an elder or chief. With spiritual acquired wisdom to guide its society through the complexities of life, anything less than those spiritual acquired requirements, would not gain the support of the spiritual Laws of Nature underwriting *order out of chaos* in life.

Clarification: Spiritual law and order, that was intuitively expressed through the evolved consciousness of the elders and chiefs, to administer and uphold social customs and traditions wisely. To supply a spiritual anchor in life for others, to cope with all the many complexities and problems that arise in life. To give spiritual guidance through the many stages of life, without becoming lost along the way of life. Spiritual authority that has nothing in common with created status authority. Alternatively, the dominant alpha quest, to acquire power, influence, self-importance, adulation, and worship in society, that leads to megalomania and abuse of acquired power in a spiritless mind.

Uncomplimentary note: A megalomania nemesis, sourced to an entity driven pathological disorder, to be found in the negative accentuated dominant alpha human being. A power and control neurosis that has now become rampant in big business and power politics. Megalomania, that is the driving force of our all-consuming material expansion sourced to greed. All-consuming expansion and consumerism that is being fuelled out of a big business created destructive life-force/entity. That has come to contaminate primordial nature's spiritual workings and therefore, human physical consciousness and the affairs of humanity. It is a contagious influence/life-force, contaminating very intelligent, powerful human beings directing all progress and the destiny of this civilisation. Namely, big corporate global business, piggy banks and the money markets, because they now control the direction of the world and its people, with their big buck, acquired power, born business acumen and spiritless minds divorced from the Laws of Nature.

Another catch 22.

We must understand that we cannot keep expanding physically and materially as a species, without ultimately destroying the planet. It has limitations in its physical resources. Physical limits to a sustainable population. A physical limit in what we can take from it that is not replaceable. A limit to the abuse and synthetic pollution, that human beings can inflict on its ecology and other life-intelligence in the name of creating progress. It is also negative structured progress, being created through spiritually divorced from nature science. In their insatiable quest to understand life and cure disease through saturated synthetic chemical pills.

Note: Along with blindly experimenting on life in the spiritless scientific laboratory, therefore, manipulating it, changing it, controlling it, exploiting it, degrading it, polluting it, destroying it, placing a patent on components of it and owning it and calling progress. That equates to thoughtlessness and disrespect for life and nature on a grand scientific polluting scale from a spiritual understanding of life that is.

Further: The science fiction dreamed-up idea that a few privileged human beings can go shooting off into the wide blue yonder, to colonise other planets when it has finished trashing this one is more ego created delusion. It is childhood acquired, and comic book, movie and education indoctrinated fantasy, operating in the unexpanded adult mind. It is coupled with incredible human conceit and spiritless minds. Because a question of spiritual logic is missing in that all-consuming quest, to conquer outer space and invade and colonise the planets as in the distances involved, the duration of human life and its fragile, complex biology. Born and evolved out of this life-supporting living planet and not, out of sterile outer space, light years, black holes or the planet Klingnong in a galaxy far away. Not forgetting to mention, the growing toxic pollution out of its technology and the billions of dollars, being spent on the space program and its spin-doctored fantasy, called creating progress for humanity. However, only for the privileged few in the top end of town … as is the way of human progress.

Another unpalatable boot camp observation: Billions of space conquering dollars that should be spent on restoring this science and technology polluted trashed planet for those who come after us. Those on its science fiction all-conquering planetary bandwagon should put their born gifted intelligence to better use. Along with the taxpayer's money, that is being used to satisfy a child's unrequited desire, in a space-obsessed so-called adult. Because surely, those lost in this science fiction delusion to conquer the planets and outer space, have yet to grow up and acquire spiritual maturity. Because outer space is unequivocally the wrong direction to go to find our spiritual potential and reach heaven. However, transcendent acquired inner space is, without polluting anything – got it?

The point to be made:

It is time to understand the words *balance* and *maturity* with our desires, aspirations, creativity, and direction in life. This through acquiring and developing, the spiritual maturity to maintain that balance in a non-trashing process of human expansion. An order out of natural chaos function, to be found at the transcendent source of nature's self-referral laws, located at the spiritual core of divine nature and its unlimited spiritual intelligence. Because there is nothing wrong with creating progress, providing we do not trash this planet, trash nature's intelligence and trash the creator's gift of life, along the way of our human progress. Comprehend we are unquestionably destroying this planet, in our present unexpanded physical consciousness and its ego-driven all-consuming synthetic creativity and immature desires. Therefore, pause for thought time required, in our existing so-called progress, because we are blindly destroying ourselves and the planet, in what we are calling progress. Along with abuse of acquired power and ego sourced delusion in clever minds in high places, that is driving that spin-doctored so-called progress.

In nature's dictionary, abuse of acquired power is the root cause of premature entropy and spiritual decay manifesting in a society, in a nation, in the world. Therefore, the exploitation of the majority by the born gifted minority from the misuse of acquired power. From the misuse of born gifted intelligence and high physical IQ but missing spiritual acquired IQ From the misuse of primordial sourced born alpha leadership power. From the misuse of born disadvantaged human beings ... the majority, that are instinctively compelled to follow the leader. A megalomania driven exploitation of the weak by the strong and a perpetuating human created nemesis that has plagued all civilisations. Pathological and psychological ancestral inherited disorders, found in those that are unconsciously compelled to conquer, control, and subjugate, everything they interact with and called success, achievement, winning and creating progress. However, to spiritless nowhere land with their evolution.

Megalomania (*king of the castle neurosis*) is linked to a contagious ancestral inherited entity, that fuels the immature ego-driven desire for status, winning, recognition, adulation, for wealth and power, to dominate and possess, to conquer and control everything. Ancestral karma driven psychological/pathological disorder, that is the visible trademark of the ambition consumed entrepreneurial dominant alpha of our species. That inevitably succumbs to the Faust enigma to achieve material success, through acquiring money and power to fuel delusional self-esteem. Because that ancestral acquired devolution ticket to no-where land, is exactly what eventually transpires at the end of the human day, spiritually speaking.

Returning to King Sennacherib and his B.C. Alpha Power Neurosis. Otherwise Known as Megalomania

It was not only the king that had access to the spoils of war that poured into Assyrian coffers, the traders were supplying the army with its equipment, its food, its horses, its chariots, its weapons, were all paid out of that acquired booty. The army were paid out of that booty. The el-Akbad Grovel piggy bank was very much into lending and credit tablets from that booty. The elite and powerful in the nation, all had access to that booty out of the coffers of other trashed nations. Thus a few, as is the way of progress, became very wealthy indeed. Palaces and extravagant dwellings became the order of the day for the prosperous traders and the elite. Thus, great affluence was not just a predisposition of that dynasty of Assyrian kings, who, over two centuries of conquering and trashing other nations, had brought the whole region under the iron knuckle of Assyria?

To compound the problem even further, the powerful elite was not predisposed towards agriculture one little bit. However, very good at tablets, exploitation, and acquisition, from out of their born gifted IQ and they began to move out into prime agricultural land that those not born with gifted IQ and called peasants, had vacated. This takeover due to the shortage of peasants from conscription to the army of its male workforce. Thus, the privileged and powerful came to acquire huge estates for freebies from the king, of course. As is the way of progress, the elite came to live the seven-star good life. With plenty of slaves with lower I.Q, to perform all the menial tasks and lord it over. As befitting the privileged status of those born with superior intelligence and highly educated cultured minds. It came to be that Assyria's economy became solely dependent on its ability to keep expanding on the backs of other trashed nations. As Assyria was redirecting their wealth and resources in the form of slaves, booty, and taxes, into the coffers of the Assyrian nation. Such is economic progress down through the ages that the ancient Roman Empire also came to excel in and pass on for posterity.

King Sennacherib, on the few occasions he was home, had cause to ponder this problem of neglect of the land and agriculture. Alarm bells were sounding in that shrewd business mind of his because he did not lack brain matter or its alpha power, only common sense, spirituality and wisdom. Which, as we know, do not count for much in economics and civilisation, for it only retards progress and economic expansion. Thus, while still out in the orchard chatting to his treetop guests from three pages ago, King Sennacherib had a sudden innovative thought bubble, also known as a, *"I know what to do,"* aberration in politics, bureaucracy, big business and others in charge of innovative progress. Yes, he would send all the residents of trashed cities holus bolus on extended holidays to Assyria … and, issue free work permits to everyone. This to restore agricultural self-sufficiency in the nation and manually aid the few talented ones, that were already working on restoration and art decor in the palaces.

"What a jolly good economic idea," he suddenly exclaimed out loud, much better than creating human signposts. Plus, as another dominant alpha brainwave and its thought bubble, he would conscript those conquered nation's armies into his own. Thus, solve the internal problem of the dwindling trashing power of the depleted army. "Yippee!" He exclaimed out loud to no one in particular, much progress comes from sitting under an apple tree. However, of course, it was not an apple that dropped on his head that caused that revelation. "Tis very strange," he

further mused, how everything falls into place at the right time when you talk to the right person. Because now, he had the missing answer to his first dilemma, i.e., the manpower and means, to sort out the pyramid dwellers of the Nile valley in Egypt, for the wrong, righteous doings of their ancestors.

About King Sennacherib's Revelations, While Sitting Under the Apple Tree in the Family Orchard

So, to start the retribution ball rolling, he would pay a timely visit to that no-good do-good Hammurabi's old city of Babylon. That had once plagued with righteousness and good doings, and for the innovative sins of that camel's cud King Hammurabi, would dispatch them and their tin pot gods and city temples to the Babylonian afterlife. Where no more will they brag about winning the tidy towns competition three years on the trot and possessing most favoured nation status for hoarding shekels as is the way of progress.

However, first things first, he would scribe a tablet and send for his lazy itinerant brother Prince Esarhaddon, to round up the city dwellers of Lachish, Beersheba, and Arad. Then, having installed them down on the farm in Assyria, he could finally take off and trash the pyramid dwellers in lower Egypt. My word, what a good day it was turning out to be, yes! He must promote one el Akbad Grovel, to world collector of other people's collectibles, as is the way of progress in high places.

Pause for Thought Time. But of Course, No One of any Standing was in the Family Orchard to Explain that Wisdom to King Sennacherib

Now when you empty a nation of its manpower on foreign acquisition projects ... as King Sennacherib had done, and then install a replacement population with a completely different ethnic background, with totally different customs and traditions ... and as they say in Hollydud and actor's equity, *"Big innovative trouble at black rock sooner or later."*

Especially when you have not asked them whether they would like to emigrate in the first place. For you cannot assimilate a repressed subjugated people on mass into a minority one and then, expect them to forget about their way of life, traditions, customs and culture. To then graciously adopt those of another nation's instead.

However, in this progress enlightened day and age, when you voluntarily emigrate to another nation, then it is the right thing that you should give your allegiance to its way of life, become one with its native people, so to speak. After all, you are the minority, and they are the majority, and because of their generosity in allowing your citizen status, you are beholden to abide by their laws and support that nation's culture and spiritual evolution. Therefore, that nation's welfare naturally takes precedence over the one you have left for whatever reason. For if you are not willing to surrender your past way of life, you will never become one with that new Nation or its people, therefore, disharmony, discord and unhappiness may well prevail.

Clarification: It goes without saying, that unhappiness and discontent will naturally become your lot, if you are not willing to embrace its culture, its language, its customs and way of life when you voluntarily, willingly, premeditatedly, take up permanent residence within another nation to find a new life. So common sense wise, if you are unable to conform to the above philosophy, then it is better to return to your nation of birth and reinstate your allegiance to its way of life, religion and culture. Thus, restore your personal happiness and cultural-spiritual evolution in the positive process.

Note: Because to give up your birth heritage and its spiritual evolution to settle in a foreign land, takes a lot of soul-searching and sacrifice. If you have come to regret its decision, then you should pack up the unhappy home and return to the land of your ancestral lineage and be of service to it. Your further spiritual evolution is then assured, because happiness and harmony are everything to acquire spiritual progress and our further evolution.

However, that natural law of harmonious cultural interaction and allegiance in an adopted nation ... most certainly would not apply, if you were uprooted, hijacked and made to become the exploited servants of another nation's people. No! That is not allowed in the scheme of spiritual evolution, because it's negative karmic influence, created out of wrongdoing to others, remains in the interactive spiritual mechanics of nature and its primordial workings. Those responsible, ultimately reaps its returning destructive karma in their evolution, in the *as we sow so do we reap* law of karma. This becomes its mandatory sentence, out of subjugating, exploiting and enslaving other human beings. There can only be one result out of that thoughtlessness eventual self-destruction, in the form of human-created chaos, premature entropy and spiritual decay in those responsible for the degradation of life.

Returning to B.C. Assyria and its Demise, from out of Trashing Other Nations

As more and more males were seconded to the Assyrian army to fill its depleted ranks, its agricultural way of life collapsed. The land lay fallow, unattended and neglected and a viable established economy destroyed as a thoughtless result. Fatherless families began to drift into the city where the good life was happening, ring any bells? Thus, karmic retribution became mandatory for Assyria. Heralded by the sacking and destruction of the cities of Nineveh and Assur, by a consortium of other nations. Fearful, that individually, when it became their turn to be invaded, they would be no match on a one to one basis with the unstoppable Assyrian trashing machine.

It came to be, that in the aftermath of that defeat of Assyria, dissolution came in the form of assimilation and absorption of its Assyrian culture, into the ever-growing enslaved Aramean culture. That, over time, had expanded to eventually swallow the Assyrian minority into its Aramean culture. Assyrian language, customs, and traditions vanished. When the Greeks and Alex marched past several centuries later, on their historic world trashing expo, all that were left of its past grandeur and affluence were a pile of mud bricks and rubble. Now that is justice is it not? However, of course, King Sennacherib was not to know of this unfolding calamity, so, we will not tell him until we are near the end of the story.

To conclude:
Much pleased with his inspirational trashing genius, King Sennacherrib arose from his royal seat under the apple tree, and replacing the inspiration from whence it had come, returned to his palace to set everything in motion and of course, much innovative progress out of the present.

Returning to Our Storyline Once More

Enter Prince Esarhaddon-the-badden' for his contribution to B.C. progress. In this version of Assyrian history, King Sennacherib is Prince Esarhaddon's elder half-brother, not father.

Prince Esarhaddon, King Sennacherib's younger half-brother, had spent a great deal of his privileged life out of the royal limelight. Being the second son of the king, as the first son of the king's second wife. Who, in turn, had been a second princess in the Babylon royal hierarchy. She had been sent from the city of Babylon to the city of Assur, as an anniversary present on the second day of the second month in the second year of King Sennacherib's reign, Hmm! I think I got that lot right, except for a possible royal apostrophe and some missing A.D. commas and semi-colons.

Note: This royal conjugal activity, was not an unusual occurrence in that patriarchal era of male macho aggrandisement and royal tribute. Along with, 'you scratch my royal back, and I'll scratch yours and forget about the others'. Now political copied, age-old 'diplomatic protocol' (official title) for cementing royal kingdoms and of course, for keeping diplomats, bureaucrats and scribes gainfully employed in the royal doings of powerful people in royal lands. The only difference in those royal romping days and our Hollywood instructed ones now, is that you are not expected to marry the tribute afterwards. Some may say it is innovative progress, but Alf has his suspicions to the contrary.

It should also be mentioned to woman's lib, that in those B.C. patriarchal days, the second wife had to play second fiddle to the first wife in most marital things. So, it came as no surprise to his birth mum, when Prince Esarhaddon was born two seconds after midnight, on the second day of the second month, in the second year of King Sennacherib's reign, Hmm! Something wrong there with the maths and not comma's and apostrophes for a change. Thus, it came to be, that playing second fiddle to everything, had become second nature to Prince Esarhaddon throughout his early trashing years.

Note: But, as we will find out in due course of our Assyrian story, the aspirations of his birth mother were firmly set on first fiddle status for her son. No matter what it took to achieve it. As is often the way of overly ambitious immature parents determined to succeed in life themselves, by dictating and commandeering the life of their offspring. That, of course, has nothing to do with teaching progressive independence and just as importantly, giving it to them. Alternatively, loving them for what they are, but rather what you want them to be. Therefore, your unfulfilled aspirations in life. Yep, not much progress made here either since B.C. in some A.D. circles.

As a male result of marital and family chaos and not a woman's lib, it should come as no surprise, that Prince Esarhaddon, ended up a right mixed up scrambled egg in the brainbox and emotional department, by the time he reached the, *'I can do what I like because I know everything,'* hormone, glossy tablet and chariot charged adolescent teens. "A prince by name but not by deed" is how the Avon bard would have eloquently phrased it … and, under his mother's watchful eye, developing excellent prospective kingship material. Thus, showing all the right sociopath traits for future trashing potential and being pleasant and considerate of others or pretending to be, was not amongst them. Which was okay for those B.C. days, because in that male macho dominated era, they had never heard of political correctness, PR double speaks or the art of subterfuge and deception, i.e., to do it in high places but not be seen to do it in high places.

Anecdotal note:

However, score one to our sophisticated A.D. era here. Enter the media delivered blossoming art of PR waffle, double speak and spin doctor spiel open to all sexes. Much progress made here for a change in the political, big business and commercial media department and even more so, in the woman's lib department. That has now caught up with the male macho motor mouth department in marital, political, public and glossy tablet affairs. Thanks initially, to Mrs. Pankhurst and her long-suffering suffragettes securing the vote and finally accepted in society, through scriptwriters, Hollybug and Co; movies, commercial television, and newsrooms cementing the previous long outstanding alpha male and female macho imbalance in society. Oh dear, Alf will get into more than node removal trouble with this paragraph, that's for sure.

It was also a B.C. fact, that Prince Esarhaddon had spent a good deal of his youth in his mother's birth city of Babylon. "Staying with the relatives," as we would say, thus, learning much about the Babylonian way of life within its royal circles, who believed in living the 'do what you like' good life in the pursuit of constitution and adolescent media tablet instructed happiness. You know, spending shekels, endless parties, a la carte scoffs, dancing girls with poles, fashion catwalk shows, cocktail parties with dates, big fancy dress rave-ups, late-night harp techno disco clubs with chemical refreshments, shekel casino's galore in the desert and its mandatory extra-curricular activity on the house, and the usual after-hours stretched chariot races in downtown Babylon afterward. Just the usual playboy stuff of the young elite and well to do, to break the monotony of being born wealthy, spoilt, privileged, and emotionally neglected according to the ghost of Sigmund?

Prince Esarhaddon Receives an Acrimonious Tablet from His Brother the King

An unpalatable tablet that had arrived in the glorious summer of Prince Esarhaddon's twenty-eighth year, most of which, had been spent on the wealthy top end of town Babylonian circuit, having a wow of a time with the B.C. equivalent of the A.D. silver spoon set. No, according to Alf's tea leaves, he was not pleased one little bit to receive a royal tablet from his brother, the king, ordering his immediate return to Assyria, for the progress creating purpose of nation building and royal trashing duties. As opposed to frivolous Babylon constitution duties. A Stephen tablet translation of which follows:

Dear Brother,

You are to return at once to Assyria and cease forthwith your idle Babylonian ways, and the neglect of your tablet duties. Our father's words laid clear your instruction in this licentious matter. "Beware of loose women and inferior wine in the marketplace and desert casinos, lest you be robbed of your shekels and tablets." In addition, I have received nothing but complaints from the Akbad Grovel piggy bank recently, with respect to excessive withdrawals in your annual allowance account. Yet again, I am forced to remind you, that family credit facilities are for human trashing purposes and not to be spent on purchasing wives and buying up gambling casinos.

Now this matter of casino licentiousness and dancing poles, has been brought to my attention by the gossiping of the palace servants. I have dealt with their gossip indiscretion accordingly and dispatched them for further trade training skills, less their wagging tongues. But, as head of the family, no longer will I tolerate your errant Sodom and Gomorrah and Babylonian ways. Thus, I will remind you as your elder brother and great king of Assyria, that not for 3000 shekels or 10 stretched chariots, will I endure any longer, the nagging of my forty wives from the complaints of your thirty wives in this matter.

In addition to all the above-named indiscretions and dalliances, there is yet another royal gripe that I must bring to your attention. My gold harp has gone missing from the tablet library. The one father gave me before he left to collect more historical tablets in the land of Mitania and accidentally on purpose, got run over by a chariot with a wonky wheel. Anyway, after questioning all the servants, it appears you were the last one seen with it before you left for Babylon. Anyway, I want it returned ... the harp that is, not the wheel.

Now, just because father gave you nothing and I got everything, is hard goats cheese and tough camels udders. I cannot help it if you are second best at everything and that I have all the brains. It's not my fault that you are lazy, or that you did not get the job of updating the family orchards, or that I can run faster than you, swim better than you, drive a chariot better than you, have more wives than you, trash better than you, have a longer beard than you, play the harp better than you. So, I want it returned pronto, otherwise I shall send your sharp-tongued mother and all her Babylonian gods and babbling priests back to Babylonia, where they can babble in their Babylonian temples to their Babylonian heart's content and not in my temples or ears for that matter. In the meantime, you are to pack your bags and return to Assyria for urgent trashing business and don't forget my harp.

Signed - your dear brother the king.
p.s. Don't forget my beard growth lotion that I lent you either.

Prince Esarhaddon Receives his Instructions and is Initiated into Proper Family Business. As Befitting his Archetypal Dominant Alpha Leadership Lineage

Having absorbed the nasty tablet, Prince Esarhaddon fumed and spluttered long into the casino night and its extra-curricular activity on the house. "Who does he think he is?" exploded the indignant prince on another clay tablet. "Why must it be me that always gets the blame for everything? Even if I did pinch his harp, so what, he didn't pay for it. No! It is always been the same, Sennacherib this and Sennacherib that. Look at Sennacherib what a fine fellow he is. Come with me Sennacherib, and we will go trashing. Yes Sennacherib, of course, you can choose which tree we shall use for the next lot of decorations, blah blah." Thus, did the words of the father weigh in heavily in Prince Esarhaddon's thoughts on the unresolved royal tablet matter.

However, a royal summons was a royal summons and not to be taken lightly. Plus, prince Esarhaddon had yet again ran afoul of the Akbad Grovel piggy bank with bouncing shekel tablets. This on top of accruing heaps of unpaid shekel bills with the merchants of Babylon. Which was no big deal of course after all, he said out loud to no one in particular, "They could afford it he couldn't." However, after weighing up all the pro's, con's and cadences along with the missing comma's, apostrophes', semi-colons, crochets, breves, semi-quavers and Assyrian swear words, prudence convinced him that perhaps it was time to return home and let his vocal mother sort the mess out once more. True, he disliked his brother intensely for always putting him down. From much past-experience, Prince Esarhaddon knew well that his kingly brother was not to be trifled with on family and Assyrian trashing matters.

Yep! he thought after much thoughtful deliberation and the tugging of his short beard, his mum would sort the problems out, she was good at that. He would have to put up with all the nagging, that always accompanied her solutions to his recidivist shekel and Hollybug disposition problems. Thus, having settled the royal dilemma of whether to rebel or acquiesce to his brother's demands, he commenced packing his personal goodies for the long desert trip back to Assyria.

Well, according to the tea leaves, Prince Esarhaddon duly arrived at the city of his birth, and after a big spat with his brother over the missing harp and the loaned but not returned beard lotion, not forgetting some sharp, caustic babble-on words from his very vocal mother. Worse still, sent to Coventry by his irritated thirty wives was much relieved, to be promptly dispatched to round up the citizens of Lachlis, Beersheba and Arad. Along with strict instructions to acquire their shekels and not spend them. Along with, the collection of their historical tablets for the family's archives, in which it should be said, had grown into an extensive library of thousands of clay tablets from the tablet libraries of Assyrian conquered nations.

Anecdotal fact:

A tablet library that had become yet another progress first for the Assyrian kings in the annals of great human academic achievements. Even though they were only made of clay, then, tablets were all the rage in the aristocracy and elite of literate nations. As their gold leafed hard backed, and glossy magazine paper equivalent ones are nowadays. The only problem being that no one seems to learn anything from tablets of all descriptions, but are forever repeating what was written on them. However, in more sophisticated A.D. up-market ways, of course. Thus, we can comment, "Not much progress made here either since B.C. times."

Well, the history archives duly record for posterity, that King Sennacherib did indeed set forth on his tablet and nation trashing mission. First to the city of Babylon, where, as good as his word, he demolished the city and duly dispatched its citizens to early retirement in the afterlife. Along with demolishing its sacred temples as a bonus, a trashing bonus that was to prove to be the instigator for his own Waterloo, down the track of our history repeating story of humans versus right and wrong and how to tell the difference.

Pause for Thought Time in Our Assyrian Story

About the ancestral karma perpetuated trashing neurosis of human beings, that was locked into primordial nature's archetypal workings and the downstairs human-created systems.

In those unsophisticated B.C. trashing days, the wanton destruction of temples and gods was considered the sin of all sins. No, most definitely not cricket as the English say. Thus, in the super logic of human beings, it was an acceptable practice for humans to trash and dismember each other in the context of creating progress, civilisation and differences of opinion on how exactly that system should work. However, desecration of the pantheon of gods that ruled supreme in an invaded nation by another nation on a trashing expo, was considered an ill omen among the population of all nations. One that warranted automatic retribution from the gods sooner or later for those responsible.

Thus, you could trash in the name of the gods, but you must observe the rules of trashing in the process. Rather like nowadays in our present civilisation and its new global corporate trashing entrepreneurs, armaments manufacturers and those peddling its destruction for big bucks on the world stage. Aided by some negative got it wrong' high tech scientists, chipping in to keep it all up to date and online for our ultimate extinction. Not forgetting a few so-called civilised governments, making billions of bucks from its lucrative official and unofficial arms market. It was coupled to hypocrisy, the nation's hip pocket and lip service talk of world peace.

The above money and death creating arms mayhem, also supplying the gun powder activity of fanatical religious and criminal political regimes. All are adding their two pennyworths into the same trashing system. Subsequently fuelling the adrenaline activity of the news media, for its worded and camera saturated coverage for the public. Along with 24/7 delivered pictures of heaps of destruction, blood-spattered images, long lines of gun-toting soldiers, helicopters, graphic accounts of genocide, collateral damage and those on the receiving end and the odd mangled corpse thrown in for visual effect and good commercial reporting. This to keep the necessary wheels of news and trashing progress turning for humankind and my word, much-trashing progress to be acclaimed here. Bigger and better A.D. pictorial recorded progress indeed ... but, to no-where land with our spiritual evolution as a species, according to upstairs.

Now the previously explained retribution belief, i.e., from the wanton trashing of temples and gods in invaded nations, may seem a little naive to cultured news and glossy magazine informed civilised person in this 24/7 media enlightened day and age. However, on reflection, it is no less a naive concept than the one that circulates at present. Namely, that God is always on one side of any conflict with another nation or religion. As in, Catholics vs Protestants, the Bible vs the Koran, the Christians vs the Arabs, the Jews vs the Palestinians, Shiite vs Sunni, the Taliban vs the rest of the cough, mutter and splutter civilised world, etc.

So just maybe, those earlier civilisations were not naive after all, in their belief of many gods involved in the affairs of human beings. After all, how can the same god be in two opposing ideologies or religious faiths at the same time, yet, only be supporting and sanctifying one faction against the other? As in, the history repeating process of its endless human trashing, to acquire and own the religious status quo in a nation and the world. No, I smell a rat here amongst the chooks so to speak. Someone is telling porkies yet again in the history tablets in the public library. Alternatively, at the very least, perpetuating those big porkies for reasons that remain a mystery or conundrum, when you apply the word logic to its religious hypocrisy and delusion.

No, Alf suspects that certain powerful, clever human beings have created a system within a system to suit their specific religious ideology and beliefs. In the pursuit of their power and ambition consumed religious deeds in it. A parallel to be found in political ideologies to direct or dictate, the direction of the people in a nation and consummate bigger and better political trashing progress. A parallel also found in big corporate take-over business, and its piggy bank ticked boardroom manifesto of greed and acquisition in the name of business. A parallel found in science and its unchallenged manifesto to experiment blindly on everything on this beautiful planet in the name of progress, acquiring knowledge and saving a life, from out of re-arranging life in the divorced from nature money making synthetic polluting laboratory now owned by big business?

Conclusion: All in all, I think it is time that we found a way to understand the real system that underwrites life. Therefore, stop creating other human systems in it, that are not in harmony with its divine perfection. Because many human-created systems/ideologies in their present expression, are a pain in the butt to nature's perfect intelligence structuring the evolution of everything on this planet.

Coming Back to the Primordial Gods

To understand the creation of many gods in ancient civilisations, along with the immense power and influence that were attributed to them, it should be explained that humankind in that epoch of uncomplicated expression, was very much in touch with spiritual creation instinctively. Simplistic and basic may have been the expression of their human intelligence in it. However, they were most certainly not lacking in the brainpower and creativity department. As the Greek civilisation and its legacy to our Western civilisation have proved.

Clarification: Therefore, having the same mental and creative potential as we have in this century. However, we could say as an analogy; those civilisations were operating from the first chapter of the book of life in the context of kingdoms, cities, and civilisations. We, in our current acquired social development and its many human-created complications and pathological disorders, are operating out of the middle chapter of that analogous book of civilisations, which has become very cloudy, muddy, stirred up and unreadable, through human pollution and 'got it wrong,' human beings in the worshipped driver's seat of A.D. progress. Thus, at their B.C. more simplistic and less synthetically polluted level, earlier civilisations could be said to have been very receptive to the primordial spiritual archetypal intelligence that structures physical creation, that structures life, that structures our chemistry, that structures our physiology, that structures our personalities, that structures our evolution. That contains and processes, our human-created cause and effect karmic influence.

Thus, within less techno complicated and spin doctor, PR, glossy magazine, newsroom and media uncluttered minds but no less gifted than ours, those earlier civilisations expressed the simplicity of primordial Nature's spiritual workings very short on sophistication and subtlety. Those last two ingredients grow, with the ability of the human mind to also grow (evolve) and expand within biological, physical consciousness and evolution. Thus, all influence (karma) we create in the spiritual system that underwrites physical life, reflects through our creative genes and procreation generation into generation. Its interactive karmic process drives the evolution of biological intelligence. However, as an afterthought, where all our current sophistication and high learning and its glowing human gene is taking us too, no one has bothered to ask, it is merely deemed as progress and must not be questioned, only worshipped by those in charge of its progress.

Explanation: Biological intelligence (physical intelligence) evolves and expands too. It is not a fixed equation but an on-going expansion. It is evolving further from the influence (karma) created out of the cause and effect of those biological parts. As we sow, so do we reap, sums up this interactive quantum structured process of evolution perfectly. Therefore, what we do with our human creativity effects everything evolving on this living planet. What we create and do as a collective via the ideologies and created realities we live, becomes very significant in that karma processed fact of evolution, for we all reap the quality of its returning karmic influence, all life intelligence.

It is true that old collective realities (lived ideologies) give way to new ones in humanity's evolution. However, once a human created reality (ideology) is lived in civilisation, its karmic influence (life-force) becomes permanently a part of the collective psyche of humanity and its specific key-signature located in spiritual Creation. In the past, that returning negative (destructive) or positive (life-supportive) karma would only affect the isolated civilisation in question. However, this civilisation is now connected globally via communication, trade, and unrestricted travel, to become a global civilisation. Thus, individual nation's karmic key signatures have now merged, in respect of its created karmic influence affecting every other nation.

Summing up the Activity of the Primordial Gods (Archetypal Intelligence) and the Deities of Nature

In spiritual understanding, the religion of many gods in earlier civilisations reflected the invisible spiritual activity of the planets in our solar system. Because biological intelligent life is a physical manifestation of primordial archetypal spiritual intelligent, that, in turn, is sourced to the spiritual composition of the physical planets in our solar system. An interactive spiritual and physical system that underwrites life, that functions through the spiritual activity of the divine self-referral Laws of Nature to create, process, orchestrate and evolve our biology, genes, consciousness, intelligence, personalities, karma and human creativity. In past human spiritual understanding, Earth, Air, Fire, and Water, have been interpreted as the dominant divine elements (cosmic energies) that sustain primordial life and this planet. From out of their divine authorship sourced to the cosmic mind, comes the innumerable planetary spiritual archetypal primordial energies, that invisibly structure biological life and its chemistry on this planet. It is for that reason; we could call the spiritual nucleus of the physical elements of Earth, Air, Fire, and Water, the deities of physical Nature and life in Alf's book of upstairs acquired spiritual facts.

Clarification: Primordial spiritual archetypal intelligence, emanates from our solar system and its planets to manifest as the biology and chemistry of life. The spiritual Laws of Nature are its government that underwrites 'order out of chaos' in its interactive spiritual primordial structure. Underwriting those self-referral Laws of Nature is Cosmic Law, that is the supreme status quo intelligence of physical and spiritual Creation. That we have also called the cosmic mind or the cosmic computer. Thus, all life intelligence in both physical and spiritual manifestation, is the sum of that cosmic mind. All biological created life is spiritually interactive with that cosmic computer, that processes the evolution of life and this universe. As human beings, we spiritually interact with that cosmic computer through the product of karma. Karma that is a creative spiritual by-product of the impulse of creative intelligence that we call thought. Karma that is the creative spiritual tool of life and its evolution, both physical and spiritual evolution. Phew, no wonder it is a verbal headache to explain the 'Spiritual System' that underwrites life, in the limitation of human-created words and incomplete human-compiled dictionaries.

King Sennacherib and the Temple of Doom.
Not Forgetting Brotherly Love and Happy Families

Now, where were we, ah yes.

King Sennacherib was feeling rightly pleased with himself, long after returning from the family orchard. Such good planning, not forgetting perfect execution of its brilliance, deserved a pat on the back. Yes, things were going swimmingly in its aftermath as a result, as they say in the boardroom and political circles. Thus, Babylon and its temples trashed, its gods departed to the underworld or overworld, depending on their plus or minus status of course. The peasants rounded up and sent for further trade training skills in Assyria. The Assyrian army doubled from reluctant volunteers and shortly, to depart to rearrange the Egyptian topography in favour of Assyria. "My word," wrote King Sennacherib in his daily trashing tablet, "our father would be pleased."

The same could not be said for Prince Esarhaddon or his mother. After all, he had been a semi-permanent guest of his mother's relatives in Babylon. Some of whom had now taken up permanent residence in the family orchards at the palace of Assur … albeit reluctantly. Worse still, he could not now repay his debts to the Babylonian merchants, and that made him very unhappy. Moreover, on top of this aggravation, his mother and her Babylonian priests had been confined to barracks. His barracks of all things. All because the king, his brother, had copped an earful of dominant alpha babel abuse from the sharp tongue of his mother for the desecration of the Babylon temples. As a result, he now had to bear the brunt of her wrath and its vocal outpourings in the family quarters. No! Thought Prince Esarhaddon; his brother would have to pay big time for inflicting that torment on him, he would not get his missing gold harp back now - no way.

Time passed in the trashing doings of Assyria. However, of course, not karmic influence. That only returns bigger and better and with interest, as the wise say. Thus, the clouds of karmic retribution began to gather over some in the trashing plot of our trashing story. King Sennacherib, having dispatched the foot soldiers of the Assyrian war machine some months prior, with orders to encamp at the first cataract on the river Nile and await his arrival with the mobile chariot divisions before attacking the Egyptians.

The Gods Decide they have had Enough of King Sennacherib and his Hubris and Vanity. Deciding Instead, to Give Prince Esarhaddon-the-Badden a Go

It was a custom in B.C. times, to consult the inside workings of a sheep before undertaking any venture. An occult divining practice called extispicy. Its modern A.D. equivalent, of course, being scientific experimentation and divining in the laboratory. Those poor animals again, they always seem to cop the brunt of the means for humankind to progress in evolution ... one way or another. In those B.C. days, they were interested in examining the liver and entrails for divining the future. A good scientist in those days could tell at a glance what was happening in spiritual creation before it manifested into physical creation as an event about to unfold on the planet. Very clever scientific dudes, no doubt about it and believe it or not, it was a very accurate means of foretelling the future of the animal in question too.

It came to be, that before the troop's departure a standard sacrificial divining ceremony had to be performed, to ascertain the viability of the global economic venture. You know, whether the trashing trip would be successful or not ... and guess what, bad news all around. It was predicted by the Assyrian scientists that the army would not reach its destination, but the sheep would. Well, King Sennacherib wasn't very interested in the latter and chose to ignore the former. Thus, there was much consternation and the writing of tablets among those who knew better in Assyrian scientific circles.

Explanation: Because if the gods were not on your team's side, then they must be on the opposing team's side. Very logical, indeed, thus should not be ignored. King Sennacherib, only having announced recently to anyone who wanted to listen, that he was "King of Kings," and "Lord of all the Lands," was not about to take a mere scientific mortals' advice. After all, he had never failed in any trashing venture, so why should he not succeed in this one? Besides, they were Babylonian sheep from the spoils of plunder, that had been used for scientific consultative purposes, therefore, in human logic, could not be trusted.

Thus, it came as no surprise to the learned scientific men of Assyria, that, three months after the departure of the main trashing force of the army, a tablet runner arrived at the palace with really, really, bad news. A great plague had swept through the main task force of the army while negotiating the marshland and swamps of Southern Mesopotamia on their way to Egypt. The result having decimated the armies ranks to the point of impotence as a fighting force. Some might say, *"that's the way the cookie crumbles in Nature, you win some you lose some,"* as politicians are frequently heard to say. However, of course, the wise know better. That's why they are wise and, the consensus of the scientifically wise in the land of Assyria, was that the King had got too big for his sandals in over trashing of late. Because, of course, the 'spiritual primordial system' will only take so much from the abuse of human beings, and then, it is time for payback with big karmic interest added on of course.

Thus, discontent began to fill the air from ordinary mortals in the land of Assyria. *"What if the plague should descend on them as well,"* echoed the talk in all the taverns, late-night harp disco's, camel shows, market places, shekel casinos in the desert and glossy tablet magazines and other publicly worshipped temples around the nation. What if, as was suspected by the worried public, the Babylonian gods were in payback mode big time, for the king's desecration of the temples in Babylon? Needless-to-say, there came to be a great shortage of sheep in Assyria, as much consultation of their interiors by Assyrian scientists was required, to work out what to do about the burgeoning crisis of public unrest in the land.

It is also a noted downstairs phenomenon, that whenever there is discontent in the air, the plotters and schemers club come alive in a nation. It becomes a golden time indeed, for all those who have been chewing patiently at the woodwork of a human created structure for many years, yet seemingly getting nowhere. Then bingo, it collapses from forces that appear equally from nowhere, and opportunity abounds among the discontented. Thus, did Prince Esarhaddon and his Babylonian mother, to realise that all their Christmases had come at once, so to speak. Accordingly, devious doings were hatched out in the orchards of inspiration. That had once proved so fruitful in more ways than one for King Sennacherib.

Heavy Metal Interlude

A boot camp detention room story about delusional narcissism, hubris, conceit, ego preening, mirror worshipping, self-importance and self-aggrandisement, where the primordial gods of Nature are concerned. Thus, sowing the seeds of King Sennacherib's demise, by incurring the ire of the primordial gods in our Assyrian story.

It was a well-known fact that the king loved statues of himself, of course. Vanity, narcissism, and ego preening, having changed little over the millenniums in high places. However, now reaching plague proportions in this promo and commercial, ego marketed consumer civilisation, through our infatuation with all things human and therefore suspected. With all its media supplied worshipping of celebrities, winners, the rich and famous and infamous, the body beautiful and its procreation whatnots and bulges and look how successful I am with no clothes on. `Cos I got a mention in the 24/7 newsroom and my picture on the television and the centrefold of a glossy magazine. Also called ground-breaking news, stunning pictures and must-see commercial product viewing. Darth ticked news, pictures and must-see product viewing that is.

Likewise, the, I love me, paparazzi picture supplied Hollybug superstar magazines, containing their karmic life history and director's cut torrid love affairs and sexual perambulations on and off the set. Along with their ego preening portfolio, procreation attributes portfolio, Oscar seating portfolio, and latest Box Office take portfolio, Oscar pecking status portfolio, and other official and unofficial out of the closet information. As in sexual preferences and more anticipated shares, property and acquisition holdings acquired on their frequent 7-star trips around the world. Information also sold to the national newspapers and glossy magazines. Along with lots of other fairy stories, from the big business financed, jet setting, millionaire sporting fraternity. Having also made it to the dizzy heights of the media created human success product worshipping mountain. Outdoing the creator by five days and the Sabbath, and my word, at the moment they do look well up there.

Spiritual fact: According to upstairs, downstairs is being exploited by a lost in ego space, very clever, born gifted minority, living the good life at the expense of the planet and the spiritual evolution of society. Who, thanks to the also, 'got it wrong,' saturated 24/7 media, are going backward with their spiritual evolution and taking us ordinary untalented mortals along with them, to its spiritually ignominious conclusion in the finger pointing departure lounge. A detention room diatribe that does not mean Alf is allergic to affluence and dislikes gifted successful, clever people. However, it does mean upstairs, and the primordial gods (archetypal intelligence) are not happy, when that material success and prosperity, is acquired through the exploitation and manipulation of other human beings, along with the degradation of human dignity in the sexual department.

Note: Because there is very little in society, that is not being exploited by thoughtless, immature, so-called successful gifted people, plagued with a social, sexual, karmic and ego screw loose, it is aggravated by the opportunism of irresponsible communication mediums and entrepreneurial big predatory business, to make big bucks out of it, driven by greed. Unconscionable greed that attracts destructive ancestral entities created out of the past, 'got it wrong,' affairs and activity of humankind, to compound the spiritual devolution problem in the present. A destructive human created *entity* that contaminates degrades and pollutes primordial Nature and therefore, human consciousness. An ancestral sourced karmic legacy of the past that grounds out in the divorced from Nature minds of, 'got it wrong' human beings in the present, to also send them in the wrong direction in life ... albeit unknowingly?

All in all, King Sennacherib's B.C. ego preening disorder (delusion) that upset the gods, has merely become normal delusion in society.

Especially with the A.D. invention of the camera, selfie cell phone, television, glossy magazines, commercial advertisements, long mirrors, billboards, neon lights, the catwalk and movie studio. Along with images of product clones, boobs, bums, abs and whatnots, stuck on everything that lights up downtown. Not forgetting to include, the input from the media baron's personal highflyer business and sports magazines. With lots of glossy touched-up picture's and up-market product spiel, on how to get rich quick at the planet's expense while playing golf. That incidentally, all make good compost in the garden according to Alf, shredded of course.

Returning to Assyria, Before Alf Gets into More Node Removal Trouble

In B.C. times, the contagious ego deluded 'I love me' and 'look how successful I am' self-esteem neurosis, was confined to those who financed palaces, not erecting them. Thus, King Sennacherib was no exception to its downstairs human ego issued permit especially as it was signed by himself. Also, because statues had to be updated every few years by following the aging process of a royal subject, much employment of ordinary mortals was required to keep up with the demand. Thus, there were always comings and goings of huge stone statues and multitudes of people called slaves. Constantly traipsing through the palaces and suffering multiple hernias, in the process of moving and updating them.

Now, one statue to a room was the bare minimum allowable, but in the king's throne room and temple annex, you couldn't move without bumping into stone effigies of the king. They were littered everywhere, all shapes and sizes and what got up the noses of the 'real gods' when they paid a surprise visit, was the king's latest proclamation that he was a winged bull. You know, a great big hairy human face, stuck on the end of a bull's body with wings on it; especially, as he had not asked for restructuring permission from the appropriate licensing body upstairs. Well, I ask you? Wouldn't you be offended, if you had spent 6 billion years getting it right and then a mere human king, decides to change the system overnight, ring any bells in science and pharmaceutical laboratories?

No! that human conceit, narcissism and self-aggrandisement from out of the deluded human ego, was the final straw in the spiritual workings of primordial Nature and the karmic influence that comes out of, 'got it wrong' human beings and stuffs it up, he had to go in other words. With a little help from other also, 'got it wrong' human beings, of course. For that is the way the, 'as we sow, so do we reap,' karma system works in our species. Because Nature's primordial archetypal intelligence, (the primordial gods), does not dictate the demise of human beings. It is the 'critical mass' of our own destructive created karma, that eventually triggers our exit through the law of cause and effect.' As in, as we sow so do we reap the influence (karma) created out of our thoughts, deeds, and actions.

Clarification: It is our human-created karmic influence, that enters Nature's interactive primordial spiritual workings, and either compliments its archetypal intelligence or degrades it. That Laws of Nature governed system will only take so much human degradation, then in boot camp language, its 'pop goes the weasel time' in the 'got it wrong' individual and collective affairs of humankind. It is only the primordial archetypal power of exceptional talent, that born gifted human beings have a say in and often, become lost in it. Born gifts and natural talent that comes out of the primordial gods (archetypal intelligence) of Nature at conception and birth and not afterward. What we do with born gifted IQ and exceptional talents etc. (that human beings immaturely worship) is our power ... our human responsibility. Thus, a double-edged sword in the primordial system that underwrites those born gifts.

Explanation: When destructive karmic influence reaches critical mass in the spiritual system that underwrites life, those responsible find out that they are mortal and not invincible after all. As they often come to believe, through much success in their field of material accomplishment and its human worship. Because accomplishment acquired out of destructive not life-supportive deeds, eventually reaps the accumulating negative (therefore dissolving) cause and effect' karmic influence, from out of its created equation. Destructive karma retribution that comes out of the exploitation and manipulation of the weak by the strong.

So, the ego storyline goes, beware of self-aggrandisement, self-importance, human worship/adulation and gifted human beings that reflect its delusional conceit especially, those lost in its adulation and bowing status from others. Because conceit and self-aggrandisement, is the opposite of humility and dignity and humility and dignity, reside in the spirit and not the fragile ego, and a dissolvable media created and human worshipped saturated image. Therefore, appreciation, respect, and admiration for another, should always be reciprocal, mutual, dignified, and never one way. When it is not, then those worshipping and idolising other human beings for their born gifts and talents, have lost the spiritual plot of life in its ego sourced delusion. The not-knowing of the true source of born gifts and exceptional talent is human ignorance indeed to the primordial gods of Nature.

Prince Esarhaddon Finds a New Personality Profile. That Does not Include Being Second Best Within its Expression

The history tablets of the day record two versions of King Sennacherib's demise. Alf's guess is that there is an element of truth in both. The first declares that one of the extra-large statues … twelve tons to be precise, decided that it did not like the position human hands had placed it in, had a big tantrum and then decided to reposition itself in the statue overcrowded temple annex where the king was saying his prayers. Unfortunately, in that confined space, the statue of the winged bull got it wrong. Needless-to-say, the king suffered the congested statue consequences.

The second version and probably the most accurate was that the workforce engaged in positioning the statue had suffered so many hernias in the process, that they had to down tools for the day. Leaving it only partly positioned on its pedestal. In that mass exodus, contravening safety regulations by leaving the statue only partially propped up. Later that night with the help of unseen hands, human hands that is, the twelve-ton monolith decided to topple on top of the king as he was bending down comparing its attributes to his own. Thus, of course, that was that. Alternatively, as they say, down on the farm, "beware of the bull," all types?

Enter Prince Esarhaddon in the kingship stakes, after conducting running repairs to the bulldozed crown that is. To finally ascend the Assyrian throne at long last and do his kingly bit for progress. This, under the glowing watchful eye and approval of his very vocal mother. Who had also risen in rank and prestige, as befitting her new-found status in the scheme of Assyrian doings. Plus, with her alpha macho motor mouth attributes, making sure that everyone in earshot was aware of this sudden promotion, including the newly crowned King Esarhaddon.

Well, true to family tradition on both sides, King Esarhaddon wasted no time in picking up where his late brother had left off. After all, he had much catching up to do in the kingship trashing department, after spending many years in the minor prince-ship trashing department. This trashing escalation, after due consultation with his mother of course, Who was also making up for lost time in all departments of royal doings. Yep, it was a real commercial buzz to be giving all the orders and, "upping the ante." As they say in the Ides of March configured corporate boardrooms and political party rooms.

However, alas, as so often happens to those in the power game that achieve high status, it eventually goes to the head, and occasionally, other parts of their anatomy. Some in the progress driving seat begin to implement what they like and not what others like, with their acquired power. Enter ego delusions of grandeur and self-importance, along with a dominant alpha, "just do it or else," philosophy. A, 'got it wrong' dominant alpha philosophy, that eventually becomes a disastrous self-inflicted pitfall into the abyss of ignominy. An ego created ignominy out of conceit and abuse of acquired power in the land. A re-occurring karmic triggered ancestral nemesis in high places, that always indicates human weakness, incompetence, character flaws, and the sprouting seeds of megalomania in the administration and responsibility of power.

Note: Along with, the inevitable saturated media conducted post-mortem of the vanquished. Headline news repeatedly played in the public ear, after the mighty have fallen off the precarious summit of fame, acclaim, status, and power. To be followed by public humiliation and ridicule. A fate that a once positive accentuated but now negative accentuated human being, often suffers worse than death, i.e., a humiliation in the public eye. The passing of time, ultimately healing the immature power consumed dominant alpha ego responsible for the ignominious exit and perhaps for some, knowledge gained from its ego crunching experience, maybe?

Time out of our Assyrian Story, for Spiritual Facts on the Profile of the Negative Accentuated Psyche. Along with Other Associated 'Detention Room' Topics

For those fallen from great heights, power afflicted with an ancestral inherited negative psyche at birth, emotions, remorse and public disgrace have little meaning because they are trapped in a pathological/karma inherited psychological disorder divorced from the *order out of chaos* function of the Laws of Nature. Where feelings and emotions have no divine spiritual connection in a negative human psyche afflicted with psychopathy. Where differences of opinion with a born positive psyche, unconsciously (instinctively) ignites instant contempt, sarcasm and malice, hate and instant or delayed vindictive reprisal. Thus, do both the born negative and the acquired negative psyche, exhibit similar sociopath patterns of behaviour in a volatile confrontation, but for different reasons. One acquires their subliminal sourced anti-social behaviour from out of an unloved damaged childhood, while the other is born with this destructive ancestral inherited bent, that triggers sociopath, psychopath and violent tendencies.

Note: The remedy to dissolve the problem is the same for both, i.e., correct meditation, some long overdue soul searching and no access to power in a nation. Especially for a born negative accentuated human being; that acquires and accumulates primordial power through the exploitation, manipulation, subjugation, domination, and forced control of others. Along with doing whatever else it takes to acquire and retain power in society, such as the 'trademark' of megalomania. A psychological disorder that always goes unnoticed in human affairs, until it is too late to stop the rot that they create in those affairs. As a negative result, all the king's horses and all the king's men, will not be able to put that afflicted nation (or organisation) back together again. It decays and collapses into chaos just like civilisations - got it?

Explanation: A highly intelligent born negative psyche with the *dominant alpha* affliction of megalomania, often becomes a magnet to the downstairs acquired negative psyche. Who unconsciously, become subservient to the created reality of a powerful, charismatic alpha mind, from out of synchronicity of similar consciousness. Because the downstairs acquired negative psyche, is magnetically drawn to the born negative psyche, through the influence of a destructive shared ancestral entity. A phenomenon, where 'like is attracted to like' in Nature's primordial spiritual workings. A destructive entity (life-force) that can also gain ascendancy in a nation's psyche and eventually, tip its collective into spiritual decay. Often leading to inhumane destructive expression in a military-dominated politically corrupt nation. Religion-fuelled fanaticism, violence, and hysteria, in a religion, dominated chaotic nation. Narcissism, corruption, and greed in a big business run nation. The common denominator, being a destructive ancestral entity that fuels a delusional euphoria. A contagious euphoria that captures the human mind and sends it off the rails of positive, structured logic and reason and into, the crowded negative entity domain of analogous Darth and Associates.

Past example:

The twentieth-century military and political lust for world power, expansion, and domination. An ancestral inherited karma driven megalomania delusion that fuelled the national psyche of Japan, Italy, and

Germany before World War II, sourced to a malevolent contagious entity, rising in ascendancy out of a powerful minority in those nations. To eventually gain political power and dominate the national psyche of a nation's people and control and influence its collective expression. *Synchronicity of consciousness* (natural phenomenon) that goes out of control in our species, when fuelled through human beings worshipping other human beings in society. Note the media and the growing phenomenon and psychological disorder of celebrity worship in our spiritually decaying civilisation.

Clarification: The accumulating karmic influence out of a human lived ideology and its created entity, is a primordial sourced power that a government or huge corporation, unknowingly possesses in Nature's interactive physical and spiritual workings. A karmic power (life-force) that influences the archetypal spiritual intelligence that is structuring the collective unconscious of a nation's people. In Nature's dictionary, it is called, 'follow the dominant alpha leader,' in a social species. A karmic influence that when negative, attracts a destructive ancestral entity out of the past destructive activity of humankind, to then contaminate lived ideologies and their created entities in the present affairs of humankind. A destructive entity out of the past that is drawn to the psyche (unconscious mind) of those who have an ancestral affinity with its human created destructive entity.

A present example:

The contagious all-consuming greed and acquisition that now dominates the national psyche of affluent consumer driven nations. The negative karmic influence of which, has grown into a powerful contagious entity, from out of greed driven big corporate global business and the money markets, who now directs the world's consumer direction and present destiny, also called the global economy. It is their greed created entities that have attracted destructive ancestral entities out of the past to claim the present. A combined destructive life-force that is fuelling greed, all-consuming expansion, exploitation, and corruption on this human trashed planet, from out of a euphoric delusion called the global economy and progress. A contagious global delusion being fuelled from out of the karmic influence of greed. Entrepreneurial big business greed driven activity that has spread like a virus around the world to contaminate all nations under the banner of the global economy. A greed created entity/influence that is underwriting the direction of big corporate business and economy obsessed socially blind governments alike. This is why they have become an amalgam in their thinking and direction.

Clarification: Greed and power consumed human beings in the business driving seat of the global economy, are fuelling this euphoric consumer delusion that is being called progress. Because making money, acquisition, and winning has come to be worshipped and followed instead of the creator on this planet. This ancestral inherited and acquired pathological/psychological disorder of megalomania drives the negative dominant alpha to conquer and win in order to acquire self-esteem and power. This contagious delusion is not normal behaviour for a human being, but ancestral inherited and indoctrinated behaviour in a human being. This re-occurring destructive nemesis (entity) has plagued all past civilisations. This greed and power megalomania and its euphoria are not found in a positive functioning dominant alpha, only in a negative accentuated dominant alpha addicted to acquiring power and control, adulation and fame. The silent means have been given, to dissolve this destructive ancestral entity that destroys civilisations. An ancestral created greed and power fuelled entity, that is underwriting the all-consuming global economy and of course, economy obsessed governments and big global business.

More About the Negative Accentuated Psyche Spiritually Speaking

The spiritual essence of a negative psyche has lost connection with its divine spiritual component and the Laws of Nature. A malfunction of evolution, that causes the spiritual essence of a human being, to become trapped in the negative planes of Creation with its evolution and rebirth cycle. Physical rebirth still takes place via the impersonal cosmic law of evolution to process and re-generate life, but positive spiritual evolution that requires divine Intelligence to augment is non-existent in a negative accentuated spiritual essence. That malfunction of human evolution is why the negative accentuated human being, instinctively opposes the positive accentuated human being. The comic book and movie never-ending plot of the goodies vs the baddies is sourced to this malfunction of human spiritual evolution; that human beings have created, nothing to do with the Creator of life.

Clarification: The inherited and acquired psychological disorder of megalomania, prevents positive spiritual development in a human being. A perpetuating devolution problem that is eventually rectified through a divine intelligence augmented, ten-thousand-year spiritual rebirth cycle. Then the spiritual evolution and rebirth cycle of a negative accentuated human being is terminated. What has caused the termination of that human spirit and its evolution, is the accumulating negative karma from not life-supportive deeds, generation into generation. The human cause and effect karmic influence of which, also becomes trapped in the spiritual family key signature located in the procreation planes of spiritual creation, i.e., the spiritual universe that underlies and underwrites this physical universe. What happens in one is bound to the other, through the karma processed law of 'cause and effect.' This inherited karma perpetuated ancestral disorder and its spiritually self-destructive nemesis, can only be rectified by the living not the dead. The silent transcendent acquired means to dissolve it, have been given.

Recapping the Ascendancy of the Negative Psyche in our Spiritually Decaying Civilisation

Subtitled: Serious stuff for those in the boot camp detention room.

A dominant alpha afflicted with this acquired and ancestral inherited karma sourced spiritual disorder gains primordial power through intimidation, control, subjugation, and the exploitation and manipulation of other human beings. A dominant alpha bullying trait, (primordial instinct), for power and control in society that is often camouflaged under the hypnotic veil of magnetic charisma and brilliance. A primordial survival instinct, (bullying) that comes in many forms of expression in our complex human species, to fuel the self-esteem of a negative psyche. When afflicted with the entity of megalomania and its psychological disorder, their whole life is geared towards conquering, possessing, winning, and acquiring power and control. They would see nothing wrong or perverse, in exploiting and manipulating others to acquire it. A delusion that becomes a destructive way of life where people and society, are all but pawns to be manipulated, exploited and used for personal gain and self-gratification. This all-conquering megalomania is fuelled by those who may well possess exceptional intelligence, but have no social conscience or sense of right and wrong. Only of winning and claiming the coveted crown of power through whatever means are available.

It is also a false premise, that brawn and muscle are the only trademark and expression of a negative accentuated dominant alpha human being. No, they come as male or female and in all psychological shades and forms of expression. When they possess the brilliant intellect and business or political acumen etc. then they are more of a devolution problem to society than their physical hands on the less intelligent counterpart. Because then, they acquire and gravitate to real power in a nation, through a destructive ancestral entity out of the past. Which invades the unconscious mind (spirit) of a power consumed dominant alpha, and that other less powerful like-minds are magnetically drawn too. To then also become the unwitting tool of that destructive ancestral entity out of the past — a phenomenon called, 'synchronicity of consciousness' in Nature's dictionary.

The past ethnic cleansing and insanity in Bosnia is a violent, malevolent example of this ancestral karma underwritten process, manifesting in a spiritually decaying nation. This re-occurring insanity is tied to a nation's past destructive violent deeds. The perpetuated karmic influence of which has the potential to ground out in a psychopathic negative psyche, especially, in those that have acquired political power in a nation. Death, destruction, corruption, brutality, and killing automatically follows. Rwanda is another recent example of this malevolent ancestral entity instigated genocide. A destructive entity that captures the negative psyche of both the visible, hands-on violent psychopath and the invisible intellectual hands-off behind the scenes psychopath. The latter, with the gift of high IQ and animal charisma, often escaping detection until it is too late and they and other like-minded individuals, have acquired the power to do what they like in a nation.

Explanation: This genocide mayhem is triggered through those who gain political power in a conflict-ridden nation through behind the scenes corrupt and violent means. Who become the alpha magnet, that attracts this malevolent ancestral entity out of the past to saturate the present population of a nation? Nor is it possible to communicate sensibly, with a corrupt regime under this malevolent influence. Those inflicted, only ever understand force, never reason. Once in a position of power, they become more and more intractable, unreasonable, delusional, paranoid, and unpredictable. It is the exposed psychological profile of the negative psychopathic dominant high IQ alpha, that often climbs to great heights of power in a corrupt conflict-ridden nation. One need only examine the often-hidden path they took to acquire power, to understand the negative psyche, psychology and destructive karma of that born gifted individual. Our history books are littered with them, books we never seem to learn lessons from, only to repeat what is in them, in more sophisticated global ideologies.

Example: Greedy all-expanding, all-consuming, all-controlling, big takeover corporate business, ugh! Comprehend that greed is a destructive created life-force (ancestral entity) that accumulates and creates a vacuum in the spiritual system that underwrites life. It is a human created destructive influence (greed) that is foreign to the Laws of Nature governed workings of life. When primordial Nature can no longer contain that destructive karma and its entity, then other cosmic forces that underwrite the spiritual integrity of primordial Nature, rush in to address it; disturbing the spiritual and therefore the physical, elements of the earth, air fire and water in the process. Thus, are many so-called, *natural disasters,* on this planet, invisibly fuelled from out of the accumulating negative, not life-supportive deeds of humankind. It is that accumulating destructive karma, that enters primordial Nature's archetypal spiritual intelligence. To then usurp the 'order out of chaos' function of the Spiritual Laws of Nature. Chaos and disorder is the result.

About Negative not Life-Supportive Thoughts, Deeds and Actions

In the spiritual system that underwrites physical life, what we direct towards others with our thoughts and intent, also returns as karma perpetuated influence on its human source. Therefore, it should always be positive karma propelled influence and not negative, destructive karma propelled influence, that returns to its human source.

For example:
    About the hidden dirty tricks and character assassination of opponents in politics. Using the Punch and Judy divisive creating news media and the gullibility of the electorate.
    Subtitled: *How to climb the political ladder but not the heavenly one.*
    Stage One: At every opportunity behind the political scenes, belittle and denigrate your opponents perceived character weaknesses. Make them up if you have too, it doesn't matter. If you persist, it will stick sooner or later, thanks to the media. Include emotional and physical vulnerabilities, past policy boo boo's and anything else your vigilant Becky Sharpe staff has dug up on them, that can add fuel to the Machiavellian plot. Then clandestinely feed its information via whisper and innuendo, to the tittle-tattle information hungry press gallery. Who will then saturate the public with its priceless information free of charge for you. Thus, do the job of long-term character assassination,

without you having to participate any further, except behind the scenes and at election time of course.

Stage Two: Make sure you use the commercial talkback radio and their guiding lights of society to spread the word. Then it gains unstoppable momentum from out of their know-all solve-all intellectual input to society. Thus, become a standing joke on the airways and byways of the big commercial business financed crap information highway. A very powerful political tool, indeed, for character assassination and destroying someone's credibility. Ask the corporations that pay handsomely for their motormouth skill at creating public perception and silk purses out of a sow's ears. Also, make sure your wine and dine the ego of the commercial shock jock or chat show host first, before implementing the campaign. Then all will go smoothly, mission accomplished.

Political postscript: Don't forget to reward, 'King of the commercial airways shock jocks' with a public achievement gong of some sorts afterward. Otherwise, you will end up on their verbal hit list next time around in the political election stakes. They are very sensitive highly-strung prima-donnas. They require much ego nourishment and public acclaim to prevent the disintegration of their created persona and bank balance.

The above political, psychological warfare conducted through the 24/7 media, has become accepted as normal in society. It is a created contagious karmic influence/entity that is very destructive to a nation and therefore, its people. Yes, it may well be considered as par for the course and something to be stoically endured within politics, but ultimately, it breeds cynicism and corrupts a nation's people with its negativity. Comprehend the workings and function of politics, must always have a positive karmic influence/entity accompanying it, never a negative, destructive karmic influence from abuse of power. That government destroys its integrity in the creative intelligence of primordial Nature, that is structuring its political entity (ideology) that in turn, is influencing for better or worse the national psyche.

In the above example, it is bad news for everyone. Because its growing destructive karmic influence, eventually attracts a destructive entity (ancestral created life-force) that lowers the collective consciousness of a nation. It is a negative political activity, that debilitates/obstructs the specific Laws of Nature, responsible for structuring *order out of chaos* in human consciousness and its thought process. Therefore, nothing positive can come of it. All in all, if we are lost in a negative devious Machiavellian activity, then we are lost to our divine spiritual evolution. Simply because there is no intuitive sense of right and wrong in its debilitation, only delusion we call winning, success, and progress. Such is the greed-driven direction of this world, led by big corporate business, carrot dangling science and irresponsible vote bribing re-election driven governments. Short term gain for long term loss sums it up for everyone because we all reap its returning destructive negative influence sooner or later.

We should understand that life is about upholding positive qualities, not creating negative, destructive qualities through abuse of acquired power and greed. It means those responsible, have lost the divine plot for being born, because trapped in that delusion, there is no evolution only devolution. Those trapped in this spiritual debilitation need to dissolve its destructive contagious karma before exiting earthly matters. At this point, the negative archetypal intelligence of primordial Nature has gained ascendancy in the affairs of humankind through this nemesis. That means, positive logic and reason, have become debilitated in the collective consciousness of humankind. That translates as no intuitive (spiritual) sense of right and wrong, is functioning in those afflicted with a negative accentuated psyche. The created reality and belief system of a negative psyche is also impossible to reason with - full stop.

Clarification: Trapped in the karma sourced debilitation of a negative psyche, those in positions of power and influence can do no wrong in their eyes. Comprehend the human being creates their truth and reality if powerful 'got it wrong' people convince everyone else that their reality is the truth, as their high IQ born gifted creative minds often do, then through its saturation on the public psyche from out of the media, it becomes perceived as the truth. That is the enormous and often abused power of powerful communication mediums in society. Therefore, able to create public perception and reality, through the saturated non-stop brainwashing of their presentations. Presentation and perception that they engineer, not the public.

That is why news and serious information should not come out of a commercial medium, but a neutral, unbiased sponsor free medium. This very grey area where self-interest is concerned is where the public paid for broadcasting medium, should come into its own. Because with its independence, it is not compromised by business entrepreneurs, politicians, and commercial corporations, whose only objective in life is in making money, winning the ratings race and advertising dollar, placating the product sponsors, being politically re-elected and acquiring power. Spiritless greed and power-driven ego activity that does not come from a positive psyche, but a negative debilitated human being divorced from the self-referral divine component of the spiritual Laws of Nature, which are responsible for creating and maintaining order out of chaos in life...and the human mind.

The Transcendent Acquired Cure for Negative (Not Life-Supportive) Thoughts, Deeds, Desires, and Actions and Especially, Megalomania, Narcissism, and Other Ego Sourced Delusions

> Note: Earplugs required again, for those not
> in the boot camp detention room.

Practice correct meditation and explore the word humility. Thus, absolution from destructive karma and associated entities must come from an abstract silence developed in the mind. Absolution is not to be found from another human being. As we have been led to believe, from the medieval papal church and its congested all is forgiven confession box. Comprehend, that no human being functioning out of the primordial structure of biologically created physical consciousness is that qualified. Absolution will come through acquiring abstract intelligence a silent transcendent acquired intelligence, that is cultured into the physical mind and spirit through correct meditation. Therefore, it is the individual that must create the silent means, not the church or the media.

In spiritual understanding, the Creator's absolute transcendent silent nature is divorced from physical Creation and its activity, even though it contains Creation and its activity. A paradox that only the *individual* can solve within them, from out of acquiring/culturing the Creator's abstract silence. To then also dissolve destructive karma and restore their positive evolution and intuitive spiritual connection, with the *order out of chaos* function of the Spiritual Laws of Nature. If we are not willing to follow that spiritual advice, then in Alf's boot camp speak, don't expect any favours from analogous finger pointing St Peter in the departure lounge at the end of the human day.

Clarification: Comprehend in the Divine System that has authored primordial life, we must earn the right to be called a human being. To then be given the spiritual divine means, to evolve further in Creation with our spirit. A positive accentuated human being does not subjugate, exploit, and conquer other human beings and Creation. They do not create weapons of mass destruction. They do not experiment blindly on other healthy life-forms and interfere with its ordained evolution. They do not manipulate and exploit other human beings and commercially prey on vulnerable minds re commercial television. They do not plot and scheme against other human beings re politics and big business. They do not prey on other human beings physically, emotionally, sexually, psychologically, scientifically, commercially or monetarily - ugh!

When we possess negative, destructive characteristics in our created persona, then we are not a human being in the all-seeing spiritual intelligence of Divine Nature. Only in this human worshipping, greed consumed spiritless world, are we considered a human being ... most certainly not in the next one. The silent means to turn this self-inflicted spiritually terminating destiny around and get on the right side of analogous St Peter have been given. Therefore, it is time to understand intelligence greater than our human intelligence and silently acquire it. Then we will come to intuitively (spiritually) understand what is right and what is wrong? What is negative and what is positive? What supports life and its evolution and what does not support life and its evolution? What is uplifting and what is degrading to ourselves and Nature? What evolves society up the ladder of consciousness and what destroys it. At this point in our spiritual evolution, many powerful, influential, very intelligent so-called successful people in the driving seat of progress, do not have a clue as to what makes them do what they do. That is why this spiritless world is in such a horrible mess. A human created mess (euphoric delusion) that is called creating progress for humankind.

Clarification:
Q: *What is meant by wrongdoing?*
   A: Human activity that does not support life and compliment Nature and its laws but unknowingly, degrades them.

   Note, as in the synthetically polluting, life re-arranging laboratory activity of the cloning, genetic, synthetic drugs, biotechnology sciences. The weapons of mass destruction, polluting space technology, and atom trashing sciences and not forgetting to include, the also spiritually blind, all-consuming private enterprise greed activity, of global corporations and the piggy banks financing it all. This ego and self-esteem driven delusion, of making money to acquire power and status, has also gone way past its use-by-date on this human trashed planet.

   Note: Because there is no such thing as big and large in Nature's spiritual dictionary, only in our human-created and incomplete dictionary; that, like human beings is dissolvable. Unlike the eternal divine Intelligence underwriting Nature and its perfect spiritual self-referral Laws, that those in the detention room on St Peter's finger pointing list, have no connection within their spiritually blind minds yet?

Postscript to those not on St Peter's finger pointing list:

To rectify this horrible human created mess (euphoric delusion) we are calling progress, we do not trash those responsible. Instead, we practice Correct Meditation as a collective in society and then Upstairs will dissolve the delusion. Without resorting to vitriolic rhetoric, malice, violence and anarchy and ending up on St Peter's finger pointing list, as another human 'got it wrong' delusion created negative result.

King Esarhaddon of Assyria Goes for Broke

Plus, social reflections on a repetitive media theme by Alf. Along with a Stephen translation of the Egyptian el Amarna historical tablets. It is politically clarified by the scholar Herodotus of ancient Greece.

Now in the meantime, back in the very affluent land of Assyria ... for some that is, as is the way of human progress, there had been much-heated discussion about expansion, innovation, progress, economics and where and whom to trash next. Spaced in between business lunches, numerous sessions with P.R. consultants (to create the right Media image) workouts in the corporate gym (to offset the business lunches) trips to the Akbad Grovel piggy bank (for investment advice). Then on to the B.C. up-market hairdressers, jewellers, beauty salon's (to pamper the ego), harp disco's and other extra-curricular activity and finally, afternoon chats in the family orchards ... or corporate boardrooms and political party rooms, as they are now called.

Note: All these very important human doings and state duties, being shared equally between King Esarhaddon, his royal mother, and the priesthood. Thus, so far so good insomuch as gaining power, but what to do with all the power. After all, unless you do something with it, what's the point of having it. No! There was nothing else for it, but to undertake a lot more trashing ... or expansion, innovation, and global acquisition, as it is called nowadays. Otherwise, it would not be right to stick the ego authorised caption, "Great" in front of the king bit, on the header of the royal tablet stationary.

However, as we know well, the great seldom learn from the past. No, they are far too busy creating the future, as is their prerogative and quite right too. After all, if you have acquired the clout in a nation, then it is your call, so bugger the rest ... as they have been heard to say in Assyrian politics. Because that's the way, the human created system worked in those far off days. Unlike now of course, in our new shining star-spangled system of democracy, image creating, spin doctoring and worshipping so-called successful/winning human beings. Where all have a say in society through its saturated communication mediums, providing, you are a worshipped winner or a commercial created product clone that is.

Thus, enter the non-stop talking Punch and Judy media circus, the St George of the masses. However, unfortunately, also trampling on everything sacred to Upstairs, in our great new-age revolution of equality and freedom of expression. Along with its do what you like, say what you like, act how you like, make up what you like, publish what you like, present it how you like, exploit it how you like, manipulate it how you like, trash it how you like ... if it grabs the attention of the public and sells that is. Compliments of the big business commercial component of the saturated media, functioning in anything goes hyperdrive. Consequently, then relayed back to the public minus integrity, social responsibility, humility, dignity and professional maturity, in the sociopath underwritten delusion of creating progress, freedom of expression and giving the public what it wants. That St Peter with the keys is highly allergic too and does not want at the pearly gates.

On second thoughts, purgatory applicable mostly to the reading, viewing and listening mediums, owned by global entrepreneurial corporate media barons and like-minded majority shareholders. Out of whom, has come a great cultural gift to society, i.e., the make-it-up-as-you-go-along gutter press and associated glossy garbage magazines, full of I love me product clones.

Along with its big brother, the equally out-of-control dead brain commercial TV, and say what you like radio stations also polluting the shared atmosphere of this beautiful planet, with its spiritually toxic influence and upsetting St Peter with the keys big-time.

Ditto, the great intellectual input of a commercial delivered plague, of I love me and my ego late-night chat show hosts. To then send humankind further into entertainment delivered chaos, psychological disorder and euphoric ego delusion. New age, worshipped, pampered, narcissistic motor mouths, that have a lot to learn from the positive, spontaneous qualities, of a past generation of night show hosts. Who were never offensive, obnoxious, and crude in their humour or maliciously sarcastic of others in society? Just plain good social/family fun and nice vibes to go to bed on. That was the golden age of television, before becoming lost to crudity, foul mouths, sexual degradation, obnoxious behaviour, anything goes entertainment and presentation, that has become entrenched in its industry.

Yep! Much glorious progress for humankind from innovative, anything goes if it sells, commercial broadcasting mediums. What a negative boon to society are commercial TV and radio stations, travelling on the Darth down-line to no-where land and taking society with them. Yes, the Assyrian kings would have been most envious of that commercial media power and its product endorsement clones in B.C times.

Interlude

My internal Upstairs fax is running hot. Hang on a minute; I will have to attend to it. Must be something important from the boss, I will just put this uncomplimentary conversation to you on hold. Unfortunately, I have not got a music tape, so this written one called, 'Media Town is Falling Down,' will have to do La La La - La La - La La La - La La La La - La La La La - La - La - La La La Oops La ... that's better La press 9 La press 1 La ... press 2 La ring ring, beep beep can I help you stop. Beep don't call us we'll call you stop. Beep get a life yourself stop. Beep it's my tea break stop. Beep Beep ... p##!!**$$ Oops!

Sorry about that, I'll switch this new age commercial promo tape off at the I.T. call on the...
...... moon ... ... splat. Oops ... Der ... La ... Corpo ... Bugge ... Wallbeet ... Foxnewt ... Skynewt...Walmat ... Pentagog ... .N.A.S.T.A ... Demcats ... Repugs.$$$$$$ ... .Oh dear, it's got stuck in the piggy bank orchestra pit again. Hang on, crash! bang! wallop! Ah, that's better. Techno peace and spiritual progress restored at last. That's got it by the bells, as they say on Notre Dame.

Normal services resumed:
Well, it appears Stephen has got his innovative techno statistics wrong. It is only if you are worshiped, gifted, talented, crude, obnoxious or a celebrity product clone, that you have a say in society through its media that carries any weight with it that is, you know, of any real importance. Because it is only the 1% of the 30% of the 100%, that is suitably gifted as a winner or suitably obnoxious as a winner, for mention in the news and tablet paparazzi. Being a distinct improvement on the B.C. of doing things ... because then, it was only 001 % of the population that had the clout in tablets. Plus, the king's wives, offspring and mothers-in-laws of course.

Anyway, the instruction from the Boss, for removing the existing exclusive top end of town playing field for winners within so-called democracy ... is, that everyone on the planet is to become a media created, famous or infamous celebrity something or other or a commercial product clone. Then we will all be equal winners, and really have a say, in how things are done on this big business commercial owned planet. Until then, we are not allowed to mention the word democracy or versions thereof, because the way the democratic system works now suites only the minority, i.e., the 24/7 media promo saturated successful winners, that fill the headlines, glossy magazines, and visual newsrooms. The opinions, lifestyles and created reality of which, directly influence the perception and direction of a nation, with its saturated visual and audio information, especially at election time.

Conclusion: A media delivered top end of town version of democracy, that has nothing to do with creating unity, equality, and progress, for those that are not media accredited winners. Therefore, democracy being delivered from a powerful media-saturated minority, living an exclusive affluent lifestyle in the top end of town. Compliments of entrepreneurial big business supplying the magic beans (called big bucks) to all the winners. Now obviously, not all the born gifted, talented, high IQ and big business and political minority running this world, are tarred with that ancestral inherited, I'm all right Jack brush, and its Darth supplied paint-pot of greed and power tinted with megalomania. There are positive accentuated, mature, empathic human beings in among them, but because of Darth and Associates taking over the progress reigns on planet Earth, they are fast becoming a minority.

The Enlightenment of Political Trashing

Time out for a translation of Egyptian tablets from the pen of Stephen, and to illustrate the current detention room topics of politics, business, power and megalomania.

Therefore, a short bedtime story for would be aspirants to the downstairs political and corporate throne. The following tall story, from a tablet translation of B.C political and priesthood shenanigans from the land of pyramids, where serious Darth doings are uncovered, in the reign of the gentle but revolutionary pharaoh Amenhotep (Akhenaten) the Fourth and his queen of the Nile, Nefretete or possibly Nefertiti (Stephen can't spell names).

The plot:

A tale of age-old courtly intrigue and of course, the usual eliminating process of some of its unfortunate participants. A tale straight out of the el Amarna collection of historical tablets washed and translated into the common English of stretched vernacular from the pen of Stephen.

Title:
　Don't just look at the hands of the clock, it's the big cogs inside that make them move. Alternatively, more succinctly, The 1353 B.C power and political game at Karnak in Egypt.

　Well, it appears that all was not well in the land of the Pharaohs around the 18th dynasty. Trashing that erupted onto front page news of the Pyramid Daily. After Pharaoh Amenhotep, had cause to write a long tablet admonishing the Egyptian god cartel, who evidently, were raking it in right, left and centre from all their entrepreneurial scarab and shekel rackets on the public? This entrepreneurial corruption via tricky dicky fiddles in the all-ordinaries temples, that formed the gathering place for the cult worship of animals and believe it or not, even insects.

　In fact, in those pyramid days, anything that moved was considered the fair game to stick in the temple as an idol moreover, if you could conjure the right chant, commercial promo spiel and keep a straight face, then it became very easy to make a few bob on the side. By removing its contaminating influence, (karma), in the scheme of the hapless happenings of human beings, who, even then, had developed that curious human lawyer propagated habit, of blaming everything that goes wrong with one human being onto other human beings.

Returning to the Hard Nose Message on Akhenaton's Tablets:

That stated bluntly, implicitly and categorically, that the vast pantheon of media created god cults, (now called celebrities), owned by the private enterprise scarab commercial priesthood, were to be disbanded. Moreover, starting from a week on Sunday, everyone was to contribute whatever scarabs they had left over after paying the tent mortgage, the chariot tax, the pyramid tax, the sand tax, the water tax and the GST on sandals and contribute to the pharaoh's retirement village. To be built up the Nile a bit at el Amarna, where in the future, everyone was to worship and chat to only one god in Amenhotep's new temple complex, that were dedicated to the sun.

Incidentally, coming back to sandal mania, if you had a sandal factory located anywhere near a pyramid maintenance site in those days, then you made a lot of scarabs and shekels indeed, from all the shuffling going on, that was all the time in those pyramid building days because they could not stop doing it in them over the millenniums. Even though they did not live in them and travel to Sirius anymore to do it, nevertheless, they still managed to do it somehow according to the archaeologists. 24hr pyramid repair business was all the rage then and believe it or not it is still in an oblique form of construction all these centuries later. However, it is now called the company structure corporate business in its new priesthood and the worship of highly paid winners.

Just like the tax on shoes, the automobile tax, the breathing tax, the taxed poor, and every other tax nowadays, we can blame it all on the pharaohs and their pyramids. Because they have the longest civilisation record for doing it and staying alive over three millenniums, and not one other civilisation from the past, got anywhere near the longevity of that one for doing it properly. So, they must have been doing something right with their Egyptian version of taxation. However, what exactly they spent it on for the public benefit, apart from those pyramid departure dwellings to the heavenly bodies, has still to be sifted from out of the quicksand of V.A.T. G.S.T. meantime big time in this century ... if you follow my progress drift?

Coming back to our gentle Pharaoh Akhenaten and the not so gentle priest cult corporate scarab worshipping brigade. Who had their piggy bank fingers in the pie of anything and everything they could make shekels on ... and who, were not very impressed with the hieroglyphic content of the pharaoh's hard nose tablet one little scarab? However, grin and bear it they had to because it was the pharaoh that had the official tablet clout in those pyramids and insect worshipping days.

Thus, the disgruntled corporate priesthood had to cease their shekel corruption of the all-ordinaries index and its innovative lawyer and accountant instructed mumbo jumbo, along with their monopoly on scarabs and worshipping them. Therefore, they had to shut up the corporate shop in their tall pyramids and adhere to the official tablet command post-haste. Otherwise, they would all be issued with government issue sandals and seconded into pyramid repair business forthwith, (Egyptian equivalent of the salt mines). Just like all hierarchical institutions that govern nations, the negative plotters and schemers sociopath club was alive and well in B.C times, among the successful high achievers in its pyramid workings. The clandestine activity of which is called unofficial clout big business as opposed to official legitimate clout big business.

The analogy of which, is like the rotating hands of the Big Ben clock, that we look at for reference of position. However, it is the unseen inner cogs, that do the work and rotate the hands. Thus, the power that drives the visual aspect lies in the machinery of big cogs and little cogs that produce the motion, and when the cogs go out of sync in a clock, then so too must the hands.

B.C. Interlude:

A further tongue-in-cheek, political and pyramid learning tablet from the ghost of the Greek historian Herodotus, not Stephen. Entitled, Wind-up Time. Alternatively, positive cogs versus negative cogs and their ticking hieroglyphics.

Now, unlike the fixed workings of clocks, in the human analogy of ticking, big cogs are constantly juggling amongst themselves for the position of Chief Cog of Works. A very high priesthood position to hold in the machinery of wheeling and dealing, fixing and unfixing, rotating and back-pedalling. Plus! Having two bob each way in the shaping of government policies, corporate enterprise and of course, the ultimate prize, namely, the power of attorney of whatever global pyramid institution or political department you have aspired too.

Note: Having overcome all opposition by fair means or foul, on the golden staircase that leads to the chamber of corporate or political cog glory, to then be crowned, (or flogged), by the truculent french-fried mischievous very political educated news media. In that glorious double achievement, to then receive its ultimate reward, which is to give all the instructions and direct the whole show, from within the ticking mire of human progress.

But, as so often happens to attain big cog potential, you must spend a political ticking lifetime, making sure that no one else beats you to its attainment ... and, it is that oily Machiavellian activity along the way, that develops those very bad and nasty human habits of megalomania, paranoia, egoism, self-aggrandisement, delusions of grandeur, pomposity, and hubris. Along with narcissism, self-importance, and self-esteem, to preen the Teflon coated ego. So that when the gold loo status of Chief Big Cog is achieved, then no effort is spared in devious enterprise and very clever manipulated doings, to retain the dual seat of fame and power. Pivotal activity that sooner or later, results in repeating the 'Humpty Dumpty syndrome' ... you know, *"all the king's horses and all the king's men, couldn't put the political clock back together again."*

Now, you do not reach gold loo status in the corporate and political fraternity, unless you have the born alpha power and control talent, the educated tablet and the gift of the product gab for it and of course, like all machinations within the collective human enterprise and its inevitable Shakespearean drama, there is pain in the butt Machiavellian big cogs versus pleasant integrity plus Queensbury rules big cogs. The former in the history books remain invisible in the clock, to ultimately acquire the upper hand over the Queensbury rules cogs in its duel workings. Ultimately, causing its workings to go out of sync and self-destruct via the following pivotal points of negative ticking character and very oily means.

About the Sprung Perpetuating Political Big Cog Business

(Earplugs required again, for those not in the detention room).

1. An impenetrable, impervious, non-denting Teflon coated ego. Acquired from a corporate diploma in the art of opportunism

and using a divide and conquer the electorate big-bucks product strategy. Example: When in high office, delude everyone in the nation including yourself, that you are unimpeachable and the pillar of integrity and honesty, then at election time, find a social issue that you know will divide the public and cause much disunity, selfishness, pettiness and small-mindedness in the public clock. Then, surreptitiously with a smiley face and Pontius Pilate hands, promote it through the commercial media. p.s. Most importantly, make sure you are on the side of the majority, or you will find yourself out on your ear when it comes to public vote counting time. National, racial, religious, ethnic, them and us and I'm alright Jack orientated issues are best for accomplishing the winning sprocket result, i.e., re-election and the orb of mandate to clout the opposition and media with, when they get up your nose at question wind-up time in the house, re your integrity and negative Machiavellian political or business brinkmanship.
2. The charismatic alpha gift of the gab to say everything in general but nothing specific, especially when confronted by those mischievous political obsessed reporters in the national paparazzi, stoned out on adrenaline and editors' deadlines.
3. A PhD diploma in negative plotting and scheming, with an acquired A+ with distinction for public manipulation and devious ticking. p. s. Excellent job credentials for post-political corporate or piggy bank life in case things go wrong.
4. Articulate well-oiled lawyer sharp lip service, coupled to the forked sprocket, double speak.
5. A hidden, "iron mask," disposition armed with concealed razor-sharp cogs, for automatic crunch rectification and removal of anyone that gets in the way of obtaining the executive /departmental/ political gold loo key.
6. The smoothed cogged diplomatic ability, to temporarily cascade over troubled waters among the irate cogs in the commercial shock jock fired-up electorate. By the PR easy fix image exercise, of throwing small increments of scarabs at complex social

problems. (From the people's purse, of course, otherwise known as the treasury). Alternatively, employ outside freelance oily product cog academic experts on a mammoth very expensive, very lengthy tablet exercise. To then complicate, confuse, and compound the ticking problem even further. Thus, wash your hands of its responsibility and pass the buck on so to speak and highly recommended.

7. The acquired art of feigning great indignity and affront when personal integrity is questioned, aligned to the back-up art of quickly capitalising on and using for self-promotion, the positive ideas that flow naturally from a Queensbury rules cog. Also, if things go wrong, then smugly and with tongue in oil can explain with Pontius Pilate lawyer precision, that it was not your fix-it idea in the first place.

8. Acquire suitable top end of town contacts from within big pyramid product business, for indirect re-election sponsorship, social invites, and perks downtown, business lunches, junket trips here there and everywhere, free tickets to the Olympics, ball games and other extras. Plus, the indirect payment of conference expenses and future very expensive election PR advertising. Not forgetting open access to the commercial image-making experts, that construct and fabricate the respectability shield within the cut and thrust, razor-sharp cogs of private enterprise corporate affairs, political business and the public eye, in glossy perception creating magazines. p.s. They tell big product porkies too on occasions, for the corporate, private enterprise interest, of course.

9. Acquire the superb smart lawyer's art, of negative inference, (reverse psychology), when all else fails to convince the public jury of your negative product winning logic. Plus, able to juggle facts and figures at the speed of light, to suit all occasions and confuse questions of accountability, questions of competence, questions of complicity, questions of integrity. Which become incidental, immaterial and unimportant, along the double ticking

path of its cerebral corporate learned game. Ultimately, come up with an unbeatable double speak cog to convince even the Arch Angel Gabriel himself, that the moon is made of pink cheese and marsh-mellows.

10. The possession of a political Oscar, for acting superbly in monochrome when under extreme verbal wind pressure, from technicolour political dust storms that suddenly appear from no-where in the media. Along with the oily vocal cords, to smoothly procrastinate and recover with superb lawyer precision and touché timing, when you make a policy boo boo and must backpedal fast on a contentious issue. Very important to develop, for survival purposes in an inevitable media conducted political post-mortem.
11. The dominant alpha bottle to implement your policies and sell-off public assets via the back door of clandestine wheeling and dealing with outside like-minded big pyramid business cogs. This, after the public has become suspicious of its intent via a departmental leak, that those nosy press cads have been supplied with from a Queensberry rules whistle-blower. Correspondingly, the front door having been temporarily closed by other Queensbury rule cogs, doing their integrity bit and shouting foul and oiled up.
12. The ability to have a sudden memory lapse, when sprung and held accountable for nefarious clandestine doings that you have not covered up properly, or that your aids have not covered up properly, due to a shortage of machinery oil.
13. The J. Edgar Hoover Bureaucrat technique of a one-way intercom system. Thus, avoid answering as few questions as possible from the Queensbury rule cogs. Plus, build your ticking warehouse to store the personal information files on anyone of any importance in the land. These to be used if any nuisance irritating nosy academic busybody, should question your absolute power to do what you like in the land. Very important to have in this corporate, private enterprise owned commercial product world.

14. Alternatively, the political alternative when in a tight spot: Grin like a Cheshire Cat and maintain a continuous, monotonous, expressionless, emotionless, low tone diatribe of long words, statistics and oily waffle (verbal diarrhea). This to wear everyone down and bore them into submission and sleep on the less than ticking opposition benches. Highly recommended at 'question time in the house' and when back peddling from political boo boo's when confronted by the media the day after its seizure.
15. Blame anything and everything that goes wrong on your predecessors. Very popular this one and highly recommended and for the very clever lawyer sharp politician, don't forget to compile a psychological weakness profile tablet on all the Queensbury rule cogs. So that you can nuke and neutralise them when debating in the house and highlighting their character flaws at media question time. Many leadership points acquired here and the Punch and Judy news media, revel in it and become excessively over product lubricated in the public clock as well.
16. Alternatively, for the bumptious, ego seized, self-opinionated ratchet-hatchet cogs, that have become heady with oily power and lost in mandate reform disease along the way, and is the eventual cause of a sudden free-fall to cog ignominy with all gold loo aspirants. Namely, the Darth ticked delusion, to blindly assume that what you are oiling the clock with through tricky dicky devious, manipulative means, e.g. clever use of the media and abuse of political ticking power. Along with a barrage of negative cog and sprocket lawyer learned inferences and innuendo, on the cog character and credibility of those who question your waffle and hypocrisy ... ego wheeling and product dealing ... coercion and hidden dirty tricks ... intellectual head kicking of honest dissenters in the clock ... bribing sections of the media duped non-ticking public for votes with big oily bucks. Along with turning a convenient political blind eye to the ticking methods used by associates, when it suites the party or company position to do so. Finally, by clandestinely covering up or verbally

whitewashing, other cronies, counterbalance mistakes and gross admin blunders. That is all done in the best interest of everyone in the clock and outside of the clock. What a pain in the public clock, the political clock and the Laws of Nature clock sums it up. Wrong oil producing wrong ticking?

17. The cog prudence and oily survival foresight, to acquiesce now and then to other ambition consumed big cogs on the dominant alpha power crunch ladder. Thus, proving you are magnanimous and not power mad or a potential threat to their cog aspirations, on the same political or business crusade to acquire the holy grail and gold loo status.

18. Acquire a special oily phone card for access to the PR fix it brigades. i.e., the verbal diarrhea, super oily, lawyer sharp, dominant alpha spin doctors. Who have built their own power pyramid inside the main pyramid and cerebrally, not physically, take care of all nasty nuisance problems of unity in adhering to the political or business cog line. Whose verbal tenacity and alpha powers of persuasion makes a party whip look like a muted tailors shop dummy in comparison.

19. Finally, when you have learned your oily craft well and reached the pinnacle of Big Hand status, then surround yourself with similar cerebral ticking cronies1, but of lower voltage, in the ambition cog stakes. Carefully selected from the supposedly all-mates together party clock for back up and to act as the quarter chimes. Along with shouting cuckoo and oil yourself to the opposition, at appropriate sprocket intervals during house wheeling and dealing time, and as a last resort, use them as patsies and cannon fodder when the Party clock finally blows up and goes boiing! This, through the clandestine antics of other talented oily cogs climbing its jewelled workings of power and sneakily, re-enacting the Ides of March. By throwing a well-aimed clock spanner in your over oiled works, i.e., doing their own thing in the political clock and not your thing in the party clock. Thus, relieving you of the key to the executive gold loo suite in the process.

In big cog conclusion:

You do indeed have to be highly qualified in the fields of bureaucracy, politics, big corporate business and the oily perception creating PR arts and crafts, to be competent to bend and oil the pharaoh's ear. Alternatively, the public's ear, as it has now become in this expanded world of gummed-up political clocks and corporate oily smooth intrigue. Hooray for political and business progress, free-enterprise and strange versions of democracy in the pursuit of happiness.

This ends the very cerebral warped cog personality profile from the ghost of Herodotus.

The el Amarna Tablets Continued ...

Returning to the land of the pharaohs and the oily doings of their big pyramid cogs, the multiple ticking from which was beginning to count down the demise of Pharaoh Akhenaton from within the political, pyramid and kingship utilities.

Now unlike today and its worshipped product and celebrity creating progress and equality and prosperity for all, in those B.C days, it was customary to physically bump-off opponents in the game of elimination in high places and kingship. As opposed to today's civilised practice, of giving unlimited free travel cards, a whopping big super with fringe benefits, a stretched limo to go to all the dignitary scoffs, sports hero admiration parties, film star and celebrity ego discos and other human worshipped product expos. Along with having a status/image place on some Q-board to keep the wheels turning in the top end of town. Plus, the feet-up time to write their political memoirs and expound the truth of over-oiled politics and reminisce on old adversaries and their oily tricks and political party shenanigans.

Therefore, a golden ex-big cog opportunity, for a pay-back time within its numerous boring politically seized-up pages, i.e., receive a crude oil contract from Hollydude or subsidiary, to write the script for the next grumpy old men sequel. Thus, set the big cog record straight in its reveal-all pages of past high office intrigue, dog eat dog political gamesmanship, megalomania and frequent perambulations to the gold loo suite, from all the official product function banquets at home and overseas.

Indeed, the dark clouds of repetitive kingship fate began to gather ominously over the land of the pyramids. Because upsetting the people living outside of the lodge and party room is one thing, upsetting the priesthood who run it, is quite another. Thus, the atmosphere was made ripe for plotting and scheming, in the truth of the following well-known statement. *"You can upset some of the cogs some of the time, but not all of the cogs all of the time ..."* and, in that political wisdom, is found the ingredients for a click oil takeover opportunity and the big cog formula, to the success of all would-be political, corporate and kingship aspirants on the way to gold loo status.

Thus, the oily dye was well and truly cast for usurpation time in the pyramid clock. The people and the commercial media and their product clones, unhappy with idol/celebrity withdrawal symptoms. Likewise, the pyramid priesthood unhappy through scarab and fiddle withdrawal symptoms. Thus, perfect conditions for the removal of the annoying top cog responsible. After all, they would definitely not be missed in the pyramid scheme of things, by all who had a piece of the product action which was just about everyone at the top of the pyramid.

A conclusion, Archeo's discovered at el Amarna three millenniums later, when unearthing Akhenaton's scrubbed over and manually inverted pyramid complex. Sealed with the not very nice hieroglyphic epitaph, *"out of sight out of mind"*, scribbled on all his inverted tablets. Thus, few questions would be asked in the aftermath of Akhenaton's departure. In fact, whoever took over the big cog ticking in pyramid land, to restore idol, scarab, product and celebrity mania back into corporate and commercial media circulation, would be able to set their own pay-check, health benefits, credit card limit and pyramid plot for the hereafter.

Now, Pharaoh Akhenaton, may have been gentle natured but he was nevertheless, a warrior king from a long line of past warrior kings, who had restored law and order to upper and lower Egypt. Therefore, he was no slouch with the tools of trade or lacking in bottle to sort the mischief makers out. However, like all royalty, he liked his tipple, cocktail parties and after dinner mints. Thus, vulnerable to the age-old drink spiking game, a terminal game that has always been a very popular elimination sport throughout history within royal circles, the aristocracy, the priesthood and political cogs. Very convenient you see, no mess or dismembered body parts to clear up afterwards. That suites the manicured cerebral plotters and schemers perfectly. For political ones, do not like a mess of any description only the cerebral games they arrange for others to enact.

A.D Political Interlude

Title: A negative peek in the dominant alpha owned chameleon mirror.

Yes, they are even more active in A.D. times. Although, soon to follow the fate of the Dodo. Unlike the genuine positive alpha Queensbury rule cogs in the political system, that need winding up and a little Upstairs spiritual maintenance, to once more gain control of the big hands in the political clock.

Cerebral alpha negative big cogs are very orderly and precision like, in their sneaky oily power and control negative deeds. That they do not end up committing themselves but, prefer to rope-in other less intelligent cogs into the plot to carry out the terminal ticking for them. Thus, keeping their well-manicured nails clean. This devious and manipulating Machiavellian activity comes from a megalomania pickled negative dominant alpha cog, functioning from the other end of Creation. You know, down there in analogous Beelzebub land. They are otherwise known as the big cog plotters and schemers club, located at the top of the pyramid.

Cerebral bad dudes are very clever in one way, but very stupid in another simply because they play the short-term game for gain and not the long-term game for gain. Because all karmic influence that we create out of our thoughts and deeds returns to us sooner or later in the real world. As opposed to the delusional world, of the power consumed cerebral delinquent plotter and schemer. Along with other negative sociopath cogs in the public and political clock attracted to them. Who firmly believe, that you must be caught to receive retribution in the scheme of mortal doings.

However, Lesson No 1. In Nature's primordial clock, because *as we sow so do we reap* in its karma ticking workings.

Therefore, when you have been a sociopath naughty cog with the exploitation, manipulation and degradation of other human beings, then its retribution always comes back with big negative and dissolving karmic interest on top. A justice that is but a spiritual law of karma operating in the spiritual evolution of human beings. A spiritual processed fact, that has nothing to do with transcendent God, but comes out of the creativity of the thought process and actions of human beings. That inescapable law of karma allows human beings, to evolve their consciousness *up* the spiritual ladder of evolution from their own actions. However, only when those actions are life-supportive to Nature, its Laws and other human beings. Summed up, as oil for thought and re-assessment for some on this human greed trashed planet.

Returning to the Final Act in our Short Bedtime Story

Thus, who did what and when remains a mystery in the plot. Perhaps best left for Agatha C. or the Pink Panther to sort out. However, seventeen years into Pharaoh Akhenaton's reign, the corporate priesthood ascended the nearest pyramid in their fashionable Nicky sandals, to announce with great gusto, the royal swan song of the pharaohs. *"The hawk has flown to heaven, and another stands in his place … it's party time"*. Albeit with a little human help along the way, of course. However, then as now, things tend to happen magically in threes, and it came to be, that Akhenaton's brother Smenkhkare (or maybe Nefertiti in disguise) came to take his place on the royal pyramid pedestal and guess what? Surprise! Surprise! Three years later they also took to the heavens on assisted passage, with a little extra Earthly help.

It then became the turn of Akhenaton's grandson (maybe?) Tutankhamen, to try his luck at staying alive. On what had become a very precarious, self-ejecting, unpredictable and terminal throne of unnatural ticking causes indeed. Inevitably then, it came to be that after reaching his eighteenth year and when Tutankhamen, would have begun to wield the real cog power on the throne, that he too departed to the increasingly congested heavens. This via a smaller chariot to the skies, also with a little extra human help along the way.

Now a strange twist of cogs began to unfold in the political machinery of our tale of many pyramids. Enter the oily chameleon character of Mr. Ay' into the throne re-circulating big cog business. A common old court official of all things, tut, tut. Nevertheless, a supposedly great advisor, councillor and chief cog of works of the royal household for many years. Who, it turns out, eventually married under much tablet protest from her, one of Akhenaton's daughters, namely princess Ankhesenam? Mind you, even though he was old enough to be her grandfather. Very suspicious indeed one might say from a safe distance of centuries of course and obviously determined to own a pyramid of his specifications one way or another.

Note: But unfortunately, Mr. Ay' must have also had a big spat with the priesthood and got up their noses. For he too, shortly after making it to gold loo status, ascended to the skies in an assisted chariot. However, I believe that he went to the other end of the big cog galaxy, where it was even more congested. Nevertheless, according to the Law of like attracts like, they took him in to help with stoking the busy Darth created boilers.

Now meanwhile in Earthly human matters, who should step into the palace grounds but the Egyptian army in the big cog attire of General Horemheb. Another one of those over the top ambitious sprocket commoners, tut tut again? This to restore law and order in the pyramid clock of course. Along with a bit of self-promotion surprise! Surprise! And conduct manual repairs to the ejection mechanism of the busy throne.

Thus, slow down the accelerating ticking of the pharaoh removal business, one that had become a bit of a bad cog joke within neighbouring nations of late.

In historical fact, it was to be a strongly worded tablet from a delegation of Mitanians, Babylonians, Assyrians, Alshians and Hittites from vassal nations, that had prompted General Horemheb, to take big cog action in the first place. The translated hieroglyphics from which, infers that they were fed up with having to hike it over the sand dunes to Cairo every five minutes, to stand in the blazing sun and have their brains addled saying hello and goodbye all the same time, with no full stops in between. Moreover, worse, wearing out expensive ceremonial stretched chariots in the sand dunes along the way. Paid for by the public purse in their nations of course as is the way of taxation progress.

Being a very smooth big cog and an expert oily wheeler and dealer to boot, General Horemheb accordingly obliged them all. Thus, did a lawyer underwritten survival deal with the pyramid priesthood and promptly restored idol, celebrity, scarab, product and shekel mania back into the public clock once more. Which, as we know through the workings of prohibition in a nation, had naturally gone straight underground into the dens of bad corporate cogs in pyramid land. Therefore, becoming even more of a hidden ticking curse to Pharaoh Akhenaton, in his royal order to stamp it out of public circulation in the first place.

Thus, it came to be, that General Horemheb having done a survival deal with the pyramid priesthood, then officially restored the previously banned corporate backhanders, big cog corruption, oily doings in the all-ordinaries temples and just as importantly, returned idol, celebrity and scarab worship back into public circulation. Thereby keeping everyone happy and content in pyramid land in the pursuit of their happiness and the good life. The only drawback being, no one made it to Sirius anymore in the afterlife and Darth and associates, have been clapping their hands in the departure lounge ever since.

To Sum up this Tall Tale of Political Intrigue and Offer Advice to Ambitious Alpha Cogs, also on the Path to Gold Loo Status in Modern Pyramids

Firstly, don't sit on the ticking throne too long, especially the political one. It may give others the impression you want to stay on it.

Secondly, do not trash anyone on the way to sitting on it. It causes public ejection problems and you are flushed down it sooner or later.

Thirdly, become a teetotaler and take along your own bottled water to all those cocktail parties, celebrity banquets and dignitary scoffs; that is a necessary stopover along the way to power, fame and status and you may reach it without terminal indigestion from the news pickled Media.

Thus, it is up to us, i.e., "the common folk" to make sure at election times in our respective nations, that we do something about the current divisive past-the-use-by-date political system and its so-called democracy, that can only function for the part and not the whole in its existing forms. Especially socially blind right-wing political ideologies that always favour the winners, elitism, egoism and entrepreneurial big business opportunism, located in the worshipped big end of town-ism. Because that inequality creating governing system, is just not working properly in its politicism, in the interest of this shared planet and all the non-winners on it. You know, the other trodden on 99%.

So, it is our responsibility as the untalented majority stakeholders in society, to shake off our indoctrinated product apathy and feelings of helplessness and ask for positive change. Change based on equality and not privilege and by so doing, create the political means to achieve that unifying status. That is your voting power, as an individual in a unified, harmonious collective, to materialise from out of an ordinary, mundane powerless existence. That miracle is the real progress, that will come out of the collective practice of transcendent meditation in a nation. Therefore, equality creating progress containing the power of divine Nature's spiritual intelligence that no primordial underwritten minority, however rich, gifted and powerful, can usurp.

That miracle is only possible, when requested from within a positive unified field. It is not possible when everyone is asking for different things within it. Along with those doing their own ego and power thing, in the divisive factions that make up our political spectrum and fuel dirty tricks and political skullduggery — along with constant political infighting, wheeling and dealing and jostling for power and top dog status. Negative activity that has become normal and par for the course in power politics and so-called democracy. Immature ego-driven activity that creates a negative *cause and effect* karmic influence in Nature's primordial workings. A destructive karmic influence that returns to debilitate the consciousness of everyone in a nation. Only in that sense, could it be called democracy in progress.

Clarification: Comprehend that Nature's Laws cannot function coherently in all that political divisiveness, manipulation, ambivalence and chaos. For chaos, is exactly what it represents to the self-referral Laws of Nature, structuring our quality of consciousness and creativity. Human creativity and expression, that is currently not life-supportive through abuse of power and insatiable greed in the top end of town. No, it is time to move on from the existing system of divisive, immature, manipulated, ego-driven party politics in governments. Its ideology has gone past the use by date in human affairs, along with the equally dysfunctional manipulated processes and hidden dirty tricks, to win an election and claim the political crown.

Therefore, the government gained from hoodwinking the public through abuse of power and bribing elements of the electorate for votes. Along with millions of wasted dollars, that is poured into saturated negative advertising of opponents. Donation money that is used to put a political party into power. Money that indirectly or directly, comes from the hip pocket of big corporate business. Aided and abetted by professional highly remunerated lobbying groups and spin doctors galore, also paid for out of the coffers of big corporate business. Thus, proliferates the age-old. "You scratch my back, and I'll scratch yours," in politics and big business.

Note: Comprehend all that big buck saturation advertising, makes the equally dysfunctional advertising fraternity, private enterprise, commercial Media barons and image creating P.R. specialists, immensely wealthy indeed. It pours into their piggy bank account from political donations from the big end of town and then, comes back as tax deductions one way or another afterwards. It is called a win-win situation any way and every way, for big global, spread your options around the transnational corporate business. Whose motto, of, *"Never give anything away unless you get twice as much back and a bit more on top,"* is inscribed in gold on its global holy grail of winner takes all.

Kind Regards from Stephen, on behalf of the ghost of Herodotus of ancient Greece.

The Perpetuating Wonky Wheel Business. Plus, another Assyrian First, the Chariot Maintenance Schedule

Now, top of the agenda on Assyrian family and priesthood business, was the appeasement of the primordial gods. After all, unless they are on your side, it is an uphill battle to go on global trashing business. So, after much discussion in the family orchard (boardroom), it was agreed that restoration of the Babylon temples and their gods, was a top priority. All that remained was to decide on the means to finance it. Alternatively, rather, who was going to be trashed to obtain the cash to pay for everything as is the way of big global business financing. Thus, you must speculate to accumulate. Thus, obey the first law of global banking institutions, that states, you must always use other people's money, if you wish to stay healthy - wealthy - wise and leader of the pack, and successful of course.

The long and the short of it all was that within a few years a new army was conscripted and eventually kitted out with the latest low-tech trashing goodies on the B.C. weapons market. Then finally, with a pained hand wave and shekel worried look from el Akbad Grovel the third, took off to pay a visit to the Nubian pharaoh "Tarhaqa" living in

Memphis ... Egypt, that is. This trashing visit, to request a special fixed basis loan with no encumbrances which of course, means you don't have to pay it back and incidentally, well worth requesting from your corporate piggy bank manager, the next time you need funds to repay your fly by blown out credit card.

    Thus, it came to be, that after a little minor trashing along the way for warm-up purposes and weapons testing only, that King Esarhaddon duly arrived at the outer reaches of the Egyptian empire. Confident, that unlike his brother, who, if we remember, had got too big for his temple? That this time around, the primordial gods would undoubtedly be on their side. Thus, make sure the deal went in Assyria's favour. After all, the unencumbered loan was for the restitution of their temples in Babylon. Therefore he, the great benefactor, wouldn't be making a bean out of its restoration. Thus, in human logic, bound to be in their good tablets and therefore, be sure of high favour within their whimsical primordial moods.

King Esarhaddon Bows Out and "King Assurbanipal" the Cerebral Tycoon Steps in

However, just like transnational global corporations, King Esarhaddon in his meticulous, careful planning forgot all about the returning wonky wheel curse. A recurring nemesis that had plagued his alpha trashing dynasty over several generations. That, of course, had nothing to do with the whims of the primordial gods. However, the whims of its family members, jockeying for top dog status and pay-back time within family feuds. Along with the karma law of, 'As we sow, so do we reap,' as human beings. It is also called, divine justice and retribution in our human affairs, if not in life, then certainly at the end of it in the departure lounge.

    Although the history tablets of the day, do mention that chariots were extremely unreliable in those days, but no reason why. Must have been too technical for them, I guess. Alternatively, perhaps, it was wise not to conjecture too much in tablets if you valued your fingers and other parts of the anatomy. I expect the departed King Esarhaddon sorted it all out when he reached the undesirable other end of Creation in the afterlife. Along with a suitable explanation to his kinfolk, for the unofficial long-term loan of his brother's gold harp and other numerous family indiscretions.

Thus enter "Assurbanipal-the-Pineapple", the last of the great Assyrian trashing dynasty, otherwise known as "the tablet worm". A great tablet collector by all historical accounts and a very studious and business-like king to boot, as well as being a cautious one, concerning chariots that is and was well-known to be very fastidious bordering on the paranoia, before climbing into them. Thus, always examined their maintenance schedule with a fine-tooth comb before taking off on trashing duties. Thus, a wise and knowledgeable great king was he.

Now it could be conjectured although some in the top end of town may disagree, that part of the reason for King Esarhaddon's rapid departure from the scene of earthly matters, was due to do-what-you-like Hollydude and Co; not being around them. With its winning input of screwball, do all, show all, how to act classes in society, from immature socially irresponsible worshipped human beings. This to enlighten, educate and guide the masses, in how to behave in any given situation found in life and to perpetuate and eulogise all of humankind's acquired pathological, sexual, emotional, psychological and delinquent disorders through so-called entertainment. Plus, as a bonus, if you trashed/acted better than anyone else on the big screen, then receive a statue of a worshipped idol called Oscar and everlasting fame, adulation and big product endorsement bucks. However, some on the receiving end of this detention room dialogue may disagree with that uncomplimentary assessment of human entertainment progress, but not Upstairs.

Therefore, King Esarhaddon had never been to the movies and learnt how to act properly, at the cerebral corporate table of big business wheeling and dealing, human trashing and doing the big buck deal. Thus, he did not possess the corporate acquired to know how, the gift of the P.R. and promo gab, the unemotional deadpan expression, the

I'm in command face, the when necessary staccato vocal chords, the right body language, the steely resolve macho look, or the long pause effect bordering on disdain, when commenting on the boardroom agenda and talking to lesser mortals. Alternatively, perhaps from the el Akbad Grovel non-macho types, the smiley insipid insincere elbow grasp and a whisper to the extracurricular activity on the house, to seal the deal of course.

No! when it came to be convincing a would-be lender of the merits of his global trashing business venture, King Esarhaddon was an abysmal failure. It could be said that the Egyptians, were hard nuts indeed to crack on the matters of finance, lending and doing the trashing deal in those B.C. days. In the end, it took the ignominious exit of King Esarhaddon, along with the incoming super business alpha brain of Assurbanipal, along with ten battering rams and their combined corporate clout and an offer they could not refuse, to finally convince the Egyptians to cough-up the funds necessary to rebuild Babylon.

Thus, it came to be, that King Assurbanipal contributed yet another first in the history books of civilisations and culture. Namely, the cerebral big business thoughtful alpha trasher, as opposed to the thoughtless smash, grab and trample big business alpha trasher. Who, by the way, still exists in many parts of the now big business owned world and still enjoy minor success; however, are considered rather inferior and decadent to the newly evolved smiley faced strain, that has sprung to life through the commercial marketing media and Hollywood education? This obvious difference recognised through not being politically correct in their display patterns of greed and all-consuming acquisition and expansion, i.e., violence and testosterone, are out and brain matter and serotonin is in, so to speak.

The Passing of the Old and the Coming of the New. Global Corporate Trashing Business that is?

As far as business progress goes, King Assurbanipal has been greatly admired ever since. For his cerebrally administered less demonstrative trashing and its smiley contribution within big business Kingship and the corporate boardroom throne. For they have become a very prolific species and greatly admired and worshipped in the new-age kingdom of big corporate business. In fact, much tribute is laid at their global feet from other envious mortals and the news Media ... and for some with additional talent, other parts of their anatomy as well. However, that is another tall story that has yet to be written. Preferably by those not afflicted with its cerebral high-flyer corporate greed disease and its pathological dominant alpha disorder of megalomania. Otherwise, it will contain bias and not be acceptable in St Peters afterlife library. Only truthful books like this one end up there, or so I have been informed by non-media reliable sources.

As to the Tablet Fate of King Assurbanipal-the-Pineapple in the Scheme of Human Trashing?

By all accounts, through keeping out of chariots in particular and by spending a great deal of his time reading in the palace's extensive tablet library. The contents of which, amounted to thousands of tablets collected from other trashed B.C. Nations ... as is the way of human progress. Thus, King Assurbanipal survived a little longer on the Assyrian throne than his more extrovert family predecessors.

However, within a few years of his departure from dominant alpha conquering affairs downstairs, Assyrian culture and all its glorious achievements obtained through trashing other nations, had disappeared off the face of the planet. As is the karma sourced fate, of all those who exploit and subjugate others for power and control, greed and insatiable acquisition. But mankind has yet to make that negative alpha conquering connection, in the perpetuated WHY of deceased civilisation's. However, there is hope that we will one day make the ancestral inherited connection and finally, create Upstairs spiritual progress for a change.

The End.

Well maybe not, if we spiritually grow up and stop trashing this shared planet out of synthetic toxic pollution, conquering everything, winning at everything, greed, consumerism, insatiable acquisition, commercial product neurosis and worshipping, Media saturated winners and big bucks instead of the Creator.

Section Two

Spiritual Boot Camp Information and Recipes for Creating Spiritual Progress

(Subtitled: Believe it or not)

Q: What is a positive life-supportive ceremony?

A: In spiritual understanding, protocol, humility and definition, it means respectful, quiet acknowledgement for the gift of life and the composite universal divine Intelligence that created it. It is fused with dignified, sincere thoughts and actions. Be it to the abstract uninvolved transcendent Creator the Absolute? Be it to a holy enlightened human being functioning out of absolute consciousness? Be it to the active status quo divine spiritual intelligence of this Creation the composite cosmic mind of almighty Nature? Be it to the impersonal spiritual archetypal primordial intelligence of Nature, underwriting the biology, sexuality, procreation and chemistry of life. Be it to silently acknowledge, the spiritual elements of Earth, Air, Fire, Water and Space that have also been called deities, in the history of humankind.

Clarification: Space, that is spiritually understood, as the inner and outer (physical and spiritual) invisible fabric of Creation. Creation that has three separated yet interconnected multi-faceted attributes/realities of intelligence and consciousness underwriting its existence. Namely, 1. physical biological intelligence and its consciousness. 2. spiritual intelligence and its consciousness and 3. absolute intelligence and its silent transcendent acquired consciousness. 1. and 2. have manifested out of 3. that is transcendent and inactive, in its silent absolute eternal value and reality. All are silently complimented, in the simple twice-daily twenty-minute practice of Transcendent Meditation.

In spiritual reality, every component of Creation, including Creation has manifested out of one absolute creative vibration the OM. That one primary manifested vibration, sources all the innumerable hierarchical arranged, individual creative non-physical vibrations, that are underwriting both spiritual and physical Creation and its duel evolution. It could be said in spiritual terminology, that the intrinsic form and substance of physical Creation is sourced to innumerable, creative, subtle spiritual vibrations. Underwritten by the self-referral Laws of almighty Nature, creating *order out of chaos* in the totality of Creation.

The spiritual interactive Laws of Nature that are the invisible *Government of primordial Nature* responsible for its physical and spiritual evolution. Continuous evolution, being the whole purpose of Creation and its diversity. Therefore, however fast, however slow, however imperceptible, there is nothing in Creation that is not in the ordained process of evolution governed by the Laws of Nature. Note existing spiritually blind science and synthetic drugs and gene and cloning technology, constantly interfering/experimenting on/changing/re-arranging/altering the physiology and chemistry of life and therefore, its pre-ordained evolution via the self-referral Laws of Nature.

In further spiritual understanding: Five of those cosmic all-encompassing elements/energies/vibrations could be called the primary divine gods (deities) underwriting the innumerable secondary primordial gods of almighty Nature. Namely, the spiritual composition of the physical planets of our solar system and its duel (Yin and Yang) negative and positive opposing archetypal spiritual intelligence; that primordial biological life and its chemistry and components, have *physically* manifested out of. All underwrite, fabricate, orchestrate and evolve, the primordial biology of life and its chemistry on this life-evolving planet, for the divine purpose of evolution of God's gods. They are the invisible interactive spiritual instruments of physical life. Alternatively, perhaps, life is the instrument of that interactive impersonal spiritual intelligence.

Either way, the above are all different active manifestations, of inactive absolute transcendent Intelligence or God, manifesting as the spiritual and physical substance of Creation and life. The ultimate unmathematical paradox, for the still-evolving human mind, to solve and be at peace with and not at war. The ceremony (practice) of transcendent meditation, eventually solves that paradox without thinking about it and without, decimating the atom and altering/polluting the chemistry of life with saturated synthetic drugs note science; that is currently locked up in their *physical-only* reality and human-created scientific words to describe it. Therefore, with only the physical half of the story/information of life missing its spiritual component of the other half?

Note: Because, as thinking creative human beings, we create all physical reality and the words to describe it, reinforce it, live it and teach it as well as create our individual and collective destiny, with its incomplete science knowledge. Spiritually speaking, science only understands and experiments on the physical component of Creation, therefore, existing science is incomplete with its acquired physical knowledge and is not, the gospel of all truth and infallible. A spiritual truth and reality, that physical science has yet to uncover, acknowledge and accept. They are far too scientifically absorbed and involved with the physical components of Creation and its reality, to acquire another non-physical spiritual reality from where everything physical manifests out of.

The 'Why' of Positive Life-Supportive Ceremony and it's Spiritual Purpose?

What quality of created influence (karma) comes out of our human thought, creativity and actions enters the creative spiritual fabric of Creation (i.e., God's gods) and causes a counter-reaction. Positive life-supporting karma in equals positive life-supporting karma back out.

Equally, negative not-life-supportive destructive karma in, equals negative, destructive karma back out, to eventually return to its human source. In further spiritual understanding, what quality of karma comes out of our thoughts, deeds and actions, is what quality of karma returns. To then either support our spiritual evolution and advance the quality of our consciousness or retard and devolve our spiritual evolution and quality of consciousness.

Explanation: Human created karma, spiritually touches everything evolving in Creation, that is our unrealised creative power as human beings. Unknowingly, we affect/touch/interact with everything, with the creative, cause and effect,' karmic spiritual influence that comes out of our physical human thought and creativity. Therefore, we create our positive or negative propelled destiny in the divine scheme of evolution. It is a 'as we sow, so do we reap,' outcome/destiny in this interactive Creation, from the quality of karma we create. In the simple practice of transcendent meditation, we are complimenting and supporting the totality of Creation with the karma created out of our life-supporting actions. We also complement and further our spiritual evolution and destiny with life-supportive ceremony. Because we create our individual and collective destiny as human beings, nothing else is responsible, for our positive (life-supportive) or negative (destructive) created destiny in Creation.

Clarification: When we observe spiritual acknowledgement through respectful and dignified ceremony (actions) to almighty Nature, then we also compliment the divine spiritual self-referral Laws of Nature, (the government of Nature) underwriting, 'order out of chaos' in Creation. We also complement Cosmic Law the ultimate law of Creation; that forms the status quo Intelligence of this physical and spiritual Creation and its unstoppable evolution. Unstoppable evolution that is the divine plan of the transcendent silent architect of Creation, the Creator or God.

In spiritual fact, we support everything in Creation with the karma created out of the positive life-supporting ceremony/action/practice, of transcendent meditation. That silent ceremony also acknowledges

Absolute and Spiritual Intelligence greater than our physical, biological created human intelligence. Human intelligence that is dissolvable intelligence, unlike the Absolute and Spiritual Intelligence, that physical Creation and biological life has manifested out of and not, the science laboratory and test tubes, computer technology and electronic artificial intelligence, the media, science fiction writers, literary geniuses, other creative geniuses, Hollywood and Co; and definitely-not, created out of commercial television reality shows and glossy product magazines of all descriptions.

Note: It could also be said spiritually speaking, that the higher the physical IQ component of the mind, the more difficult it is for the ego to accept, that there is Intelligence greater than itself. Especially, if that mind/psyche has no unconscious spiritual connection to the self-referral Laws of Nature in its thought process, that is also, the unknown spiritual basis for a conscience. Along with humility and dignity in the born positive accentuated empathic human being. Spiritual qualities, that come from out of the divine component of Nature and not, the impersonal primordial component of Nature that orchestrates life.

The spiritual self-referral Laws of Nature are indeed man's and women's best harmonising friend into eternity. They also go hand in hand, from within the domesticated canine and feline species perfectly. Ask any animal lover they know? That special harmony is only evident when bought up from scratch together, within the family environment of learning to give and take and respect for each other. They are primordial jungle predatory adversaries yes, but the Laws of Nature functioning in them when we tend to their survival needs, is their silent bliss, their joy that we allow them to experience through the interactive karma created influence created from out of that kind act. A joy that they return to us, from the interactive spiritual level of life because of it. Thus, is love born of love, as respect is born of respect, as giving is born of giving in this interactive Creation.

As a dog is often a man's best friend, then so is a cat, often a woman's best friend. Allegorically, one represents the cosmic male component of Creation, and one represents the cosmic female component of interactive Creation. Moreover, when the Laws of Nature are functioning coherently within them, (as they should be within us) then they are each other's best friend when brought up together in a loving, harmonious household environment. Yes, they have their canine and feline tiffs but, two minutes later it is all forgotten, and then harmony returns, via the spiritual, 'order out of chaos,' function of the Laws of Nature, operating in that human domesticated harmonious environment.

Clarification: That then, is how those animal species should function in a domesticated family environment only. The primordial Laws of the predatory jungle are different, they must be, for the preservation of each animal species and we must come out of that primordial physical jungle and move on to another spiritual plane of life to experience that. This spiritual accomplishment is created from out of the long-term application of transcendent meditation. That short practice is ceremony too absolute silent personal ceremony using a specific mantra. The dignified application of which becomes the transcendent gift of the Creator's abstract silence and eventually, spiritual enlightenment on the long path of human evolution.

A Further Ceremony to Spiritually Connect with Nature

This is what to do at least once annually in summer. It is also positive ceremony via physical acknowledgement and positive actions that, create positive life-supporting karma. Have a trial run first to its pre-designated location, so there are no timing hiccups on that special day. Parents? Take your children with you, as you should for every ceremony, as they will teach you much through their innocence. As you, in turn, will teach them much through including them in its ceremony. At the first practical and well-planned opportunity families in particular, rise early before dawn. You need to be on site, (even if it is in the back garden) just before the dawn chorus commences, and pick a calm day, to conduct this simple ceremony.

Find a tree amongst the trees. Approach with dignity and follow the spiritual instructions given. Therefore, raise your hands high in the air and touch the trunk feelingly with care, and attentively listen, in the darkness, what do you hear? It should be nothing if your timing is right. That nothing is the silence and stillness of the Cosmic Creator. As the dawn comes up, what do you begin to hear that grows in volume? That dawn chorus from the birds is life acknowledging the dawn and the joy of life through song. That joy and harmony is also to be found in our children's innocent, spontaneous expression, for they too, when they are happy, carefree and mutually loved, are the song of Creation, the joy of Creation.

Mutually love, nurture, guide and play with your children always. Then they will remain the joy of Creation throughout their lives.

About Bereavement.
From a Spiritual Perspective and Understanding

Spiritually speaking, it is time to get our act together on this one. Passing on means just that, passing from one reality to another. Birds do it and bee's do it, everything living does it on this planet sooner or later.

IT IS A QUESTION OF WHAT YOU ATTACH TO IT?

If you attach yourself to it, then 'you' become stuck with your spiritual evolution ... because we are not supposed to when it is not our turn. It is merely freedom of the spiritual component of life from the physical component of life at death. What we are going to do is gain freedom from our physical body while we are still alive. Won't that be something to write home about? e.g. "Hi mum and dad and aunty Mabel guess what? I got here before you, but I have reserved your seats. So, hurry up and listen to Alf and not the media, commercial television or Hollywood for directions."

First, we must gain freedom from our mind, from our emotions, from our thoughts, from our material attachments, from our ego and of course, Hollywood and commercial television, saturated products and promo's. Along with freedom from our existing created reality, that binds our thoughts to its human created reality at this point of our human evolution.

Q: *Does this mean we do not feel anymore when we are alive?*
A: No, not if you are normal and are not afflicted with psychopathy. You feel more; you feel everything. You are everything so how could you not feel it, if you are a positive functioning normal human being?

Q: *Does this mean we do not cry when bereavement comes along?*
A: No, it is perfectly natural and healthy to cry. It is Nature's way of releasing enormous emotional energy, and I do mean enormous, from our mind, from our body, from our nervous system. If you do not cry, then it becomes stuck in our mind and body as residual stress. Ask your children they know, but of course, you tell them not to cry because only babies cry? Therefore, they keep quiet about it, and they eventually suffer because of it.

Q: *Does this mean we spend our lives in fits of crying?*
A: No, but when we feel like crying? Then you jolly well must have a good cry. Otherwise the Laws of Nature, cannot do their emotional repair job properly in our mind and body. That means big repressed trouble for you and depending on your disposition, everyone around you as a projected result. SADDAM. H. (Nebuchadnezzar personified) was born with this pathological disorder of not being able to feel or cry ... and; he took it out on everyone else because of it. He was permanently stuck in his ancestral inherited non-feeling, non-empathic psychopathic reality, exacerbated through a loveless conception. His personality, spirit and evolution, was the property of Darth and Associates because of it. However, had you told him that fact, he would have bumped you off, or locked you up and not allowed you to play or cry anymore because he was afflicted with

an unloved miserable negative childhood. That made this born psychopathic disorder even worse and he was determined to take it out on everyone else around him because of it. Just like those with power in other nations, with the same ancestral inherited psychopathic disorder that plagues humanity from out of the ancestral past.

Interlude:
   Now, King Saddam H. and his carbon copy psychopathic male offspring, had become well and truly stuck in the negative planes of Creation with their evolution ... and because he did not sort himself as he was supposed to do in this life, his people suffered the terrible consequences and reaped much death, destruction and misery because of it. Along with its perpetuating destructive karma, still locked in that nation's spiritual key-signature in the primordial system that underwrites and orchestrates life.

Why?
   *   Because as we sow, so do we reap the karmic product/influence created out of our thoughts and actions individually and collectively. e.g. When we are the boss of a nation giving all the orders, then everyone under him/her, also reap its returning negative or positive returning influence in that nation.
   *   Because of the negative logic and destructive ancestral karma, that drove King Saddam's dysfunctional desire, megalomania, violence and intent and born psychopathy.
   *   Because he wanted power and control of everything and everyone in his nation. The only way he could achieve that was to bump anyone off that got in the way of that all-consuming negative, dominant alpha power agenda. Simply because he had a born negative spirit trapped in an unfeeling human body. Along with a powerful, charismatic alpha dominant mind, afflicted with megalomania and devoid of empathy and a social conscience. A negative accentuated mind, missing the *order out of chaos*

function of the Spiritual Laws of Nature in its thought process sums it up.

Thus Saddam H. as the ruler of his nation had never learnt to practice correct meditation, to be able to stop bumping people off all the time. As a devolution result, according to Alf's tea leaves, he, along with his equally psychopathic sons, got kicked out of this Creation as poor excuses for human beings. Had he practiced Transcendent Meditation and grown up as an adult, then instead of trying to kill himself and his people and destroy his nation in the megalomania afflicted process, he would then have used his born dominant alpha leadership power, to make them all happy, healthy and prosperous as a ruler and not, utterly miserable, unhealthy and hungry. As a lot of other powerful people are doing, in other dysfunctional, corrupt nations. Also doing what they like with their acquired power and obscene wealth.

So, because of growing corruption, greed, inequality, chaos and abuse of power within nations, the powers that be Upstairs, have stated that we are to grow up in the 21st century and understand the 'Real System' for a change and stop worshiping human created realities/ideologies and other human beings and big bucks, that prevents us acquiring spiritual consciousness. Note the top end of town within nations, creating and directing our collective human destiny with their creativity and acquired power. It is sourced to big bucks, big ego's, intractable belief systems and dissolvable realities/ideologies and incomplete information. Otherwise, the other, 'powers that be', will start all over again on this human trashed planet ... and, it has taken a very long time to create the primordial sourced physical human being. So, its small wonder the boss Upstairs is suffering from gout, from out of the horrible polluting greedy chaotic mess we humans have created on this planet and that we are calling progress and success. As Stephen knows well, when he accidentally stepped on the gout bandaged toe of the boss, in his Upstairs office last time he was there.

Bereavement and Dealing with it Sensibly and Maturely

Coming back to our original plot.

So, we experience the humongous emotions of bereavement; we must not repress it or ignore it. Thus, we feel it and accept it and then move on from its emotionally painful legacy. Thus, we perform a respectful, dignified ceremony (actions) to honour the departed. Ceremony conducted with respect for the dignity of both life and death and its purpose and function in our human evolution. Therefore, to progress further up the ladder of evolution - yes? However, then, we must move on with our own life afterwards. This absolutely must be so, as soon as possible after bereavement and must be top priority for our well-being and evolution.

About the aftermath of the taking of life. Another human being's life through whatever circumstance and the deep unresolved emotional wounds that it leaves on the family, relatives and friends. At this point in the incomplete evolution of the human being, nothing said, can offset that sorrow, that pain, that emotional wound, that is carried by the bereaved from senseless killing and on occasions the perpetrator when its killing has not been planned/premeditated through a psychopathic debilitated mind devoid of empathy. Because contrary to the belief of many, it is most abnormal to wilfully hurt/harm another human being in our highly social species. When killing/harming/maiming is not pathologically sourced, it comes from a complete lack of self-control in a delinquent undisciplined, immature mind. From a lack of maturity, through a lack of parental love and firm but kind discipline in childhood. From not being taught/shown respect for life and the values of others.

Explanation: If we are not born a pathological sociopath/psychopath, then committing unconscionable violence on others, has its roots in immature parenting, inappropriate upbringing and poor parental example in childhood. A growing problem exacerbated and made worse, by the irresponsibility of scriptwriters endlessly eulogising and perpetuating mindless violence and calling it drama and entertainment. The buck stops with the immature actors, scriptwriters, authors and directors, responsible for its saturation in society through entertainment mediums as does the divorce rate, sexual degradation, and behaving how we like in society. Big greedy business and its all-consuming neurosis for profit, is the entity underwriting its anything-goes escalation in so-called civilised nations.

Note: Thus, do the growing sociopath and immature element in the acting, entertainment, newsprint, television, computer games, marketing and advertising media, score well here in the chaos creating department, and making life extremely difficult for conscientious parents to do their job properly. Most communication mediums are unknowingly fuelling a dysfunctional, irrational society, through the saturation of wrong superficial values, poor-quality creativity and presentation. As a corrupting result, the long media mantra of *anything goes if it grabs the public's attention*, has become the new age norm in this spiritually decaying civilisation. Aided by the additional unbeatable double mantra of, 'freedom of expression,' and 'I've got my democratic rights,' to then sanctify its contagious delusion in society.

What can be said about bereavement brought about through killing and its devastating emotional pain to those left behind, is that the bereaved must move on with their spiritual evolution. Using the regular twice-daily short practice of Transcendent Meditation, to dissolve its residual stress and resentment trapped within the physiology and especially the mind. Therefore, we must move on from its emotional devastation as soon as possible after bereavement. i.e., from the emotionally shattered remains of our lives. Comprehend when we grieve continuously for our departed loved ones, they cannot continue with their further spiritual evolution. They are liable to become stuck in no man's land in the afterlife, as a karma created consequence from those endlessly grieving for them, that creates a potential for the departed to become lost from the light of Creation.

Why?

We are tied to the departed in more ways than bloodline. We are also tied to them in spirit and karma. Comprehend that when our spirit is continuously saturated with grief in the physical body, then the departed cannot leave you and become lost in ethereal space as an afterlife result. They cannot see the light of Creation and step into another reality, because of your unresolved grief and its powerful emotional created karma clouding their afterlife spiritual vision. Therefore, you have a great responsibility to regain your happiness, so that the departed can leave you and continue-on with their afterlife journey for their happiness.

Thus, learn to meditate consistently, and you will acquire the spiritual maturity, to rise above that seemingly insurmountable grief. Also, the spiritual maturity gained and acquired through consistent Correct Meditation, will, after experiencing bereavement, naturally help return our emotional body, our mental body, our physical body and our spiritual body, back to this physical planet and to positive expression in life once again. It is knowledge that does not come from the science laboratory, 24/7 non-stop talking newsrooms, books, glossy magazines or commercial television reality shows and quiz programs for winning big buck's downstairs but, from spiritual creation and divine intelligence.

About Bereavement and the Spiritual Laws of Nature

The self-referral Laws of Nature should function effortlessly through the eldest of the family, be it son or daughter when parents are incapacitated or have moved on in the scheme of physical evolution. The spiritual knowledge of the family tree is latent in the oldest sibling, to intuitively allow them to function through serious crisis for the survival and wellbeing of younger siblings. It is an automatic process in Nature's spiritual workings as a survival instinct at work. Assuming it is not a dysfunctional, chaotic family, lost from the order-out-of-chaos function of the Spiritual Laws of Nature. It could also be called automatic leadership at work in the family structure. The eldest will intuitively know what to do without thinking about it, as an instinctive survival reflex activity. Therefore, all family problems created through the loss of parents are in the hands of the eldest. They will intuitively know what to do in the family structure, in the absence of parents through bereavement. However, only if the family unit has been functioning in harmony and not disharmony and chaos with the Spiritual Laws of Nature.

Bereavement and Tears and Dealing with Emotions

If we are not afflicted with psychopathy, we will cry, which is perfectly natural and psychologically healthy to do so. It is also sensible as a mature adult, to have somewhere private to release those bereavement tears, i.e., not hysterically in front of our children or insensitive, irresponsible news reporters, to create ground-breaking attention-grabbing wailing news on the television. When this tear release happens, then afterwards, we are to dry those tears of emotional release and then concentrate on willing our departed over the line and into the light of spiritual Creation. As well as making a firm commitment to the departed and yourself, to move on from its trauma through accepting and not repressing or denying its emotional pain.

Repeat: We direct our departed with our loving thoughts to enter the light of Creation. Therefore, to whatever spiritual plane of Creation (strata of consciousness) their spiritual essence is bound for with their further evolution in the afterlife. This duty to perform is important for your physical wellbeing and their spiritual wellbeing. Because initially after passing-on, the spiritual essence of the departed are lost in ethereal space without direction. Their spiritual thoughts, when undeveloped, are back here on the planet, mostly on unfinished business. They will remain in spiritual limbo because of it. Thus, you must do your spiritual duty and after every bout of tears, *visualise* them crossing that metaphorical line into the light of spiritual Creation with your emotionally charged thoughts. Once there, through family affinity, they will unquestionably meet up with a loving member of the family who has departed in recent times. The Spiritual Laws of Nature, operating through ancestral family key signatures in spiritual Creation, takes care of this afterlife confusion in the departed. Providing, you do your bereavement duty after each bout of tears and with your concentrated thought, you *will* your departed into the light of Creation. Spiritually speaking again, the created karma from that concentrated loving desire, forms the spiritual communication channel between you and your departed.

Therefore, we perform this special duty after each bout of sudden memory attacks and tears. As in, when you are suddenly drawn to think of your loved one and of all the beautiful things you shared, of shared personal struggle and of enduring the trials of life together. Shared experience that makes for eternal friendship in a mature, harmonious marriage. Therefore, of all the joy, laughter and ups and downs you shared, of the shared love that brought your children into this world, because that love is eternal with its shared karma. Thus, let these bouts of tears come and go but do not become lost to them or in them.

Understand if we do not consciously block those emotional thoughts and tears off, then eventually they will diminish in intensity and frequency and dissipate naturally and healthily. More importantly, its energy will not become trapped in the mind and body, because thought is created energy. When it becomes trapped in the physiology, then it becomes residual stress that debilitates both mind and body, eventually causing problems with the immune system and making it vulnerable to disease in a sensitive human being, but not an insensitive, unfeeling, negative accentuated spiritually debilitated human being.

So as soon as possible after bereavement, we must get on with our life and all the necessary activity required for our well-being, for our family's well-being, for our other children's well-being. That then is true family responsibility and spiritual maturity in operation. So, we must do our duty to them, to our departed, to the Laws of Nature, to God. We perform a dignified, respectful ceremony to finalise that departure. Therefore, a formal, dignified funeral and then afterwards, an informal wake, to then rejoice their past life and their future life in the afterlife. Therefore, eternal spiritual life in quantum Creation and eventual, physical rebirth of our spiritual essence on this living planet for our further evolution.

We must always release the great floods of emotion from bereavement. This does take time to dissipate. However, if we do release and not suppress tears, then the Spiritual Laws of Nature will always honour us with peace of mind, in the years we have left to live upon this earth. The sun will indeed return in due course of time and renew our life as it does in springtime to all of life-intelligence. For that is how bereavement, though very necessary in the cycle of life and death, must eventually fade and be replaced with new life new goals new loving friendships. That special relationship that you have had with your departed will always be honoured once a year with a beautiful ceremony, a simple ceremony. By just sending them your quiet love with your thoughts on that very special day, and what is that positive day? The anniversary of your child's birth. The anniversary of that very beautiful day of your wedding. That joy is eternal in its created karma from your loving thoughts. That joy will find them in whatever afterlife plane of existence they reside and help further, their positive evolution and yours - guaranteed.

About lingering sorrow?

Q: *What to do about this necessary process in the chain of emotions that follow bereavement?*

A: We do not shut it off. We do not deny it. We do not ignore it but live with it and accept its necessary experience, as the dissolving attachment to another's psyche. For how could this deep sorrow not be felt in an empathic human being? Because sharing, giving, caring, loving, and the great friendship that comes from life-long companionship, is a beautiful process of a human being evolving in their journey through life and beyond. Rest assured; you will meet up again in a future life. You are a family tree, which means just that within spiritual creation as well as physical creation.

The Conclusion of Bereavement

The spiritual advice is to develop your spiritual awareness through consistent twice daily Correct Meditation everyone. For once we have developed its expansion, then we will be able to handle all our bereavement emotions and gain maturity from its traumatic experience. In that spiritual awareness, you will also not know that person you have loved so dearly when they and you return to this beautiful planet in future life. Because all things are possible for the human being in the divine scheme of spiritual evolution. That forms part of the divine plan of Creation, from transcendent, eternal silent Intelligence greater than ours.

About the Initial Void, the Pending Loneliness, the Emptiness, the Emotional Vacuum in the Aftermath of Bereavement

Q: What to do about it?

A: Again, do not deny it but experience it. Work through it and move on from it. Everyone is different in this lingering department. There is no definite signpost to refer too when temporarily lost along its cloudy path. Someone will come and fill that void have no doubt. The kindness within the intelligence of divine Nature is endless. This must be so, for it is God's active intelligence functioning through the Laws of Nature, but unless we overcome, accept and acknowledge that loss of our loved one, we will stay blind and not know, not see, not realise that person when we meet them.

Note: So as soon as possible after bereavement has run its course and we have lost our emotional vulnerability and regained spiritual maturity, then look to someone else for loving companionship in your life. Then you will know them for they will surely know you. Because in Nature's eternal intelligence, the laws of affinity run deep to address bereavement, and we should never be alone in life. Unless almighty Nature has ordained the recluse way of life to complete our spiritual evolution, to then move on to absolute existence as an eternal result at death. Where the part becomes the whole and the whole becomes the part for eternity. Thus, we release that great emotion and natural tears when Nature prompts us to do so from bereavement. Then this transition from great loss to positive gain will be the divinely ordained outcome in due course of healing time and spiritual maturity.

Clarification: It is not natural for the average human being to live on their own in isolation. Human beings are conceived out of duality, a sexual interaction, conception and duality, underwritten by male and female love note spiritually blind Science. Not from test tubes, harvested eggs, frozen sperm, syringes, freezers or glossy magazines and masturbation in a cubicle, compliments of entrepreneurial big money-making business, but through a male and female loving bonding sexual interaction. Because, how could this natural affinity and mutual love not exist within the differing genetics of male and female fused in sexual union? Thus, its created positive karma to be passed on naturally, (and not synthetically in the laboratory), to their offspring, as a Nature structured ordained natural result.

We should understand that natural happiness in our species is everything in life. It is the ordained path of our human spiritual evolution. It comes naturally through loving, caring, spiritually mature, responsible parents. It also comes naturally through following the transcendent path of Correct Meditation. If we have missed out on the former, then follow the latter and catch up. Spiritual love is never acquired by money, acquired status, downstairs gongs, celebrity worship, ego preening, acting and living the commercial product good life, at everyone else's and the expense of this planet. Therefore, definitely-not through acquiring fame, worshipping celebrities, commercial television, big business and big bucks and other human so-called successful beings note the unprofessional media, as the opportunistic cheerleader. Big noting themselves in the sycophantic ego deluded human worshipping process.

When we depart this physical planet having developed our spiritual potential, we are given free will to enter the light of Creation and continue our spiritual journey, or if it has been a strong desire at death, to step back out of that light to be physically reborn. Because one day, everyone, (assuming they acquire its spiritual reality), will have to show trust in what is being explained in this boot camp lecture, to acquire its miracle out of death.

Q: *What miracle is that?*
A: The path to acquiring eternity and a divine spiritual reality, within a fully active life on this physical planet.

Postscript. Do not forget always to keep your house in order?
Which means, do not leave a chaotic mess behind within your family affairs for your offspring to have to cope with in addition to your great loss to them. You will have passed onto a different spiritual reality, but they must pick up the emotional pieces in their physical reality. So, keep your physical affairs in order throughout your life, to avoid leaving chaos when you move on from it. Therefore, wills and requests etc. It is reassuring for your offspring to know that you have taken care of family responsibilities and not left them with a mess to sort out.

Clarification: Through that parental thoughtfulness, family duty and concern for offspring, the Laws of Nature responsible for the process and reality of life and death, then maintain harmony throughout its necessary transition to another plane of existence. For we all must move on from this physical planet, in the process of our species continuing evolution. Comprehend also, that it is what we move on too that is under our authorship on this planet. Because we create our individual and collective destiny in evolution, as a very creative species, nothing else is responsible. From that spiritual understanding, it is best to find and subscribe to a reality that compliments out individual and collective evolution. That should always be a positive life-supporting reality that complements life and never degrades it. Whatever our personal beliefs are - yes?

About Depression and a Growing Contributory Unknown Cause

Note the new-age *anything-goes* creative extroverts in the media, entertainment, music, movie, acting, directing, author and script-writing fraternity in society audio, visual and literary. That creates a negative desensitising or positive, uplifting influence, reality, direction, illusion, delusion and destiny, for those following and worshipping them through the saturated media. They are also referred to as media created pied pipers and commercial spin doctors, in the spiritual boot camp manuals.

Further thought for the day, especially for 24/7 newsrooms:

It is not necessarily what we say, but the way that we say it, present it and saturate it, that determines its negative or positive karma and destiny value to society. Re- Hollywood educated commercial newsrooms and news readers. Saturating the public with drama scripted, unprofessional presentation and delivery, of non-stop negative attention-grabbing information and therefore, its cause and effect karmic influence that invisibly touches everyone. The influence from which, can either raise our collective consciousness when positive, or lower it when negative, to the entry point of depression. Note that commercial media and Hollywood are the worst offenders. With their poor quality contagious, *anything-goes* creativity, divorced from the Laws of Nature and heaven. According to St Peter with the keys.

More ground-breaking unpalatable news from Upstairs:

It is time for positive quality, not *negative quantity* from all communication mediums and especially, saturated news, print, television and entertainment mediums. These have become so influential and powerful in the 21st century, through the non-stop 24/7 saturation of their content on the public psyche. The media, has a great social responsibility, not to corrupt and desensitise society with their non-stop information and creativity. Because when it is continuously negative, (not life-supportive), in its content, its saturated *cause and effect* influence (karma) creates and causes depression and negative creativity to grow in humankind. The boot camp spiritual advice to those unknowingly contaminated and depressed by its contagious karma is to learn to turn the radio, TV, internet and Hollywood celebrity entertainment switch off and set yourself some positive goals. Activating that off-switch will also create positive influence (karma) in the spiritual workings of primordial Nature to return to you for a change.

Start your rehab with a sensible, inexpensive, simple fitness program, because both mental and physical activity is very important to climb out of the black hole of negative karma, that sources depression with its destructive cause and effect contagious influence. A growing negative karmic influence in humanity, that artistic geniuses and the entertainment and commercial fraternity are adding to. From out of their media saturated creativity and its sociopath mentality, of, 'anything goes,' and 'I can do what I like,' in the public domain, in the name of freedom of expression, entertainment and acquiring fame. To counter that got it wrong, socially irresponsible, media saturated thoughtless creativity and dissolve, its growing contagious negative karmic influence we initiate a positive implemented, socially interactive and constructive wellbeing programs. That includes Transcendent Meditation and its back in sync with the spiritual Laws of Nature program with our thoughts and desires.

Therefore, not a Darth authorised nightclub dancing pole program. A non-stop movie entertainment program, featuring anything goes in the sex, crudity, foul mouth, violence, emotional hysteria and chaos categories. Big-buck greed underwritten immature commercial television reality-show program. Fred's casino and extra-curricular activity on the house program. Trash, bash, smash and obliterate the other party computer games program. A cell phone selfie, ego authorised, celebrity copied, look-at-me program. Collecting glossy product magazines program. Shop spend and consume until you drop commercial product program. Catwalk fopsville fashion and bling galore indoctrinated program. A sociopath authorised, verbal and character trashing of others program also called, freedom of expression on commercial radio. Along with avoiding a blame everyone else but yourself program. A commercial television product, promo, celebrity and *anything* goes behaviour program. A non-stop talking 24/7 saturated newsroom program. Shut yourself up in your room anti-social program. Shoot the rapids program (drugs). Blow out the fly by credit card program. Alternatively, any other negative, sociopath underwrote, spin-doctor propagated, pain in the butt to our further evolution program. i.e., trashing the self-referral spiritual Laws of Nature, that are responsible for creating order out of chaos in the human mind and life.

Therefore, we initiate a positive boot camp spiritual program, life-supporting program, interacting with Nature program. So as soon as sensibly possible, divest yourself of other spiritless material programs and go on holiday. A country holiday, not a 7 star live it up jet setting holiday emulating the commercial TV product clones not yet. Nature will heal you in this depression department unquestionably if you come back in sync with the spiritual Laws of Nature with your thought process and creativity because divine Nature is your progenitor, the progenitor of us all. However, we must structure a further transcendent acquired silent consciousness to operate out of with our thoughts, to experience that spiritual truth and a lot more besides.

The positive boot camp directive is to learn how to meditate correctly twice daily. Then go somewhere where there are animals and interact with them, domesticated animals and pets of any description are preferred. Talk to them, touch them, stroke them, care for them, love them. A very important therapy for a damaged heart and mind and the unhappy subliminal child locked up in the adult mind, and we all have a hidden subliminal child as adults. That caring interaction with animals will help dissolve that depression, no doubt about it because animals respond to the spiritual vibration of love and affection and return that vibration to the human being, from the interactive spiritual level of life. Within that shared spiritual vibration of love, functions the Spiritual Laws of Nature and Divine Intelligence. That spiritual connection helps dissolve entrenched negativity, especially depression. However, we must first open-up our mind and expand our spiritual

Self, through the regular twice daily simple practice of Transcendent Meditation.

As an analogy, put a new film in the camera ... with you in it participating with Nature in it. Then you will have introduced another positive element into your dissolvable black hole of depression. A positive element, that will dissipate that invisible karmic ugh influence that has engulfed you, saturated you, mesmerised you. Along with your spirit, your thoughts, your whole physiology and your way of thinking. Thus, you snap out of it with your awareness. Awareness that is expanded through consistent Correct Meditation and move on in the scheme of human evolution with your spiritual essence. Understand that nothing is impossible when you understand and master yourself and not everything else around you.

In conclusion, pull yourself together with positive intent, to tackle this depression problem with determined resolve and perseverance, to overcome the negative sourced karma causing/instigating depression. IT WILL PASS, as clouds do across the sun ... sooner or later. Thus, hang in there with the consistent practice of Transcendent Meditation and the real you, will eventually emerge once more into the sunshine, back into life and its positive participation with Nature and its Laws.

Bonus from Stephen Musical or Not?

Pick a musical instrument and practice the scales often, regularly, every day, anytime. Note: anywhere out of earshot of others. We do not want them depressed as well - right? If you have access to a keyboard, then so much the better. Scales and patterns left and right hand, this helps to stimulate both hemispheres of the brain into coordination with each other, less traumatic than electric shock treatment and the old scientific method of lobotomy. Therefore, we stimulate the left and right of your creative potential, the independently functioning left and right components of the brain. Have those communicating positively and not negatively and you will help Nature restore equilibrium to your nervous system, chemistry and biology and dissolve the black doldrums.

Note: Persist with that musical enterprise work at it, even when you do not want too. That is called self-discipline, perseverance, personal enterprise and creating the means to come out of your transient created tunnel vision, your black hole that is sourced to the Negative strata of Creation. Thus, start putting something positive in and then you will automatically receive something positive back out. If not? Then write to Stephen, and he will take it up with the boss Upstairs when the boss has recovered from his gout, that is. Repeat: Correct Meditation, plus positive creativity, plus perseverance - okay?

About Spiritual, Sexual Expression Within the Human Being and the Laws of Nature.

Because if we wish to evolve up the ladder of spiritual evolution to claim our harp, then mutual, mature, shared love for each other, should always underwrite the sexual act not primal lust, ego gratification and loveless sex. Also, anyway and every way the *first time* we sexually mate, is a no, no, to the archetypal intelligence of primordial Nature. Spiritual intelligence that underwrites and orchestrates our physical biology, chemistry, sexuality and procreation. So, if we want to spiritually compliment the invisible primordial Intelligence responsible for sexuality and procreation, and therefore our future children, then a complimentary to Nature sexual ceremony the first time we mate, is always the life-supportive positive way to go, but it must be initiated by the female, not the male. To then create the right and not the wrong karmic (cause and effect) sexual influence to return to us, and our future children and their destiny.

The second seemingly impossible boot camp directive to teenagers is to abstain from sexual activity until we have acquired the spiritual maturity to create sexual maturity. It is called, being officially given the keys to the car, in the sexual procreation spiritual department of Nature. An acquired sexual and emotional maturity that should come naturally through the growing intellect in the mind, after we turn twenty-one. So contrary to the current entertainment, internet, television and movie introduced *anything-goes* sexual norm, no playing doctors and nurses in the closet or the nearest motel, or one-night stands after *all-night parties and rock concerts and night clubs*, until we gain freedom in our mind from Nature's sexual chemistry, in the teenage and adolescent haywire physiology and undeveloped intellect.

Thus, the euphoric phenomena of falling in procreation love and its biological and chemically activated euphoric sexual fireworks, taking control of a yet to mature adolescent mind. Therefore, being lost in that teenage/adolescent sexual space accompanied by another, who is also on the new age Hollywood/author/scriptwriter instructed and actor/entertainment/media/television/internet visually promoted sexual promiscuity ego blink? Far from any spiritual connection with the, *order out of chaos*, function of the Laws of Nature, called a human created and contagious delusional, *anything-goes*, sexual reality in boot camp, but not in Hollywood, the internet and elsewhere in the top end of town.

Clarification: Comprehend to complement our spiritual evolution and divine Nature, we must first understand, acknowledge and respect the immense procreation forces of primordial Nature that underwrite sexuality, before blindly diving headfirst into its domain. Because, it is those humungous procreation sexual forces/energies, that have become activated in a still growing adolescent mind and causing it to go starry-eyed and oblivious, to everything else around them. In that delusional teenage/adolescent sexual euphoria, the mind becomes lost in the emotional body and the physical body, to the total exclusion of the thinking body i.e., the thinking intellect that discriminates reality. Therefore, they are very vulnerable to making stupid decisions and falling into an irreversible sexual pitfall, that mature loving parents should see, but teenagers and adolescents and other immature adult minds do not see. So, memorise the following words until you can say them backwards, SEXUAL and EMOTIONAL MATURITY first because we are still growing and maturing within our mind, body and intellect before twenty-one. Understand in the *spiritual department* of our evolution, we are not emotionally or intellectually mature enough for a sexual relationship under the age of twenty-one. Physically yes, but spiritually no – got it?

The Unpalatable Boot Camp Spiritual Advice:

Kiss, cuddle and caress that's fine! However, if we want to evolve in the spiritual department of life, we must learn to respect and master our primordial procreation sexual instinct and immature ego, before jumping in bed with each, other note the entertainment brigade? In the 'Spiritual System,' (and not the Hollywood sanctioned system,) it is called gaining spiritual maturity through correct meditation, to acquire sexual and emotional maturity in adulthood and not delusion, denial and conceit. Accomplish this unheard-of miracle of mastering our sexual thoughts, instincts and desires, and it will enable us to have a life-long happy sexual relationship in marriage, with our equally spiritually evolved life-long partner.

Also, avoid the following disrespectful to Nature negative words, to describe the sexual act. Words that demean degrade and destroy the divine spiritual element of sexual intercourse with their use. As in the crude sexual connotation of fuck, bonk, root, shag, screw, laid, scored, get it up-her, mother fucker etc. etc. etc. Loveless words and influence (karma) that desensitise, obliterate and destroy, all-important spiritual sourced sexual dignity in a human being. The created contagious karma of which is influence alien and destructive to the spiritual self-referral Laws of Nature structuring our spiritual evolution.

Comprehend that a maturely loving husband and wife and not promiscuity, infidelity and unfaithfulness, is divinely meant to be in the spiritual evolution of human beings. Marriage and its loving sexual interaction, bonding and commitment, is sacrosanct in the divine Intelligence responsible for our spiritual evolution in the family structure. Along with ensuring healthy children in the psychological and emotional department, that promotes their happiness and not misery in life — unhappiness and misery, created through sexual immaturity, infidelity and divorce. As promoted, saturated and eulogised through actors, directors, scriptwriters, authors, movies and so called entertainment and freedom of artistic expression. Along with making big reputations, (downstairs and Upstairs), in our *new age* media, movie and internet promoted, *anything goes* in the sexual department of life.

Saturated Clarification, of the above Unheard-of Unpalatable Sexual Information

Not least on the list, is that reciprocated love, empathy, tenderness and a committed relationship, should underwrite the sexual act in the human species. The spiritual advice is to forget all about Hollywood and the actor's hall of fame and their spiritless sexual portfolio. Along with other sexually immature adults on the TV and their also scriptwriter authorised, ego preening acted out sexual antics in front of the television camera. Ditto, the saturated porn on the also *anything-goes* Internet, attempting to outdo everyone else in its, 'got it wrong,' visual sexual education.

Spiritually speaking, a woman is the decider of her mate in the procreation sexual department. Notably, when the seeds of conceptual desire and love flow in her female procreation sexual physiology; that has been stimulated/triggered through interaction with a Nature compatible male. Comprehend the male, unlike the female, is a natural wanderer by primordial Nature in the sexual procreation department. However, when we reach spiritual maturity as males, we have gained control of the primordial sexual instinct/lust/ego and learnt to respect sexuality and Nature. Unlike new-age authorised and media-saturated, sexually delinquent actors, scriptwriters, authors, directors, singers and porn stars on Darth's sexual payroll. Certainly not St Peter's. Therefore, no role model for society to copy and especially, highly impressionable children and teenagers.

Note: Along with other entertainment and book club saturated sexual fantasies, from out of sex-obsessed spiritless minds. As in, descriptive worded fantasy sex, one-night stands and a change of sexual partner every other week, to preen our immature ego and self-esteem and earn Darth's brownie points and not Upstairs brownie points. Comprehend immature sexual fantasy/imaginative thoughts, may well arise in the primordial structured mind and ego, for we are all very vulnerable human beings, in the unstoppable procreation sexual department of life. However, we do not become lost to crude undignified sexual thoughts, words, crudity, fantasy and desires when we gain spiritual maturity in our mind. Those immature sexual thoughts and fantasies come and they go. No problem at all, if we let them come and then let them go, without its detailed description through literature and books or demonstrably acting them out in public in movies, on television or the Internet. It is called adult sexual, spiritual maturity in Nature's self-referral dictionary and not, media, internet and entertainment authorised, *anything goes* in the sexual department for public viewing, reading and our children's education. As in the current entertainment, media, glossy magazine, internet and book club authorised and saturated sexual indoctrination/brainwashing reality for everyone.

Comprehend if we desire a successful, lasting loving happy marriage, we have a great responsibility in its marital contract, to honour and respect our partner ... support, our partner ... love, our partner ... fulfill our partner's needs; because it is that positive created shared karma, that allows the Laws of Nature to function coherently in marriage, its commitment and the family structure. When we are intuitively/spiritually, connected to those self-referral spiritual laws in our thought process, both parties, then our marital relationship is automatically harmonious and happy. Our thought patterns become unconsciously attuned to each other. Thus, within spiritual acquired maturity, there are no childhood leftovers of jealousy, ambivalence, insecurity, denial, mistrust, emotional chaos and adolescent sexual immaturity, eroding our procreation physical love and respect for each other, and respect is as important as love in the sexual department.

Therefore, do not become brainwashed, mesmerised and desensitised, by scriptwriter, author and actor perpetuated, immature, delinquent emotional and sexual behaviour called acting and adult entertainment. Delinquent adolescent behaviour that has come to be saturated in society from thoughtless, socially irresponsible viewing mediums. Notably, the movies, internet and television, where *anything goes* has become an unchallenged norm and awarded plaudits and gongs, to those who write it and those who do it best in front of the camera. Then forever regurgitated and saturated by the news media, to also big-note themselves and grab the attention of the celebrity mesmerised public. It may be normal behaviour for the writers, actors and producers, swamping society with its acted-out *anything-goes* behaviour. However, it is not normal behaviour for a socially responsible mature adult. It is only a thoughtless, socially irresponsible behaviour for an attention seeking immature adult, that has become divorced from the, 'order out of chaos,' function of the Spiritual Laws of Nature in the mind. When the adult thought process and creativity is in sync with the spiritual Laws of Nature, it is natural to function with emotional and sexual maturity, integrity, dignity, empathy, respect and consideration of others in society, especially impressionable children.

The repeated un-heard of boot camp advice is to give viewing glossy magazine and book mediums saturating delinquent undignified emotional and sexual behaviour a big miss. There is a much more productive sexual reality to aspire too. One that will enable us to evolve spiritually with our evolution and collect our harp and not a shovel. Along with creating a happy sexual life in marriage and not a delinquent, miserable, unhappy and unfulfilled life, through adult immaturity, unfaithfulness, infidelity and divorce. As promoted and eulogised through scriptwriters, actors and movies and called, gripping adult drama and entertainment. Along with the now mandatory sex scenes in every new age entertainment script, to receive five stars and accolades from the equally ego deluded media. No wonder St Peter has locked the gates and thrown away the key, because we have lost the spiritual plot, in the new age saturated Hollywood/internet/entertainment/media promoted sexual plot of life.

Recapping the Spiritual Reality of Sexuality and Mating and not, the Internet, Book Club, Scriptwriter, Movie and Television Anything Goes Entertainment Version for a Change

Most have watched other animal species and not just the human species, in the instinctive sexual function of procreation. So, understand in Nature's primordial workings that orchestrate sexuality and life, this position the *first time* we mate, was once the natural procreation position of our evolving animal species too. Not bouncing around on top of the female and not anywhere, everywhere and with anyone, in one-night stands and in front of a TV or movie camera for public consumption. As instructed by Hollywood, the book club, actors, television and the porn doused Internet known as entertainment and freedom of sexual expression.

Clarification: We are of the primordial animal species as human beings. Therefore, we should respect this Laws of Nature governed and primordial ordained sexual position the *first time* we mate, consummated in emotionally mature love for each other. To then spiritually compliment, the specific archetypal intelligence of primordial Nature orchestrating sexuality and procreation in the human being. Along with the female's permission, (by her initiation), for the male to enter her reproductive space, as it is her divinely ordained procreation right, as the child bearer. So, having *first* spiritually complimented the primordial Intelligence and Laws underwriting procreation with its natural primal sexual position, after that any mutual sexual position, is open to our human sexual creativity with Nature's blessings. The evolution gone-wrong problem of pathological sexual disorder in our species, that is locked into the ancestral inherited karma and genes of human beings, is compounded by not respecting this natural procreation position, the *first time* we sexually mate. This ceremony/action and it created sexual karma, will contribute to dissolving that evolution gone wrong pathological problem, of growing sexual disorder in our species. Notably for those who come after us.

Repeating the above, 'Believe it or Not' Spiritual Sourced Sexual Information:

If we wish to spiritually evolve to reach our spiritual potential, then emotional and sexual maturity and shared love must underwrite sexual union. Then its love created sexual karma, compliments the divine Intelligence that has authored life and returns, to support our spiritual evolution, wellbeing and happiness. Without that shared love underwriting sexual union, sexual intercourse has no divine connection with the Laws of Nature, only an impersonal primordial connection fraught with unknowns. Without that spiritual acquired loving connection, the male should not enter the female on top of her, especially during the fertility cycle. It becomes a position of domination, in the primordial spiritual workings of Nature, (archetypal Intelligence,) structuring conception, procreation and sexuality.

Explanation: Comprehend, when we do not respect the primordial archetypal Intelligence underwriting sexuality and procreation, then we become divorced from the Laws of Nature responsible for creating *order out of chaos* in sexuality and life. As a negative, not life-supportive result, we create an *ancestral inherited* potential, for sexual disorder, sexual delinquency and sexual disease to manifest in our biology. Comprehend that sexual union, is the primordial sourced means to bring life into this world and should always be underwritten by respect and love for each other. Comprehend that acted out sexual intercourse in the movies for public entertainment, is far from spiritual love and respect for the means to bring life into this world. However, it is everything to do with spiritual ignorance, in those creating it, promoting it, performing it and watching it.

Clarification: What the public and especially teenagers need to know, is that sexual intercourse comes with lasting destiny ramifications. Because, as we sow, so do we reap, with our sexual creativity in Nature's interactive primordial workings. Therefore, up or down on the ladder of our spiritual evolution, from out of its negative or positive created returning sexual karma. Comprehend, the created karma that comes out of sexual intercourse and orgasm is incredibly powerful and reactive in the negative and positive primordial Intelligence and orchestrates physical life and its evolution. Comprehend that sexual union devoid of shared love, empathy, affection, intimacy and respect for the means to bring life into this world, is an absolute no, no, to the divine Intelligence that has authored the spirit of a human being. Because the human being is a special creation in this Creation. Born with spiritual potential, to evolve with its positive, (life supporting), created karma, to reach a divine destiny with its spiritual essence.

Repeat: It is the quality of the created karma (influence) from out of our actions, especially sexual actions, that determines our up or down destiny during life and in the afterlife at death. Note actors, authors, scriptwriters and other sexually deluded human beings in the media, Internet and elsewhere, who are promoting and saturating, a different spiritless sexual reality in the public arena? Where sexual dignity and respect for procreation, do not exist in its desensitising, undignified, spiritless sexual reality. Where the sexual union has no divine meaning, only primal ego fuelled self-gratification divorced from the Laws of Nature. It is time to come out of the primordial jungle and dissolve that delusional entertainment saturated sexual reality and its contagious euphoric entity. That becomes a dead-end sexual reality, where our divine spiritual evolution is concerned. Note Hollywood and Co, scriptwriters, literary geniuses, the media, the internet and the growing porn brigade?

More about the Female Gender Spiritually Speaking and not Hollywood Speaking

Females understand by the maternal instinct/nature of your female gender, i.e., the biological and archetypal energies directing motherhood, means you are the divinely ordained maternal nurturing and tenderness of Creation. Always should this be so, underwritten by instinctive nurturing female maternal love? Then your children, are always the beauty and tenderness of Creation too. If you do not wish to prescribe to this divine reality, then do not procreate, for you cause chaos to arise in the primordial Intelligence underwriting procreation, by not acknowledging your maternal instinct and its natural female tenderness and love. Therefore, your divinely ordained female creative function in Creation, to bring life into this physical world from out of the spiritual world that underwrites physical life.

Repeat: The sexual act, is a perfectly natural instinctive preservation function (procreation) that contains physical and spiritual fulfilment, at least it should do. Providing we do not degrade sexuality, ourselves, our evolution and Nature, through participating in loveless sex. As promoted through entertainment acted-out sex for public consumption. Note those promoting its delusion in society as artistic expression, crazy? Because when we do not respect sexuality and the means to bring life into this world, our divine spiritual evolution becomes lost to us. i.e., as boot camp analogy, expect big trouble at the pearly gates from finger-pointing St Peter if not before, in the form of lingering unhappiness and unfulfilled life.

Q: *What is the fullness of the female function to bring life into this world?*

A: Natural, spontaneous dedication and devotion to your children and husband and vice versa, when the Spiritual Laws of Nature are functioning coherently within you and the loving father of your children. Then love, harmony and happiness, permeates the family structure from its created marital karma. Then marriage is always fulfilling and joyful and not destructive, devoid of love, unhappy and miserable. Because the positive karma/influence created out of that shared love, sexual bonding, commitment and devotion, saturates the Spiritual System that underwrites life and invisibly returns to its physical source you, your husband and your children – got it?

More unheard-of spiritual advice:

Males within adult spiritual acquired maturity; we do not bombard the female with big macho mouths, sexual advances and crude verbal sexual innuendo and sleaze not in the real world anyway. If you live in TV sexual entertainment la la land or Hollywood, then maybe. They cannot help themselves within any aspect of the words, sexual dignity, sexual maturity, social responsibility and respect for Nature. This Hollywood/actor copied, ego prompted motor mouth sexual behaviour, is a sign of male macho adolescent immaturity, to say the least. Thus, it does nothing for our spiritual dignity or our spiritual evolution.

Comprehend that in real life, we do not have to be a sexual prima donna, a strutting peacock or a farmyard rooster or an adolescent retarded, sexual fantasy created James Bond. A mature female always knows her mate. Her procreation prompted sexual desire arises in her maternal female thoughts because of it. That is Nature's procreation archetypal Intelligence, functioning in her sexual biology/chemistry naturally. In that spiritual understanding, the male does not have to sexually bombard the female to catch her attention, but respect her biological right as the child bearer, to initiate sexual activity through love. It is time to come out of the primordial jungle and delusional Hollywood/author/scriptwriter and male authorised sexual fantasy land and spiritually grow-up.

Note: Then we are behaving maturely, respectfully to Nature and with sexual dignity as the male and not stooopid as the male. Comprehend the female when *emotionally* and *sexually mature*, is naturally faithful to the father of her children. That is when the male is also mature and caring of her female needs too, when he acknowledges, respects and honours her positive wishes and unique position in the family structure. Because a mature loving woman, intuitively knows what is best for her kids and her man. Being a male, we are fickle by primordial sexual survival instinct and therefore, acquiring spiritual maturity and control of our sexual desire is a must before marriage. Then, if we are mature and not lost in Hollywood, internet and TV sexual entertainment la la land, we will know the female's procreation love, her maternal tenderness and inner strength. That is the gift of divine Intelligence for the excruciating pain that is biologically meant to be, that she endures when bringing offspring into the world. A birthing pain that causes her to love instinctively, nurture and bond with her child when free of psychological and ancestral inherited karma problems. That spiritual bonding maternal love is given from divine Nature, to conquer all her fears, pain and misgivings when giving birth. The male should know this and the need, to respect her constructive wishes and security needs in the family structure.

Young inexperienced females: When the procreation seeds of conceptual desire arise and possibly, you turn all colours of the rainbow, but your intended does not lovingly (only lustfully) respond to your glances, to your smile, to your subtle hints? Then sensibly move-on, he is not right for your happiness. He will cause you much misery and pain If you share his bed without reciprocated male love only self-gratuitous primordial activated sex. Understand in the primordial jungle of procreation; men can be fickle and thoughtless in the sexual department. Instant sexual arousal and gratification is locked in the male biological primordial sexual instinct. They cannot help themselves if you offer it without sensible checks and balances in the love and commitment department. So, understand this male primordial procreation trait, then you will not cause eventual misery, unhappiness and pain to yourself, by pursuing the male through euphoric sex and not reciprocated love, tenderness and a committed relationship.

It is also spiritually unproductive to dwell or obsess negatively, on the lost causes of love that arise when growing up. Understand if you meditate consistently and correctly, then you will acquire the spiritual maturity to handle this painful experience to your female anatomy, emotions and self-esteem, from male rejection and broken relationships. When this happens, as it does for both males and females, know that it is normal to feel rejected, angry and vulnerable. So, do not dwell on its rejection with unproductive negative, destructive thoughts that create, unproductive negative, destructive karma, the influence that returns to you and perpetuates its misery and unhappiness in your life. Know you are making the right decision, to walk away from a situation causing this emotionally painful experience. It is a necessary part of growing up and becoming a mature adult for both sexes.

Repeat: Contrary to new age author, scriptwriter, entertainment, Hollywood and internet instructed sexual education, sex without mature male and female love and tenderness underwriting it, is a spiritual no, no, for our spiritual evolution and our future children. Therefore, consciously accept that some things are not meant to be where relationships are concerned and then move on with your precious life. Do not become sexually involved if your love is not truly/honestly reciprocated from the male or female. It creates humongous karmic problems within Nature's genetics, structuring our evolution. A loveless sexually created karmic influence that returns to you down the track of life and beyond. Understand it is necessary to observe this sensible spiritual instruction, for your future partner's wellbeing and that of your future children's wellbeing. Comprehend that painful rejection, is a very necessary part of growing up and mastering, (not denying,) our emotions and learning, through accepting its experience, how to deal with uncontrollable primal emotions, the fragile ego and instincts. Therefore, that word maturity again - yes? We will never find spiritual happiness, without its adult intellect acquired acquisition via the Laws of Nature.

More Spiritual Information for Adolescent Females Moreover, Males.

If you can see through the confusion between sexuality and spirituality, that all encounter along the path to sexual union, and you can maturely step away from having sex without love and a committed empathic relationship, then know this secret. The female will eventually find the right male to share her body and life with, from out of its painful lesson. Because a mature empathic, loving male, will not pressure the female with sexual demands, but respect her female sexual vulnerability out of his genuine love and respect for her and patiently, wait for the right time. Therefore, her time and place to surrender her virginity and sexual innocence. So, consciously accept the very painful learning experience of rejection both parties, as a spiritual test from divine Nature. If you pass it, then you will find the right marital partner from scoring ten out of ten in the spiritual department of life. It is the way the system works within the *spiritual evolution* of a human being, towards higher states of consciousness. A male must show through his sincere, respectful, loving, dignified, honest actions and not just words, that he is genuinely, (not just sexually/lustfully), in love with the female. Because sex without love, is a no, no, to both parties in the karma destiny department of life, especially for the female, the child bearer.

Q: *Was the first unrequited lost love the wrong one?*
A: Not necessarily, it could just be the wrong time in both of your lives. However, it is likely you are not evolving through the same spiritual planes of Creation together on life's physical journey. A criterion, i.e., similar/compatible shared consciousness and archetypal qualities, necessary for natural harmonious natural bonding in marriage. Not all those you are attracted to and fall in physical/sexual love with will fulfil that requirement for lasting marital compatibility and happiness. Therefore, learn to meditate correctly and consistently, then your developing intuition will override your confusing female emotions and scattered thoughts. Because in adolescence, females are sexually vulnerable with their immature emotions and procreation driven sexual desire to find a mate.

Eventually, you will master this hormonal, emotional, procreation driven sexual euphoria, that is mistakenly called love. Then, when you do meet the right male to share your body and life with, you will have acquired the spiritual maturity to know that it is the right one. For as you are to him so will he be to you, in the commitment and happiness department of a loving, empathic relationship. That must underwrite the eventual sexual department of that relationship, where your future happiness, children and spiritual evolution is concerned. The same for the male, because contrary to new age entertainment promoted and saturated *anything-goes* sexual and dating education, promoting one-night stands, promiscuity and sex without love, is a negative karma no, no, for a human being, in the spiritual evolution and destiny department of life.

Repeating the Missing Spiritual Facts of Life:

If you adhere to the positive spiritual advice that has been explained, then you will eventually find the right partner to share your life with. Through not creating disharmony to divine Nature in the sexual procreation department of life. Comprehend it is positive life-supportive actions, desire and intent and its created karma, that makes this miracle of finding the right mate possible for 99. 999% of human beings. To then acquire its potential soul-mate destiny, through complimenting the invisible spiritual workings of divine Nature in the sexual procreation department of evolution.

For the 0.001% of females that do not incline men, marriage or children, but are perfectly sane, loving and empathic with others? Therefore, without psychological, emotional, sexual or ancestral inherited karma problems?

Q: What is wrong with me?
A: Nothing at all, you are still maternal as a female. However, like Mother Teresa, your bonding is with God, the absolute. Thus, no man can fulfil this transcendent acquired criterion. That was your desire in a previous life and its karma … overwhelming desire a pure desire, to know and serve the Creator in your present life.

Know this: If it is your one and only desire in your present life, then follow its non-sexual path and you will reach your one goal in life to serve the silent transcendent Creator? Remember, we always have free will in Creation as human beings, that is God's Law, to change your sexual abstinence path in life if you so desire. Because a female was born to create and bring life into this world and to give of her female magic, of her instinctive tenderness, of her bonding love, of her nurturing procreation qualities. The spiritual advice is to consult the 'JYOTISH' astrologers and pundits, for advice on this clarification of your destiny. Because with that born desire to serve God, you are spiritually highly evolved and marriage, is not meant for everyone in their evolution and destiny. Comprehend that marriage and sexual involvement, is one of the most important and far-reaching of steps in life and beyond, with its powerful perpetuating karma.

Clarification: The positive suggestion is to consult the JYOTISH pundits/astrologers before entering any love relationship leading to marriage and children. Preferably, after you reach twenty-one or before if you are mature and its thought keeps arising in your mind, then treat that spiritual advice from those Vedic scholars with great respect. It is always correct for that situation then in your life. However, it is not an absolute, unchangeable statement, because individual destiny can change during your life. If it is said that you and your loved one, are not spiritually compatible in your birth charts and consciousness, then you will run into big trouble and unhappiness down the track of your marriage. For you will not be evolving through the same planes of consciousness in life — a necessary criterion for long term compatibility, bonding and lasting happiness in marriage and children.

Understand that Vedic knowledge and advice is never wrong, no matter how those involved may disagree with its finding. Because their information comes from the centre of complete knowledge the self-referral field of spiritual Creation the Veda. That is why respect should always be accorded to those with its Upstairs born gift, that comes from the divinity of Nature to help humanity's evolution. When we approach the Jyotish/pundits with dignity and respect for their Vedic knowledge, we are respecting the intelligence of Divine Nature that sources its knowledge and far removed, from the foibles of the creative fickle human mind and daily newspaper horoscopes. Along with big commercial business organised self-proclaimed psychics; that now litter the internet, making big bucks out of snared vulnerable human beings called clients. An internet supplied avalanche of new-age money-making opportunistic so-called psychics, far from the rare genuine article. As a self-deluded result, far from the divinity of Nature and the Spiritual Laws of Nature and spiritual knowledge.

Repeated Spiritual, Sexual Facts

We need to spiritually understand, that emotional and sexual maturity and a loving, empathic relationship must come first, before jumping in bed with each other. Especially where sex, pregnancy and children come into its karmic mix and where a positive destiny and a happy fulfilled married life is concerned. Comprehend that the future of our children's happiness depends on establishing harmony, compatibility and a committed empathic, loving relationship with another first before sexual activity. Not short-term sexual infatuation, all-consuming obsession, one-night stands and other Hollywood, commercial television and Bollywood promoted sexual fantasy and promiscuity and children, should always take precedence in the female's thoughts, even when they are not yet conceived. If we want long term happiness in a marital relationship and a sexually fulfilled life free of growing STD, then do not sleep around with all and sundry before marriage. Sexual and emotional maturity, empathy and establishing compatibility and commitment in a relationship comes first, before any new-age entertainment, media, movie, television, scriptwriter, author, glossy magazine and internet and porn instructed/indoctrinated/saturated consideration called, sexual liberation and freedom of expression.

Through acquiring sexual and emotional maturity from out of the consistent practice of correct meditation, we will acquire the intuitive spiritual means, to know when to walk away from a euphoria clouded, but incompatible, volatile emotionally immature obsessive/possessive/delinquent delusional relationship *before* becoming sexually involved … not afterwards. If we do not make that mature, sensible decision, then the potential for relationship trouble and emotional grief is inevitable down the track of life, therefore misery and unhappiness. Do not bequeath your children an unhappy childhood through adult bickering, arguing, infighting, sleeping around, hidden affairs and of course, divorce. The disharmony and misery you create for them returns to you sooner or later as a perpetuating influence. To then retard/stagnate your spiritual evolution with its negative, not life-supportive karma as well as your offspring. A life wasted, through short term physical self-gratification gain for long term spiritual loss, sums it up. If you are already locked into its karmic created misery through a divorce or whatever, then correct long-term meditation is the spiritual path to eventually dissolve its perpetuating negative returning influence (karma) in your life. Because contrary to popular opinion, there is a lot more to life than death, taxes and of course, sex.

Repeating the unpalatable spiritual facts:
    Understand that spiritually sourced and acquired maturity, must come first, before sex and marriage. If you are hopelessly infatuated and besotted with the wrong person, then understand it is not a mature, lasting love but temporary euphoric delusion. So, have a good cry … by all means, but move on. The sun will return guaranteed. Because by moving on, you will not cause pain to Nature and yourself by not complying with your intuition, rather than your overpowering sexual, physical or status attraction to another. Understand a happy marriage and family is sacrosanct in the Laws of Nature. Our further positive spiritual evolution depends on it being spiritually respected and honoured and not trampled on, through immaturity and lack of introspective thought and respect for life and Nature.

About Finding a Life-Long, Happy, Harmonious Empathic, Loving Marital Relationship Naturally

In my spiritual understanding, if harmony and balance is returned to the spiritual workings of life through the collective practice of transcendent meditation in a nation, then the above complex difficult problem will disappear in society. As by the time we leave home at age 21, spiritual orientated lasting love … and not, just primordial sexual procreation orientated physical dissolvable love, will be the evolved mature love that comes along to share with our equally evolved life-long partner. Then the deplorable marital, sexual, family and social chaos, that currently plagues nations will be no more. Specifically, ensuring our offspring's happiness and maturity when they leave home. That spiritual acquired family happiness is a potential acquired from out of Correct Meditation and a top priority for this civilisation's wellbeing and survival. Everyone should understand that for a successful marriage, then compatibility and emotional and sexual maturity must be established before marriage, before sexual entanglement and the children come along.

The repeated boot camp advice is to consult the JYOTISH (Vedic astrologers) first, before sexual activity and tying the knot. Before you become too emotionally, sexually, and karmic entwined to walk away from each other. If you are long-term compatible, yet you still make a chaotic mess of your marriage, then you have not grown-up out of adolescence. To solve that childhood acquired immature problem, practice Correct Meditation and work on accomplishing your spiritual maturity. If you both accomplish that maturity, then your marriage will automatically come good, as a positive acquired Laws of Nature, *order out of chaos*, adjusted consequence.

Note: Along with giving a big miss, to watching adolescent developmentally disabled actors and their sexual antics, emotional hysterics, foul mouths and acted out sex on the big screen, called gripping drama and explosive entertainment. Ditto buying sexually explicit book-club promoted novels and glossy product celebrity garbage magazines, with other ego preening, in-love-with-themselves, so-called adults. Notably selling their sexual and facial anatomy, ego sourced delusion and closet information for big bucks and big reputations. The devolution result being, an invisible Darth issued ticket to sexual purgatory in the departure lounge, unknowingly of course. Note all those on the new age, money-making, sexually explicit, open house and anything goes in the sexual department of life, such is innovative money-making sexual progress but, to no-where land at the end of the human day.

The equally unpalatable bottom line:

According to ground-breaking news from Upstairs, our media, movie, internet and entertainment sexually instructed global civilisation, has degraded the Laws of Nature responsible for sexuality and procreation, to the point of, *'no return to normality'*. It is time to do something constructive in the form of a positive ceremony, to restore equilibrium to the primordial spiritual intelligence responsible for procreation, sexuality, and bringing life into this world. The following procreation spiritual ceremony and new spiritual instruction on the, 'facts of life', will help dissolve that contagious growing devolution karmic influence destructive (entity) our species has created in Nature.

Note: Primarily from out of growing sexual degradation and the resulting loss of sexual dignity and respect for the sexual means to create life. Because at this point, (note Hollywood, actors, celebrities, scriptwriters, literary geniuses and the porn brigade), you are sending this civilisation to the 'funny farm'. With your stupid cupid love and sexual fantasies and its saturated interpretation of the, 'facts of life'. An ego-preening immature spiritless sexual education that we will never get through the Pearly Gates with - guaranteed. Time to dissolve this contagious, delusional, entertainment proliferated sexual reality, now saturating this spiritually decaying civilisation. Along with updating its, 'got it wrong,' media, internet and entertainment version of the sexual, 'facts of life'. Ugh!

Procreation Ceremony to Compliment Ourselves and Nature for a Change

Find a tall tree approach with dignity and follow the instructions thus given.

Before starting on this 'boot camp' status free instruction and spiritual ceremony to compliment procreation, comprehend that sexual union is private property. You and only you as a loving couple, share your procreation organs. Therefore, sexual union, whether in bed or out of it, is between one loving male and one loving female and the spiritual progenitor of life divine Nature?

Note: Sexual activity that is not meant to be taped on video for public or private viewing or scientific purposes. Alternatively, acted out on the big screen for the benefit of adolescent retarded immature minds, from narcissistic actors with a creative screw loose and no respect for Nature in the sexual department. From having lost all connection with the Spiritual Laws of Nature underwriting sexual dignity in the human being. Understand that sexual union, whether for procreation or bonding, is something very special that you share that you create together. It is a perpetuating, 'cause and effect,' powerful karmic influence that you are creating in the spiritual workings of Nature and its archetypal intelligence. The influence that returns to us to either support our spiritual evolution or eventually negate it, if it is not life-supportive in its quality of expression. Moreover, believe it or not, our spiritual evolution is the whole purpose for being born on this life evolving planet.

Clarification: We should never abuse our spiritually sourced sexual dignity, we individually and collectively, ultimately pay its devolution price for abusing the Laws of Nature in the sexual department. When we debase and degrade those Laws structuring sexuality and its procreation function, then we create chaos and disorder in the primordial archetypal spiritual intelligence underwriting our life note Hollydude and co; Out the back door with our spiritual evolution, is the eventual price to pay for doing so. Yes! We should always lovingly share our bodies and organs to create sexual bonding in marriage, but not with others and not on camera. If we respect this spiritual knowledge, when we make sexual love to each other, we will then compliment and fuse, with the archetypal intelligence responsible for sexuality because we will have respected and honoured them with our sexual union underwritten by love. Not loveless sex, sexual degradation, lust, ego preening, conceit and its immaturity and, a Darth issued one-way ticket to no-where land as an unknown consequence. That eventually, always produces unhappiness, misery and unfulfilled life, as its negative karma acquired product.

Firstly, when conducting this procreation ceremony, find a private location for the reasons explained above. i.e., absolute privacy. So, let's have some common sexual sense and spiritual dignity functioning for a change in the sexual department of life. Therefore, do not conduct this ceremony in a public park in the city precincts of a concrete jungle. That is polluted to high heaven, with more things and in more ways than most are currently aware of. Thus, we go to Nature's pristine forests, where the atmosphere and surroundings, are not saturated/polluted by humankind's negative deeds and its corresponding devolution karmic influence.

Note: A growing destructive influence (entity) that has become concentrated in our cough, mutter and splutter sexually liberated cities. Especially from promiscuous promoting commercial television entertainment, sexually gyrating dancing pole night clubs, extra-curricular activity on the house casinos, massage parlours, brothels and other traditional male sexually liberating establishments, called the money-making, tax-free sex trade. All are going at it hammer and tongs any way and every way for big bucks, and a ticket to no-where land at the end of the human day unknowingly. Such is wrong progress in the evolution of human beings.

Females: In spiritual understanding and its knowledge, it is wise not to engage in intercourse during menstruation … never. In that monthly female cycle, your body is being prepared by Nature to conceive a beautiful gift one day, therefore a child. Honour, respect and accept, this biological procreation Intelligence at work in your body and abstain from sexual intercourse, but still make sexual love with your loving husband and vice versa. Also, when you are most fertile, your body temperature peaks. Its temperature cycle can be visually monitored and recorded through a high-tech thermometer and a graph, know this fact, along with the corresponding days of your fertility cycle. Then you and your considerate husband will come to know when your body is safe from conceiving both sides of the fertility cycle and mutually abstain from sexual intercourse, but not from making sexual love. If you conceive, even when you have taken the above advice, then know that it was right for you to have done so.

Why?

Because the spiritual intelligence of Nature underwriting conception knows best and not, science created synthetic chemical contraceptive pills. When the female is spiritually mature, there are positive forces at work guiding their spiritual evolution. Far beyond our present scientific physical understanding of the biology and chemistry of life's very intelligent invisible forces. Trust me; I know what I am talking about through experience and not imagination. Alternatively, the creative, *anything goes*, pen of a scriptwriter or author, functioning out of their sexual fantasy land and writing, the sexual script for others in society to copy and act out, (especially our vulnerable children and teenagers).

Know also, that in the scheme of spiritual evolution, both males and females are responsible for applying the above spiritual acquired knowledge. Including the spiritual fact, that the female has the procreation right to initiate sexual intercourse during the fertility cycle, not the male. That is if we wish to collect our harp at the end of the human day and not a shovel. Note: The commercial and entertainment created male sexual prima donna and stubble beard macho adolescent pin-up brigade and marketing geniuses, that believe it is their primordial caveman right, to dominate the female in sexual matters, to preen the immature male ego. Along with other, 'got it wrong,' females with ancestral inherited pathological problems, that want to be sexually dominated, disrespected and trashed by the alpha male GROW UP ALSO. For you also, have *got it wrong* in the sexual department of life spiritually speaking, as well as psychologically speaking.

Repeat: In the spiritual department of human beings, it is the female's procreation right to choose the right time and place for honouring Creation with their maidenhood, their virginity, their sexual innocence.

Because in the spiritual system of life, the female is the organiser of this procreation ceremony, not the male. That choice of the right time, the right place and the right male, is the female's procreation right, as the child bearer in the workings of spiritual evolution. Also understand, that this very first occasion is unique with its created returning sexual karma to both male and female. It is a sexual ceremony to compliment life, procreation and the Laws of Nature and not, the self-gratuitous, primordial driven human ego, note the entertainment brigade. Therefore, it is not to enjoy but to give that first sexual union and its karma to Creation. This first sexual bonding also comes as a shock to the nervous system and this procreation ceremony, invisibly grounds that shock into the Earth and not, into your nervous system and mind. Then there are no painful memories to contend with in the marriage bed. Just shared male and female love and its powerful bonding karma, always underwriting sexual union.

Positive Sexual Ceremony for Newlyweds in the Appropriate Surroundings.

So not at parties, the television studio, the movie studio, the boardroom, other rave-ups, the back seat of automobiles, public stairways, back alleys, airplanes, public conveniences, trains, buses or at kitchen sinks, i.e., attention-grabbing Hollywood and Co and big narcissistic deluded ego's as usual. Therefore, in private, dignified, complimentary to Nature, pleasant surroundings.

Males? This initial act of copulation can be painful if you have not been circumcised, but not harmful. We will deal with this simple problem later. We were not born circumcised, so, do not go and have a circumcision performed on you; it is not necessary if you observe daily bodily hygiene with your sexual organ. Now, we came into this world naked, and we should always sexually bond together naked. It is most natural and mentally and spiritually healthy to do so, for **you have nothing to hide** from each other. Plus, you are fused as one with its created positive bonding sexual karma when you do so.

Having removed your attire, the female then places her hands on the tree and takes up the primal procreation position. i.e., legs comfortably apart and body arched. The male must then support her waist for there is initial thrust required from the male organ to penetrate virginity. Therefore, the female must hang on tight to the tree. Your husband will support your body gently, lovingly and most importantly, honour you with great respect. When you feel it is right to do so ... perhaps when your seeds of conceptual desire flow? Then release one hand from the tree and insert his organ into yours. Then hang on tight to the tree again or you may lose your balance in the ensuing thrust from your husband. Copulation will be very short. Then he will take you in his arms and love you dearly. Cry if you need to, it is not wrong to do so, it is a very healthy emotional release for the female. Just bond together until you are ready to return home.

Males? Treat the female with genuine love and respect during this spiritual ceremony and throughout life for that matter. She is giving you her life, her female love, her trust, her total body. Respect her entirely for that sexual surrender and trust, or big invisible trouble for your spiritual evolution from the Laws of Nature. Your wife is beautiful; she is tender; she is total lovingness in her maternal instincts. Therefore, you act accordingly, not like a bull in a china shop. Make sure your body touches hers through-out this ceremony so that she feels your organ. For she ... and she alone, initiates this act of copulation the *first time* you sexually mate. Plus, your gentle touch is security for her throughout its process of surrendering her maidenhood, her sexual innocence. A very emotional delicate time indeed for the female, yet one she will treasure for eternity in her reciprocal female love for you.

Both Parties? If you are not completely successful the first time, as in premature ejaculation from the male? Then forget about it. Try again later. You are on your honeymoon, at least you should be for this ceremony. Because once upon a sensible time, that is what a honeymoon was for. Therefore, coming to know each other all over again, sexually, intimately, completely, lovingly. Much long-term sexual happiness and lasting trust in your marriage from this spiritual ceremony, have no doubt.

Positive Sexual Ceremony in Cold Climates or if You Do Not Have Access to Nature's Pristine Domain

Slightly different ceremony required here for cold climates, or you will freeze in the process. You will have to bring divine Nature into your first sexual union, by honouring the deities of Creation with flowers in the bedroom, which is also highly recommended when trying to conceive. Comprehend in its action, you are acknowledging the Intelligence responsible for the reproductive organs and procreation. Thus, for their blessings, i.e., healthy children conceived then, or later in your marriage.

Therefore, this first sexual union and its ceremony is very special. Along with both your thoughts centred around that intent, that request, that pure desire to honour Creation with your future children, along with a desire for their happiness and natural harmony with you. Then, assuming you are physically and psychologically healthy in body, mind and spirit? Then that is what will return to you - guaranteed, that positive influence and its created karma will accompany your seeds, your deeds, your needs, for everyone, would want healthy, happy, beautiful children. Know this spiritual knowledge that makes all things possible, from within the creative intelligence of divine Nature and yourselves, and always remember, that respect is born of respect as love is born of love, in the spiritual and physical workings of life.

About conception/conceiving:
Our intent for children must be mutually agreed before marriage in Nature's interactive workings. i.e., not ambivalent or one-sided after we are married, thus, both parties should be in harmonious agreement for children, otherwise, abstain during the fertility cycle. Men must respect and honour their wife's wishes always in this maternal department. She

and she alone as the child bearer knows when the time is right for her to conceive, not the male. A man's seed is primarily the physical catalyst for conception. However, the spiritual ingredients for that child, are within the spiritual attributes and pure desire contained within the female and divine Intelligence. Males are the physical means - yes, but that means must contain mature love in its expression and delivery. Re- the impersonal spiritually blind artificial insemination laboratory and its frozen sperm and harvested eggs.

Note: Because spiritually blind science, are unknowingly damaging Creation, with their misplaced genius for tampering with life and altering its Laws of Nature ordained evolution. Understand that male and female love, is the influence (karma) that should accompany sexual union and conception in our species and not, thoughtlessness and a total lack of respect and consideration for the Intelligence underwriting life. Nothing else but that combined male and female love is required for her desire to be fulfilled from the Intelligence of Nature. Then no negative karma from other realms of existence may enter that mature, shared, bonding procreation love during conception. Note: The impersonal cloning and artificial insemination components of medical science and the entrepreneurial money-making big business promotion behind it. To make big bucks and fuel the economy of course.

Clarification: The female, (when not damaged in childhood), is the maternal tenderness of Creation, the nurturing divine aspect of Creation and perhaps before we go any further, we can dispel any doubt about the other archetypal attributes contained within the female species. i.e., tenacity, great stamina, the strength of purpose, courage, the ability to rise above all hardship for the love of her children and the warrior spirit contained within her feminine essence. For truly, they are all contained, (however latent), within the female gender. Note: Male macho dimwits and immature alpha males with crude sexual jokes and female derogatory put-downs, i.e., dumb blondes and bimbo brunettes etc. Who themselves, obviously function from everywhere else in the human body but the brain in the head?

Clarification: Adolescent males need to understand that your future children need all those archetypal spiritual qualities found within the female's creativity, that is fused by your mature love for her contained within your seed, in your sexual deed, within her need. Comprehend and honour the Laws of Nature as the male catalyst for conception, when you control your sexual drive with spiritual maturity and respect, the female and the Intelligence underwriting procreation and sexuality.

If possible, when possible, consult the JYOTISH Vedic astrologers for the best time to conceive. Therefore, which equinox of the year to compliment both your archetypal astrological qualities. A very sensible consideration to bless your future children with, for on-going harmony within the family structure. i.e., Consideration of natural affinity between you and your yet to be born children within your birth signs. An astrological factor, but not the sole factor, for compatibility within the family structure.

Further Knowledge for Continued Happiness Throughout Your Married Life

Sexual union throughout our married life with our soul mate only - full stop. Sex with others, even if your marriage partner is not aware of its infidelity, brings negative influence (karma) to invisibly contaminate your marriage and sow the seeds for family chaos and unhappiness. It is a devolution cause and effect karmic influence that your offspring reap too.

We bequeath them that destructive karmic influence through thoughtlessness, immaturity and selfishness in marriage. So, 'think about others first', instead of, 'I can do what I like,' in the sexual department of life. Therefore, do not applaud and emulate the sexual promiscuity that is being saturated into society through its current entertainment mediums. Comprehend those acting out and eulogising sexual promiscuity on the big movie screen, the internet and television, have got it seriously wrong in their spiritless minds. If they persist with this negative bent to corrupt society and send our children in the wrong sexual direction, then its good night with their spiritual evolution at the end of the human day. Therefore, do not go with them. Prescribe to a different sexual reality, one that compliments life and the institution and sanctity of marriage and family not degrades it.

More unheard of serious sexual stuff:

Never engage in group intercourse called orgies. Alternatively, repeatedly jump from one man's\woman's bed to another, also called, casual sex and sexual freedom. We bring sexual disorder (STD) into the world by doing so, and it is the male, that has created, (and is still creating), sexually transmitted disease in our species. In Nature's primordial procreation workings and our human species, many females may have union with the same man without creating sexual disorder in Nature, but never vice versa. When more than one type of male sperm is present in the reproductive organs of the female, then sexual disease will eventuate. Perpetuating disease in the biology of Nature's genetics structuring life and sexuality is the outcome. The procreation fluids of the male and female are powerful creative fluids in Creation biologically and spiritually speaking, because they combine to create life. Male sperms of different opposing spiritual qualities, (negative and positive), invisibly clash in the creative reproductive biology, (archetypal Intelligence), of the female. A clashing invisible to microscopes, until it manifests as a disease within the reproductive organs of the male and female. Knowledge and understanding found within spiritual acquired consciousness, not physical consciousness or the science laboratory. Also, do not believe that condoms are the saviour of humanity where STD is concerned, it is a fallacy.

Explanation: All diseases of the sexual organs are born from not life-supportive, disrespectful to Nature, wrong sexual activity of human beings. Understand all contagious diseases of the sexual organs, have come into existence through past sexual malpractice in our species.

Wrong to Nature sexual practices and its created sexual karma, that is alien to the archetypal spiritual Intelligence structuring sexuality and procreation. It is that human-created destructive karma, that enters the primordial creativity of Nature underwriting the biology of life and procreation and causes it to malfunction.

Growing sexual disease and pathological disorder is but one physical returned outcome of that human-created self-destructive sexual karma. Because, as we sow, so do we reap with our human creativity in the creative workings of primordial Nature. Human garbage creativity in equals primordial garbage creativity back out and returned to its human source. Therefore, once we know something is wrong and harmful to ourselves, life and Nature, then always avoid doing it and those promoting its wrong to Nature sexual behaviour. They are going in the wrong sexual direction in life and taking the rest of society, especially our children, along with them to its dead-end conclusion in the spiritual evolution department of life.

Clarification: When we turn 21 and become an adult in Nature's biological and spiritual workings, then we become responsible for our actions. Therefore, as grown adults with matured intellects, we are fully responsible for all of our actions and deeds and the returning karmic influence that has been created from them. When we regularly practice transcendent meditation, it becomes natural to intuitively function by Nature's Laws with our thought, creativity, desires and sexuality. However, it is the individual that possesses the faculty of conscious free will, that is the creator's gift to the human being. Therefore, to make the positive life-supportive right choice or the negative not life-supportive wrong choice with our thoughts, actions, creativity and sexual expression. Therefore, the individual freedom to personally choose our course of action and its created up or down destiny with our human evolution. Individual and collective destiny, that is created from the negative or positive quality of karma we have created out of our individual or collective actions. Karma, being the creative tool of evolution into higher or lower structures of consciousness as we sow, so we reap sums it up.

Recapping Sexual Expression in Accordance with the Laws of Nature

Therefore, the understanding and necessary respect for the sexual means to bring life into this world, namely, the composite physical and spiritual intelligence and natural Laws that underwrite procreation and sexual union. Along with dignified intimate sexual expression, underwritten by shared love a between male and female, that compliments the function of sexual union to create life. That has nothing to do with making big reputations, big bucks and big egos, under the delusional banner of artistic freedom of expression to the public of our sexual anatomy and misplaced talents. Along with other sexually immature attention seekers, afflicted with the ego need to constantly make crude sexual jokes and sleazy conversation in public and are often called, comedians.

Clarification: All undignified crass and crude sexual behaviour, also called entertainment, comes out of acquired and inherited negative karma, (an entity), attached to the human psyche. It is time to understand the life-supportive way to honour Nature, life and Creation when sexually interacting with each other. We have a responsibility to future generations to remove that negative, contagious, not life-supportive sexual entity, from the procreation genetics of Nature via this spiritual knowledge. Surely, enough is enough of inappropriate sexual crudity and anything goes sex, coming out of communication mediums and sourced to immature attention seeking adults with poor quality creativity, bumptious egos and media sourced and saturated acclaim. All are having no regard or respect, for the responsible family values of others in society, especially impressionable young minds. The attention-grabbing saturated media, being the worst offender.

Note: Notably from out of entertainment mediums and the porn doused internet, both writing the contagious, *anything goes*, behavioural sexual script for society to copy. A new-age, ego wrote, attention-grabbing, sexual and foul mouth script. That has no respect for the Intelligence of Nature that creates the means for sexual expression. Therefore, its primary purpose of conceiving and bringing life into this world through loving sexual union.

Comprehend, doing what we like, when we like and how we like in the sexual department of life, merely causes human society to unknowingly spiral into sexual chaos, sexual crudity, social decay and spiritual devolution. Because as we sow, so do we reap with our creative thoughts, actions and deeds. That not life-supportive sexual influence (karma) into primordial Nature's creative workings, equals not life-supportive sexual repercussions back out and returned to its human source. To then manifest as growing sexual disorder, social decay and disease (STD) in the human species.

Those responsible for promoting, endorsing and eulogising sexual promiscuity in society for whatever ego, celebrity, fame, attention seeking or monitory pay-off, are blindly going backwards with their spiritual evolution in its human created and promoted reality. Along with corrupting the function of the spiritual and physical Laws of Nature responsible for creating *order out of chaos* in life ... and therefore, the human mind. The non-physical root cause is from an ancestral inherited destructive entity attached to the spiritual psyche and therefore, the human mind also. Trapped in its contagious entity, makes it impossible to experience the divine of sexuality and the fullness of its spiritual expression within the sexual union. Therefore, promoting loveless sexual promiscuity lifestyles in society, in no way compliments our spiritual evolution, primordial Nature and the divine source of life. Reluctance to open the mind to this subject matter healthily and with maturity, causes the degradation of sexuality in the those afflicted. A sexual delusion sourced and fuelled, from an ancestral inherited and karma created destructive entity. An entity/influence that is locked in the ancestral family tree of those afflicted with its nemesis. As we sow, so do we reap sums it up.

Explanation: This perpetuating karma created destructive entity, one of many, is sourced to the wrong to Nature sexual practices of our ancestors. An inherited nemesis compounded through the frigid sexually repressive Victorian era and puritanical purges of sexuality by religious authorities in earlier generations. Succeeding generations have inherited its perpetuating specific ancestral entity bound to its source human beings. Comprehend those afflicted, have inherited the potential of sexual abnormality and wrong to Nature sexual practices. The means have been given to dissolve its karma created ancestral nemesis, locked into the impersonal primordial Intelligence responsible for procreation and sexuality.

Anecdotal notes:
1. Sexuality should always be open to complete frankness, (with a delicate touch), to our children when they request information on its subject. Also, if we are gentle and loving with our sexual expression towards each other, then its observation by an infant (one to three years), will unconsciously endow them with similar behaviour when they sexually bond with their future mate. Their psychological health in the sexual department will then be assured, so too their happiness. That should always be our primary consideration if we bring children into the world, i.e., their welfare, wellbeing and happiness, underwritten and structured from out of unconditional mature parental love.
2. About a solution to the initial pain experienced by the virgin male when penetrating female virginity and vice versa. Anoint the male organ with the specific body oil type of the female. i.e., pure plant extracts, not synthetic substitutes. Consult the Ayurveda holistic health physicians for this knowledge.
3. The male, if not circumcised, should always keep the area under the foreskin washed and clean every day. Make it a healthy habit each day. Many nerve ends are connected under the foreskin, so it is an extremely sensitive area of the male anatomy as it should remain, because we were not born circumcised. However, always pay special attention to its cleanliness before sexual intercourse. A very important consideration for the female's vaginal health.
4. It is not wise to use synthetic contraceptive chemical pills. Especially if we wish for healthy children to complement our

offspring and their offspring ad-infinitum. Saturation of synthesised chemical pills into life, will ultimately cause the demise of life on this planet. Science cannot subjugate the Intelligence of Nature underwriting sexuality, procreation and the chemistry and biology of life. To do so contravenes the function of the self-referral Laws of Nature to create order out of chaos in life.

5. The spiritual advice is to understand the workings of the menstrual cycle and use its knowledge, to map your fertility cycle. Comprehend we must understand, respect and work with Nature's interactive intelligence, not fight it, subjugate it or blindly pollute it. As some creative components of science and its synthetic toxic pollution are currently doing, albeit blindly.

6. To compliment the Laws of Nature, the female should always positively acknowledge and respect their unique gift to give birth to life. How beautiful is this monthly gift that comes from the divinity within Nature to conceive? You are honoured as a female in this reproductive department of Nature and its privilege, to bring life into this world, underwritten by mutual male and female love.

Understanding for Those Females that suffer from the Effects of the Menstrual Cycle

From a spiritual perspective, this monthly re-occurring misery is linked to an ancestral inherited entity, causing *chemistry imbalance* in the female's procreation biology. Because this biological/genetic/ karma created and perpetuated malfunction, is not meant to be in the, 'order out of chaos,' function of the self-referral Laws of Nature in the biology of life. Laws that have ceased to be self-referral in processing the chemistry of the female's menstrual cycle. This inherited and perpetuated procreation malfunction is linked to an ancestral created destructive entity. Its lineage inherited misery is compounded, from the karmic influence created out of resentment for the menstrual cycle. Those negative thoughts have also become a monthly returning habit locked, into the menstrual cycle. Therefore, understand the invisible cause of its re-occurring monthly misery and neutralise that negative cycle, through regular twice daily correct meditation and do not hate your body or the menstrual cycle with negative thoughts. It is a no, no, in the interactive workings of primordial Nature, that returns what quality of influence (karma) we create with our thoughts. Also, see the Ayurveda holistic physicians, for a natural plant extract to help address the chemical imbalance in your female reproductive biology.

Explanation: It is time to understand that existing science, has no comprehension of the Spiritual System that underwrites and orchestrates life and its biology. Therefore, they have no comprehension of the invisible root cause of pathological inherited disorders. The synthesised chemical drugs that science is creating are only addressing the manifested physical symptoms of entrenched spiritual located causes. The public must understand this spiritual shortfall in their physical acquired science knowledge, in addition to those experimenting blindly on life in the spiritless laboratory. Because incomplete experimenting on everything science and drug companies are unknowingly taking future generations to an unhealthy conclusion, with the saturation of this synthetic drug technology (pills) into life. Because all perpetuated biological malfunction and disease that plagues our species, has come out of humanity's wrong-to-Nature creativity, contaminating the function of the Laws of Nature to create and maintain *order out of chaos* in life.

More spiritual observations:

If we respect the intelligence of Nature and its Laws, and the sexual means to bring the life into this world, then Nature's *order out of chaos* function will naturally flow through our sexual expression, conceiving and giving birth. If we do not wish to have children or any more children, then use the knowledge of medical science to have the fallopian tube tied (female) and the vasectomy method (male). Not synthesised contraceptive chemical pills. In this non-polluting to Nature method of contraception, we are helping Nature, not contaminating the biology of life with synthetic chemicals and other thoughtlessness. As in bringing unwanted, unloved children into this world, with perpetuating negative karma repercussions for those responsible and the offspring. That in turn, breed potential pathological problems to arise in humankind. As we sow, so do we reap?

Where pregnancy has occurred from unconscionable rape or where a genetically malformed fetus is concerned, abortion is not a crime to the divine intelligence that has authored life. In spiritual and physical fact, terminating the pregnancy prevents the procreation perpetuated pathological malfunction from repeating its cycle. In further spiritual understanding, when we take our first breath at birth, then do we become recognised and treated as an individual within Nature's spiritual workings of life, not before. Understand that we cannot destroy the spiritual essence attached to the unborn child, through terminating a pregnancy. However, we can certainly destroy the quality of life for that child and eventual adult, by not doing so. It is also wise, to avoid using wadding of any description inserted in the female anatomy for menstruation. Perhaps well-meaning in its original idea, but spiritually blind people and big bucks, are responsible for promoting this wrong method of dealing with monthly periods.

Comprehend in primordial Nature's creative workings underwriting the biology of life, the above method is asking for trouble. The potential for disease is a possible negative outcome not necessarily now, but later in life. Therefore, do not insert anything synthetic into the female sexual organ other than the male sexual organ. Sexual disease is the possible end-result, unhappiness is the possible end-result, misery is the possible end- result. Those manufacturing, promoting and marketing synthetic so-called sexual toys, should stop brainwashing others to use these toxic to Nature synthetic products. Nature's intelligence is perfect; our human intelligence and creativity is not. Note, sex shops, the science laboratory and drug companies. We must understand and respect Nature and work with Nature, not keep usurping the Intelligence and ordained natural Laws, that are processing life and evolving our physical and spiritual evolution.

More spiritual facts: It is time for immature males to spiritually grow up in the sexual department and master the primordial sexual instinct and its drive. That includes implementing the meaning of sexual dignity and respect for the female within its expression, along with the necessary thoughtfulness required towards your wife's wellbeing and happiness within the family structure. Because your children's happiness and wellbeing depend on it also ... they go hand in hand. Thus, demanding sex when you feel like it, and she does not or is monthly indisposed, is not only selfish but a glaring sign of immaturity. In the 'spiritual department of life,' this thoughtlessness and inconsideration leads down-hill to the negative planes of Creation with our spiritual evolution.

Comprehend also, that sexual intercourse and orgasm, creates powerful returning karma to both male and female, this is why sexual union should always be underwritten by shared love. That shared love, in turn, contains a spiritual potential to create an unbreakable harmonious bond in a mature marital relationship. In further spiritual understanding, sexual union is for the eyes of you and your loved one, never anyone else. So private property always, if we wish to evolve our spiritual evolution and as analogy, if we want to collect our harp at the end of the human day and not a shovel. If we respect the primordial intelligence that underwrites sexuality and life, then, in turn, we will be respected by its divine source. Therefore, grasp the importance of positive ceremony, personal acknowledgement, kind thoughts and sexual dignity, towards the composite spiritual Intelligence that underwrites physical life and procreation.

A Spiritual 'Facts of Life' Extra for Young Adults from old Alf

Boot camp handy hints time for young adolescent bloods, sometimes hot blooded, but hopefully never cold blooded. Therefore, spiritual rules of engagement with each other within sexuality and that elusive word MATURITY.

Q: What's it all about Alf?

A: Well, it has nothing to do with sexually gyrating, *let it all hang out*, pop idols and unintelligible trashy lyrics. Alternatively, the latest also commercial media-saturated, must have high tech teen status product gizmo. Alternatively, strutting weirdo fashion fops dressed in the latest synthetic 'horrible designer clothes, underwear and cosmetic bling, but not much else. Ditto, brain numbing, decibel shattering, plinking plonking dancing pole music, with chemical pill refreshments at every three thousandths monotonous techno beat.

Alternatively, media created, fame intoxicated, I'm a success and legend in my own celebrity head TV movie, music and sport's idols. That are cloned to big bucks, big egos and big commercial business pied pipers all? Most of whom, have fallen in love with themselves and their equally superficial upmarket lifestyle of material excess, adulation, big bucks and fame.

Along with other acclaimed business geniuses, dreaming up the next money-making marketed pop culture trend, so that you can also join them in the delusional image creating product of la la land. Therefore, they are playing way out of tune with the Laws of Nature and its subtle music, to the detriment of their spiritual evolution and yours.

More: Neither is it about fashionable self-mutilation with rings stuck on the end of your nose and other bodily protrusions. Alternatively, indelible tattoo *look-at-me* ego advertisements on the body beautiful and other delicate parts of the anatomy. Alternatively, becoming a zombie clone of the, oh so beautiful, also a legend in their own head and infamous, sorry, I mean famous, top of the twang-bang-dang rot world, sorry, I mean rock world.

However, it is about you becoming you in this world, and not, a copied clone lost in a delusional marketing genius and commercial media created world. Therefore, not a carbon copy of those that have become lost in a superficial world of created images, promo's, self-obsession, products, narcissistic egos, big bucks and called, being a winner and success and taking you along with them in the media-saturated pied piper process. At the additional expense of your piggy bank ... or your parent's piggy bank. That has become their piggy bank and grows and grows and grows and Oops! *Pop goes the weasel* in the departure lounge, from out of its big business greed and unproductive life degrading karma.

If you do not agree with Alf's boot camp delivered assessment of the euphoric human worshipped celebrity world, then take it up with the boss Upstairs. However, remember, he's got chronic gout from us lot downstairs on the commercial media and entertainment created sexual blink.

So, if you have got lost in all the above new age top end of town created progress you know, I can say what I like, do what I like, when I like, how I like, with who I like, (*as in the exclusive media created world of worshiped winners),* then you have not grown up yet and learnt the meaning of that new fashionable in-word MATURITY. So, if you have not learnt the meaning of that Upstairs in-word before you have left home then, it is very difficult to learn it afterwards.

To use a Greek mythology metaphor? You will fly too close to the sun and melt your teenage/adolescent wings and likely as not, find it very difficult to fly ever again as an adult. The boot camp directive is to throttle back on this dipstick hypno, hypo, psycho, media-saturated delusional image-created way of life and its pop culture. Along with its also saturated consumer products and sexual instruction, coming from those who have lost the spiritual plot of life and are functioning out of commercial media created la la land — also called, delusional no-where land in the boot camp manuals.

Clarification: According to Upstairs spiritual information, the above media-saturated pop culture garbage is being directed at your impressionable age group, making big bucks for ruthless big business and so-called winners from out of your innocence, vulnerability and naivety.

Also, just like the commercial media, those entrepreneurial money-making geniuses, are using your teenage and adolescent vulnerability, to feather their own nest and to get rich quick at the expense of equality in society, morals, ethics, integrity, social responsibility and our spiritual and social evolution. Those positive, life-supporting, integrity sourced qualities, should always underwrite and propel the actions of those who have acquired power and influence over others in society. To then positively and not negatively, influence a society's direction, culture and destiny.

Note: Because it is that top end of the town acquired *pied piper* power, that young minds have become sucked into and mesmerised by. Through that greed underwritten and commercial driven exploitation of society, you have unknowingly handed your spiritual evolution and destiny to marketing geniuses and Darth's commercial media empire lock, stock and barrel. What is more, they are high on it, your power that is. As well as big buck megalomania and stretched limo ego disorder, that goes with it.

However, to delusional no, no, land in the departure lounge, not to spiritual happy land in the departure lounge. It is time to dissolve this big business greed created destructive entity, that is invisibly powering that exploitation of your vulnerable age group, as well as adult society. So, give that delusional marketing genius promoted lifestyle and its magic wand a big miss, for a little while anyway. It will not take long if you listen to Alf for a change, instead of marketing geniuses, commercial television, dead-brain reality shows, saturated promos and commercials, glossy product magazines and those starring in them and called, celebrities or winner's downstairs, but not Upstairs.

Note: Then you can carry on enjoying yourselves with the positive life-supporting element, that will be left over after the big spiritual shake-up on this human trashed planet. The new mantra to learn that has nothing to do with the commercial media and entertainment negative mantra of *'I can do what I like in society.'* is called, *'positive, harmonious life-supporting activity at all times even in your sleep.'* A positive life-supporting mantra, that automatically promotes that in-word maturity and the power that comes out of it, from the untapped spiritual essence located within you, not outside of you. Therefore, not from worshipping and copying the, 'I can do and say what I like,' behaviour of media-saturated celebrities entrenched in television, newsrooms, glossy magazines and the big movie entertainment screen. That unknowingly, you have also become swallowed up in. Also called, a human created delusional reality on the devolution blink in Alf's spiritual boot camp.

Explanation: That means start respecting Upstairs, Nature, yourself, society, family rules and acquire self-discipline and maturity along the positive way of life. If you find that boot camp directive difficult to accept? Then book yourself in at a behavioural boot camp in your nation and learn to, *'verbally take it as well as give it,'* if you get Alf's new age cool drift?

Highly recommended, for all the out of control alpha young bloods of both genders. For you will surely *come out* a lot more MATURE and knowledgeable of yourself than when you *went in*. By doing this, have a good start to adult life and eventual marriage, kids and happiness down the track of adulthood. Therefore, you will make sure your kids do not fall into the same adolescent pitfalls of irrationality, delinquency and dysfunctional behaviour that you have. Those commercial media, scriptwriter and entertainment distributed, teenage/adolescent euphoric pitfalls you have fallen into, can also be dissolved through the simple twice-daily short practice of correct meditation and not, 'I can do what I like in society,' attitude.

About New-Age Fashionable Sexual Promiscuity, Casual Sex, One-Night Stands and Foul Mouths?

No! No! No! No! No! No! No! No! No! and No! Have you got that urgent spiritual message from Upstairs? Therefore, avoid the above no, no, Hollywood/movie/internet/television entertainment promoted fashion like the plague. That is, if you want to attract the right male to share your life with and not, the wrong male to share your life with, and eventual unhappiness and much regret.

Also, do not go around busting at the seams with your new-found sexual attributes and their magnetic hormone power on the male circuit. Remember, there are negative alpha male delinquents, that cannot help themselves in this sexual department. In their testosterone glazed eyes, no means yes and you become fair game when you let it all hang out on display.

Along with its female sexual message of, *'come and get it,'* tagged on. It's *'look but don't touch'* is just not fair to the positive adolescent male element, trying to hang on to their sexual urges and sanity. Plus, you should be looking for a mature, respectful, considerate positive male to share your life with. Not a one-night stand sexually charismatic prima donna, or a smash grab, you're the weakest link and goodbye after they have notched up yet another, 'James Bond' victory and one-night stand, to tell all their mates about on the internet and elsewhere in public.

Recapping Spiritual Rules of Sexual Engagement and Acquiring that New In-Word Maturity

Therefore, the path to a happy, sexually fulfilled life within marriage and its combined loving commitment. So, do not use your female power and its new-found sexual accoutrements, to tease, tantalise and excite the immature male macho brigade within the marketplace, never not ever. There are some very negative sociopath delinquents among them, that will break more than your heart if you lead them on and do not deliver - got it? Now, according to Upstairs, YOU are the new boss in this procreation department from now on. Therefore, what you say goes in the sexual intercourse department. No means no, the time is not right and not yes, if I persist a little longer. As the alpha male population, Hollydude and that stooopid babbleitus marketing media have come to believe.

So, be much more discreet, subtle and sensible, with your female sexuality in the marketplace and how you use its magnetic power. However, do not go silly and dress like a frump, because as a female, you are automatically sexually attractive to a male. If not to every male, then most certainly through Nature's procreation workings, to some male somewhere, and you should show off your feminine beauty. However, unlike the media, actors, pop stars and celebrities, learn the meaning of subtlety, dignity and natural and not ego acted out sexual sophistication in the marketplace. Along with saving your sexual beauty and its gifts from divine Nature for your future husband after you are married, not before - got it?

Comprehend if you want to attract the right male to give your procreation gifts too, then that right male is the one that will be attracted to your inner qualities, not just your outer qualities. Plus, will understand, respect and honour your female vulnerability, sexual responsibility and dignity in the sexual department and not, have a juvenile tantrum and proceed to emotionally blackmail you, when you put the sexual brakes on before marriage. Thus, if he genuinely loves you, he will respectfully accept that no means no, but not forever, just right place and the right time ... your time. When that time is right, you will give him everything and more. As a result, he will probably walk round in a daze for a week and then ask for a divorce, only joking, okay?

So, how do we bring out these inner spiritual qualities that you latently possess and that will naturally, attract the right compatible, harmonious male. Very simple, we learn to meditate correctly twice daily every day. Then the true you, the real you ... and not, the Dill's and Loon, Barbara Larland and Hollydude days of our dysfunctional lives fantasy make believe you, will develop and radiate your inner qualities to invisibly attract a partner with the same inner qualities. A mutual attraction that needs no words and is sourced, to natural compatibility through Nature's interactive invisible spiritual workings. A shared compatibility phenomenon that is a prerequisite to acquiring a harmonious long-term happy marital relationship. Understand in Nature's dictionary, if physical euphoric sexual attraction, (that is often confused with love), is the only attraction that you have in common, then you are in for heartache and misery in your relationship down the track.

You also need to have duel interests and hobbies in common before marriage, not afterwards. Sexual euphoria and all the fireworks that go with it, eventually diminish down the track, perfectly natural. However, your inner spiritual qualities do not; they keep growing within acquired spiritual maturity. It is those *shared* inner qualities with your lifelong partner underwritten by shared love, that will grow into a karma created spiritual bond, that will be unbreakable through all the inevitable ups and downs of marriage. For marriage, comes with adult responsibility and commitment, to always do the right life-supportive thing within its complex domain, especially where children are concerned.

Note: That parental responsibility often brings great pressures and stresses to a marital relationship. Therefore, you need a mature, harmonious, loving relationship that has shared spiritual foundations, to prevent cracks turning into chasms and everyone ending in the divorce courts down the track, including your vulnerable children. That expensive lawyer easy-fix avenue is a no, no, if we wish to evolve further with our spiritual evolution. It is also time to grow up and understand, the trapped, unhappy child within the subliminal mind, causing all relationship problems in the immature adult. Personality and emotional defects that have been acquired out of a dysfunctional childhood, poor parenting and an unhappy family environment.

About Self-Development, Self-Realisation, Acquiring Adult Maturity, True Freedom, and Finding the Real You. Along with Developing a Lasting Quiet Happiness in Your Adult Life

Now, having put the boot camp verbal stops on any delinquent out-of-control behaviour, i.e., doing what we like, when we like, how we like and with whom we like, then what to do, to fill in that vacuum while you change paths to learn that new in-word *self-discipline* that goes with that other new in-word, *maturity*. Simple, no problem at all. You find out what you are good at, that you do not know about yet, and it is not entertainment copied dysfunctional delinquent behaviour and foul mouths either. A lot of you have already acquired that Darth authorised talent, from out of the television, the internet and movies and its ego sourced self-gratuitous garbage creativity called acting. No! Give that saturated media, internet and entertainment distributed instruction and behaviour a big miss and develop your positive creativity and hidden spiritual potential.

Clarification: So, we dig deep and find out what you have a natural talent for, e.g. fun sport, not winning the sport. Acting? Woodwork? Metalwork? Sewing? Embroidering? Music? Writing? Helping others less fortunate? Wholesome cooking, not new age yuppy cooking. A most important skill to acquire before the kids come along and don't expect the average male to come into the marriage with this talent. You will be lucky if they can cook bake beans on toast without a kitchen disaster I know? Gardening? Create a kitchen garden like in the Victorian days? And use and preserve its produce.

Highly recommended in this century of great change to acquire self-sufficiency and true economic rationalisation and not, material consumer excess and waste. Therefore, investigate and acquire the ancient crafts, the skill of, which are locked up in your genes from your ancestors. Thus, traditional home crafts and anything else that has not been mentioned that is positive and allows you to express yourself creatively and happily. Got the new spiritual age drift? Because *you* must develop *you* to find your elusive spirit, not copy and worship someone else on the celebrity-worshipped blink.

About Finding the Right Partner to Eventually Share Your Body and Life With?

The boot camp directive is to find and develop your specific hidden talent and use that very special free time, that comes with being single and unattached and very precious, to develop it. Therefore, do not become lost in the talent and expression of others called stars, winners and celebrities, pied pipers all. That through commercial exploitation and media saturation have become worshipped trendsetters and role models in society, especially for young minds. Because *follow the leader*, is a natural survival instinct that is milked for all its worth by marketing geniuses and commercial television. Along with ruthless, opportunistic big money-making business, that owns, controls and underwrites the greed-driven treadmill of pop culture and its contagious delusion. A contagious delusion that is sourced to a growing, not life-supportive entity/influence that is contaminating those living, following and identifying with, in its *anything-goes* pop culture.

Note: The spiritual definition of delusion, is anything that has nothing to do with Nature's Intelligence only humanity's dissolvable intelligence. As in high technology and all its science created synthetic wonders and must have techno products. That makes for living the good life spent on a permanent electronic high, but are devoid of Nature's Intelligence and empty of life and spirit because of it. Comprehend the processed substance of all that synthetic material technology, comes out of this precious planet's never-to-be-repeated, irreplaceable, natural resources. Plus, along the polluting way to that fabricated synthetic transformation, has created a destructive entity/influence out of the insatiable greed underwriting its all-consuming expansion. A technology-driven progress that is unknowingly, polluting this planet and its life intelligence and destroying the future for this civilisation.

To help dissolve the above top end of town promoted delusion called progress, we dig deep and connect with and develop our positive, natural, uncomplicated, non-polluting expression and its creativity, not synthetic creativity. Therefore, positive life-supporting creativity and expression, that keeps us in touch with our spirit and the Intelligence of Nature underwriting life on this living planet.

P.S. Do not write to Alf and complain that you have no hidden talents to express yourself through. You must dig deep and find it in other words. This positive process and its spiritual path is called sublimating your sexual drive. That comes booming helter-skelter out of puberty and adolescence and takes over your life and body, there is nothing wrong with it either. It is primordial Nature at work within your body, to make sure the human species survives through procreation. However, we must learn to channel that sexual energy into something positive and expressive and not sexual, until after we are married and settle down in life.

Note: Because it is that sexual energy and its development and sheer power, that causes many of you to go off the rails during adolescence aided by the irresponsible media. You know, *'I can conquer the world, I'm the greatest, I'm a winner, I am invincible.'* Alternatively, perhaps, *'Stop the world 'cos I want to get off even if you don't, so hard cheese and get a life yourself. Because I can do what I like and what's it got to do with you anyway? And you don't own me.'* etc. etc. etc. However, a wrong! Wrong! Wrong! Scriptwriter, actor, movie, commercial television and entertainment introduced philosophy (delusion) into your vulnerable age group. Understand when we live in a society, there must be childhood learned, positive self-administered rules of behaviour operating in it. Otherwise, there is social and family chaos, there is social disharmony, there are unhappiness and misery, and a society/civilisation commences to disintegrate and decay spiritually. It eventually self-destructs and goes out the back door of evolution in chaos, and we don't want that. You have your precious life ahead of you - right?

So, having dug deep and as a result, found out what you are positively and naturally good at, you then need to join other like-minded individuals and develop it further and that is called, positive live social interaction and not synthetic impersonal interaction with your shared creativity. Therefore, join an existing hobby club ... or form your own? This way, you will mix with people of both genders, that have similar interests in life. Out of that interaction will come good friends to share your dreams and aspirations with, to go out on outings with, to have a good laugh with. Plus, sooner or later down the track, you will find a like-minded soul mate of the opposite sex. That also has the same interests and hobbies, likes and dislikes, therefore a similar structure of consciousness that is a variable in human beings. Also, sharing similar consciousness is a must for a harmonious relationship. That positive, giving, caring, sharing socially interactive and not the synthetic lifeless environment, is a good place to find a life-long partner - yes?

Clarification: Therefore, not at disco halls with chemical refreshments, not at all night rave-ups, not on the commercial television, not in glossy magazines, not in blind dating on the porn doused internet, not going kerb crawling, pub crawling, nightclub crawling or any other commercial advertised searching for a future partner. It is wise not to go looking for a life-long partner consciously, its preoccupation contains a potential, to create obsession that clouds sensible judgement. So, let that serendipity miracle from Nature happen naturally, from out of the blue, as it will do if you follow this spiritual advice. Therefore, place its unrequited desire in a compartment of the mind and then forget about it. Let the invisible spiritual workings of Nature take care of the complex details through karma. Because that is how serendipity works – got it?

Comprehend also, that males and females are individual creations in their birth-right, so forget about Adam's rib and the biblical version. When the male and female are not dysfunctional and lost in adolescent immaturity, fantasy and Hollywood and glossy magazine delusion, then the natural negative in the male compliments the natural positive in the female. That ultimately, finds its consummation and further evolution, in a Laws of Nature structured sexual union and spiritually, very beautiful. However, comprehend that Nature, only reveals that perfect sexual chemistry when we are spiritually mature, not before. The non-delusional transcendent path to acquiring that spiritual maturity has been explained. Practice correct meditation.

Note: The marketing genius, commercial television, internet, entertainment and Hollywood path to not accomplishing that serendipity miracle, has also been explained. Along with dysfunctional sociopath, *'I can do what I like,' behaviour* in society, that also does not compliment you or Nature only social chaos. As an analogy, come back to the starting line and wait for the *starter's orders* contained in the word maturity. You have left the blocks prematurely in your quest to grow up, especially in the entertainment and internet endorsed sexual department. If you keep going in that media promoted direction, you will be disqualified at the other end by Nature - got it? In a sensible conclusion, do not trash each other but learn to respect and naturally harmonise with each other. Learn to give and take happily and maturely with each other, then your further spiritual evolution is assured along with a happy, active life and not, a miserable unfulfilled life down the track of adulthood.

Postscript:

Do not go into the habituated childhood acquired state of denial and counter accusation, because your present top end of town indoctrinated euphoric lifestyle and created reality, has been challenged for logic and sanity. As those thoughtless adults responsible for creating and promoting its delusional lifestyle in society will surely do, especially commercial television, entertainment and the media in general. Instead, practice Correct Meditation, and you will find a silent path out of its superficiality and delusional euphoria, that leads to no-where land in adulthood as well as the departure lounge. There is a much more productive reality to find and subscribe too. This spiritual acquired reality will release the full spiritual potential of your precious life. So, do not waste your birth-right, going down the wrong, not life-supportive superficial dead-end path. That has been explained in depth.

Section Three

Revisiting Alf's Spiritual Boot Camp Soapbox Oratories

Oratory No (1)

A Story about Karma

I awoke the other morning to find the alarm clock in a million pieces at the far end of the room. It's still a mystery to me how it got there, but I do know Science and God move in mysterious ways.

Anyway, I will put it down to him/her and God and then we can move on with the rest of the story.

So, having retrieved all the pieces, I then put them in my 'gizmo fix it later cupboard,' (which I might add, is very congested at the moment), and plugged in the kettle for a cup of tea to cheer myself up ... and guess what? It went up in a puff of smoke, the kettle that is. So, having stuffed that also in the, 'fix it later cupboard,' and after engaging in a wrestling match with the cupboard door to get it shut, proceeded to turn the television on to find out what was happening outside in the rest of the world ... and guess what ... nothing happened, in the television that is. I was not sure about the rest of the world, but mine was beginning to look very bleak indeed. No alarm clock, no cup of tea, no television, and guess what? I broke the cupboard door as well trying to squash the television in with all the rest of the broken techno product gizmos.

Anyway, I did not put the door in the cupboard not because it would not fit, but because it had started to rain, and the roof had a hole in it. Where did the hole come from? Good question. Well, to cut a long karma story short and keep it brief, I was up on the roof the other day fixing the television aerial that the birds all sat on at five o'clock in the morning arguing amongst themselves who could make the most noise, (like human beings), and had previously got broken when one of my boots hit it. How did my boot get up there? I threw it.

Anyway, I got the ladders out of the cupboard, (different cupboard that is from the broken gizmo product cupboard), and while trying to fix the aerial, I accidentally fell through the roof and made a hole in it, the roof that is ... not my boots, I'm still wearing those.

Anyway, coming back to my bad karma day ... otherwise we will never finish the story. Well I fixed the hole in the roof with the busted door ... because it was far too useful to put in the fix it later gizmo cupboard. Then I went and got my bicycle out of the shed to go down to the village and see old Bob, (my mate), and have chat about my misfortunes over a cup of tea, and guess what? Two flat tyres and as everyone knows, you cannot work on an empty stomach. So, I shoved it in the broken gizmo cupboard too, the bike that is. Which was easy now there was no door on it and then took off on shank's pony, (my legs), to have a chat with old Bob about my unfortunate happenings.

Anyway, the long and the short of it was that I managed to reach old Bob's place without further mishap, and over a cup of tea, which was very important, he proceeded to explain that all my unfortunate happenings were all to do with the Karma Suture's. Karma means, "action" and "suture" means weaving or stitching. Well, I understood the karma bit, but for the life of me, I could not see what my misfortunes had to do with sewing. I mean I can fix most things, but when it comes to darning holes on socks and sewing buttons, I'm hopeless. Coming back to what old Bob was saying:

All actions are seeds of influence (karma) that we sew into time and time has cycles too, but nothing to do with push bikes no, but influence contained in those cycles of time that return from the Universe.

Because in that past time, is contained all influence (karma) that we have created from all lifetimes on this beautiful planet. So evidently, all my past misfortunes from that cycle of time had arrived at my house all in the one go. Because I have never had a calamitous day like this one before and that, according to old Bob, was a reason for it. Anyway, old Bob said I should stay with him until it all had blown over, (not my house that is but the Karma Suture's), and gone on its way once more. Otherwise, at the rate I was busting gizmo's, I would become a clear and present danger to others and a public liability, whatever that is. I will let you know after I find out from the top end of town. In the meantime, I must fix a few of old Bob's gizmos, because he's got quite a few too. However, at least, his cupboard has a door on it ... at the moment that is.

Postscript:
Q: *What are your thoughts on karma? (also called, as we sew, so do we reap).*
Q: *Have you all got broken gizmos in cupboards too?*
Q: *Are you any good at sewing?*
Q: *Have you experienced karma recycling? (also called, a bad day at the office).*

Old Bob' says not to take the writer too seriously, only seriously enough. Otherwise, you will end up in the cupboard for broken techno gizmos too. Therefore, don't forget to read in-between the lines of this story on karma.

Alf's Boot Camp Oratory No (2)

About Creating Spiritual Progress for a Change

Therefore, not all-consuming economic and big greedy business progress, corporate predatory takeover progress, piggy bank owns everything progress, global power and control progress. Along with making billions of bucks progress, saturated product and promo progress, marketing genius progress, acquiring tall buildings and shares progress, corporate boardroom progress and grossly overpaid bonus progress. Ditto buying up the planet progress, Hollywood acting, image and fantasy creating progress, catwalk and fashion fop progress, ego preening and euphoric winning progress, obsessive spiritless education success progress. Not forgetting, media non-stop talking progress, celebrity worshiping progress, Barbie doll and macho Ken progress, selling weapons of mass destruction progress, flying to the moon progress, conquering the planets progress. Along with atomising the atom progress, polluting the Earth progress, rearranging life in the laboratory progress, experimenting on animal's progress, synthetic technology progress and other science laboratory divorced from Nature progress. But, about creating spiritual progress ... family progress ... social progress ... adult maturity progress ... world unifying progress ... Upstairs progress.

Clarification of the above: Therefore, not exploitation and manipulation of others progress, entrepreneurial mogul buy-up-the-world progress, telemarketing annoying progress, glossy magazine tittle-tattle progress, coming out of the closet progress. Ditto do what you like in society progress, act stupid now and pay-later entertainment progress, adolescent-targeted commercial television progress. Hollywood presentation of news and information progress, product and promo brainwashing progress. Not forgetting saturated advertising consumer progress, image creating progress, the worshipping of winning human beings progress, I love me and my ego progress, the body-beautiful progress. They are collectively summed up, as delusional progress to the Funny Farm for a winning consumed, commercial TV and entertainment and techno product addicted nation. Otherwise known as living a human created delusional reality called progress. No wonder Darth is clapping his hands, and St Peter is wringing his.

Conclusion: Some of America's founding fathers and dignified statesman (presidents) embedded on Mount Rushmore, will be turning over in their graves with utter dismay at where big corporate owned America has ended up; after all their constitutional hard work and political Endeavour to make a better New World long ago, take another look at the Constitution?

Professional note of caution when dealing with this contagious media promoted delusional reality called progress. Now gone global under the banner of democracy, freedom of expression and I've got my rights to do, say and create what I like in the world. This self-gratuitous progress comes in the name of individualism, capitalism, free enterprise, winning and realising my childhood dream. But, at the expense of society and the planet and collecting our harp at the end of the human day, note the top end of town in the driving seat and the majority shareholder of so-called progress. Also included in the caution, is commercial television, saturated promos and products, celebrity worship, anything goes entertainment, violent computer games, anything goes sexual freedom and dollar withdrawal symptoms. That may all be very traumatic to give up.

The suggested boot camp remedy for withdrawal symptoms. *Therefore,* stay off the café latte and drink tea, to neutralise the media, internet, entertainment, TV and glossy magazine 24/7 delivered cocktail of boobs, abs, bums and whatnots. Along with human winning and worshipping neurosis, commercial product toxicity, stock market information overload, saturated promos, advertisement delinquency, the late-night ego and sex shows, celebrity worship inebriation, catwalk fatigue, spin doctor and scriptwriter delusion and synthetic pills, café latte and fast food saturating the human brain.

The bottom line: We create lasting happiness from inside located spiritual sources; we only create a delusional fleeting, temporary happiness from outside physical sources, image creating, material possessions, worshipping ourselves, big bucks, commercial television, being a winner, acquiring status, fame, adulation, gongs and dissolvable public acclaim etc. etc.

Alf's Boot Camp Oratory No (3)

About Relationships and Social, Family and Cultural Decay

What exactly has gone wrong in the world with the way we treat each other? The way we treat our loved ones, our families, friends, strangers and society. Because the cause of this scriptwriter, celebrity, actor, glossy magazine, media and entertainment channelled behavioural problem, is fuelling endemic divorce, single parents, miserable, unhappy families, social decay and psychological disorder in society. Its invisible cause is from a contagious destructive human created entity/influence coming out of the so-called successful top end of town. This not life-supportive entity/influence sourced to greed, is fuelling endless miserable spiritless existence within so-called progress. A progress that is but a delusion, when it is unaccompanied by spiritual integrity, family values, respect for society, respect for life, respect for Nature.

Along with respect for each other and respect for equality, harmonious interaction and spontaneous not acted out, natural empathy with others. Surely enough is enough of this socially unproductive, media/entertainment delivered, delinquent behaviour and ego sourced king of the castle message to win at everything, to be bigger and better at everything, to conquer everything, to possess and own everything and claim success in society through being a worshipped winner, a dysfunctional society that is. This delusion in society, is born out of a 'got it wrong,' ego-driven ideology to be successful and a winner in life, through acquiring material, winning, fame and status accomplishments to fuel delusional self-esteem. A primordial ego sourced delusion that is being eulogised out of, 'got it wrong,' scriptwriters, entertainment and communication mediums, that include our incomplete Education system.

Comprehend as the mature adult; everyone is a winner if no one is a winner. Because under that past-the-used-by-date ego driven ideology for acquiring self-esteem and fame, there can only be one winner, therefore everyone else is a constant loser. Understand in the 'Spiritual System', life is not about pursuing power, fame, adulation and winning to acquire a dissolvable material sourced self-esteem, it is about spiritual living and its accomplishment to acquire an Upstairs lasting spiritual acquired self-esteem.

Note: Because it is this education/media indoctrinated all-consuming material success neurosis acquired in childhood, that prevents us from acquiring spiritual success neurosis in adulthood and that, is the correct neurosis to acquire if we want to get past St Peter at the gates, not the other media and education promoted one. That is a recipe for creating unhappiness and dissatisfaction in society, especially in the untalented bottom end of town.

Clarification: We do not constantly give one child in the family all our love, attention, praise and accolades, and none to the others, it inevitably creates an unhappy fractious discontented family. Likewise, we should not constantly give born talented children in the classroom and on the sports field, all the accolades, awards and attention and none to the others. It inevitably sources inadequacy, disillusionment and loss of the child's self-esteem in those of average intelligence, who happen to be the vast born norm on the planet and not the other way around. It is an immature education and media ego practice, that leads to creating a psychologically damaged, inadequate, disadvantaged, worthless, lost, depressed, unhappy, dissatisfied adult section in society that do not know why ... and are constantly chasing and worshipping the winners and products to find out why and claim a piece of the action. Spearheaded and driven, by the obliging non-stop talking, winning news of day, socially blind, thoughtless media.

As mature adults, we should understand that worshipping and showering adulation on a born gifted minority creates disharmony in society, it sows the seeds for inequality in society, and it fuels underlying discontent in society. It unknowingly creates misery, unhappiness and a lack of self-worth in its ordinary citizens, the losers. It also fuels ego delusions of self-importance, superiority, euphoria and invincibility, in those that are being immaturely worshipped for winning at everything. That, in turn, leads to mental disorder, conceit, ego sourced narcissism, megalomania and delusions of grandeur, especially in the corridors of acquired power, study our history books for confirmation.

The bottom line: Psychological disorder in both family and society, is the negative outcome from this immature worshipping of born talent, high IQ classroom distinction, sport distinction, the body beautiful distinction and other so-called material success accomplishment, to acquire self-esteem in childhood ... that is then, carried forward into adult life. Unknowingly, we end up with a psychological recipe for creating social problems in the losers as a result. All because we must endlessly compete and become a worshipped winner, to receive adulation, fame and accolades and claim success in society, that is not true. Adults have merely created it to be true, by creating its reality/ideology for acquiring self-esteem and fame and worshipping it in society, remembering that children learn by adult example.

Clarification of the endemic problem in verse.

Relationships

Do not dominate another's personal space
Understand and realise
This unnecessary human mistake
From out of childhood does this come
And all power, winning and ego-fuelled habits
Can be realised dissolved and undone

So love and let live
With honesty supreme
Power and winning over another is most immature

And not in the Spiritual Scheme
For we have twin roles to play out in life
Know them as the ingredients of husband and wife
Both must be balanced and never weak
For they are part of our psyche
So make them complete

This duality is part of the human norm
For both masculine and feminine
Are within our Earthly form
Fuse them together in harmony and love
Then through the silence of Meditation
Share and give
The offering of the dove

Then the relationships we form
Will be sustaining and warm
That will nourish another
Whether it be sister or brother
Possessing another's innocent space
Is far from love
And most definitely not of grace

Then shall all beauty flow our way
To compliment the fullness of our ever-active day
For when we touch and acknowledge
Another's heart
Friendship will play a lasting part
In the meaning of life and a working connection
Complimenting Creation with kindness and perfection.

Alf's Boot Camp Oratory No (4)

Alf's Uncomplimentary Message on Trashing, that we are Calling Progress

SPIRITUALLY WAKE UP or go down the cosmic gurgler within both physical evolution and more importantly, spiritual evolution. For that is the way to eternity within this beautiful ever diversifying shared Creation. Dead end devolution is the bottom line if we persist in calling what we are doing on this planet progress.

This delusion is not progress it is unmitigated trashing, the trashing of the planet and the trashing of ourselves and Nature in the process. A mindless thoughtless trashing created out of incomplete education, poor parenting, and pursuing wrong social values that do not compliment society or life. Those not-life supportive spiritless values fuelling society's negative direction and destiny, are coming out of the top end of town and saturating the bottom end of town. Where the primordial sourced instinctive, *follow the leader*, rules in a highly social species.

Comprehend if we keep up all this so-called progress, then social and cultural decay and growing psychological disorder is inevitable, the polluting bottom line and the negative outcome in society. Created from the media sourced and saturated worshipping of material values, self-image, fame, status, greed, products, winning and so-called successful human beings called winners and celebrities.

We have the gift of life, priceless gift of life, from the Creator, yet many are pursuing all the wrong values in life. As in movie and television entertainment promoted lifestyles, they sleep around and call it sexual liberation and pursue superficial material values, that do not respect life and Nature but unknowingly, degrade life and Nature and Upstairs.

Note: Therefore, in that spiritless lifestyle, we do not cherish our children, each other or family values merely acted-out pretence at going through the superficial motions. Family spiritual values, that should make a family sing into eternity, share into eternity, love into eternity, when we are in harmony with the spiritual Laws of Nature structuring, *order out of chaos*, in life and not the endemic greed and winning, that is fuelling the global consumer economy and its so-called unstoppable progress.

Q: *What has gone wrong in affluent, product saturated, entertainment swamped, economy propelled nations?*

Q: *Why are our human-created material ideologies/realities that we live and called progress, unknowingly so socially destructive?*

Q: *Why have we become self-destructive, self-absorbed, self-gratuitous and uncaring of each other and devoid of respect for spiritual values and empathy for this planet and its well-being?*

Note: Because self-destructive we are, in families that have no spiritual based harmony or joy within them, only commercial and material indoctrinated superficial values. Those families merely exist as the very poor training ground for the next generation to go out and trash the planet, as their commercial brainwashed, product saturated, status, image, success, greed and winning consumed parents have.

Q: *So why is this sorry state of human affairs, endemic in affluent so-called civilised nations?*

A: We have lost contact with our spiritual essence and the Laws of Nature, creating order out of chaos in life. Therefore, we have lost intuitive connection with the divine source of the Laws of Nature contained within our spiritual essence. For the spirit does not conquer, does not possess, does not dominate, does not trash, does not exploit and manipulate other human beings, does not degrade life and Nature, does not trample on everything for big bucks, power and self-esteem. The spirit loves, the spirit gives, the spirit cherishes everything that belongs to the transcendent creativity and intelligence of the Creator.

Spiritual fact: The accumulative, negative cause and effect influence (karma) coming of our destructive material consumed trashing progress on this planet, equals the following: We must snap out of the euphoric spell of greed, winning, fame and self-gratuitous behaviour, that we have been saturated with from the, 'got it wrong,' communication mediums, economy obsessed governments and big greedy corporate business. It is time to swallow Alf's uncomplimentary boot camp words and understand the spiritual knowledge contained within them.

Alternatively, accept the dead-end consequences of not doing so for this, 'got it seriously wrong,' global civilisation and its future.

Note: Because it is our so-called progress, that is creating these dead-end consequences for our spiritual evolution. Nothing to do with God, nothing to do with the Devil, nothing to do with Fred Nerk, Joe Bloggs or Alf; but everything to do with those who are creating and in charge of this greedy civilisation's all-consuming polluting progress to no-where land.

It is time to move off the platform of material evolution and move on to the platform of our spiritual evolution for a change. The transcendent acquired means has been given, to collectively dissolve this human created delusion we are calling progress. Because when our human intelligence is back in sync with Nature's interactive spiritual Intelligence and Laws, we will have acquired the spiritual means to dissolve this delusion we are calling progress. A created miracle that will come out of our positive charged and not negatively charged human creativity and intelligence. Note the born gifted minority in top end of town creating and in charge of progress, with the acquired power to make this miracle of change happen.

Clarification of the above in verse.

Progress

**It is time to introduce new elements to life
This spiritual knowledge
To help neutralise all strife
Positive inspiration forming the collective key
Let us draw together
And learn the meaning of harmony**

Nothing is impossible
Of this, you can be assured
The attributes within the universe
Are 'divine' and very pure
So let none deny another's personal space
To understand the scheme of things
Within the divinity of the human race

Let those who have the power
Unite in a common cause
To expand their integrity
And understand Cosmic Law
Acknowledging their gifts in this unity combined
Dissolving old habits
That complicates an intelligent mind

Then let us progress to another plane of life
One that is uplifting
From knowledge of what is right
That is naturally acquired
Without ego or praise
Through the simplicity of Meditation
Dissolve the perpetual haze

Of ignorance and discontent of poverty
And malefic malcontent

For nothing is more detrimental
To the progress of evolution
Than the negativity of trapped
Suppressed unresolved emotion
Realising this is our personal due
Within the field of awareness
That lies within you
Thus never, not ever upon milder dispositions
For this negativity returns
And permeates all motion

So, in the knowledge of the archetypes
That manifest as our deeds
We will understand Nature
To the Nth degree
Then knowing our self in subtle content
Fuse and use our evolution
Towards Divine intent

Thus, Education must be holistic
And not consist of one source
Our children must learn the rhythms
Of Nature's discourse
This is found in the science of inner understanding
By knowing what motivates intellectual blinding

Thus, schooling should provide
Spiritual knowledge of the Universe
Knowledge of the planets
Knowledge of their influence
For everything is related

On this Universal plane
Through the understanding of the heavens
There is much to be gained

So it is time to make all progress our way
For spiritual Intelligence to manifest and stay
For both humanity and Nature must join as one
To acknowledge Creation in harmony and fun
So let's chart a course and come together
Thus understand ourselves
Understand each other
Through activity that unites
Now and forever
We will always honour
Our sister and brother

Then shall we progress
To all that is meant.

Alf's Boot Camp Oratory No (5)

About the Subliminal Child within the Adult and a Feedback Comment from a Wal-Mart Enthusiast:

Oh yeah! what do you mean the subliminal child within me? I'm grown up, got kids and a mortgage and whopping big credit card blow-out and a live-in partner. I've got the latest talking fridge, the latest 90-inch flat screen smart TV that makes hamburgers and café latte in-between commercial breaks. I got the latest fashion Barbie and Ken I-love-me clothes off the ego catwalk at Fopsville, the latest brain matter transporter mobile-phone with sanity recall on hold, the latest you beaut super-duper electronic gizmo cluttered vertical take-off automobile, the latest DVD zonc player with multiple free instructions in twenty-five languages. Not forgetting my new three hundred horsepower chip-blown remote-control ride on lawnmower, with electronic lunch-pack, ear-pod and internet extras.

Oh yeah! and I've accumulated enough in my overseas Wall Street share portfolio, to fly to the moon and examine its craters next year. Then the following year with all the frequent flyer points from my moon trip and credit card binge, I will have enough to take a big buck trip to Mars in my Wal-Mart, do-it-your-self and assemble at home inter-galactic techno 'Tardis'. To then collect all the scrap from those dud probes and other remote-control techno junk from N.A.S.T.A. Because someone at commercial Foxnewt and Skynewt, said there's big bucks in it and a celebrity contract and a trip to Fred's Casino in the desert, if you get in first at their commercial newsroom with its junk along with all the other junk.

Oh yeah! Nearly forgot to mention my newly installed big buck triple glazing in the house. This to keep the noise pollution out from my loudly complaining neighbours, when I'm listening to my ten thousand-watt, ninety-eight-decibel techno hi-fi and twanging and jumping up and down, on my electric guitar and techno-amplified electro fortissimo jungle drums. That I brought last week on, have now and go deaf later, terms of biological credit, and to keep my new-age live-in partner happy, I've ordered the latest duel-purpose time-saver washing machine with internal ironing circuitry and multiple home-entertainment facilities. With internet connection for the kids, while she's washing and spin drying them together at the same time.

Anyways, what subliminal child are you talking about, because I ain't got one on me? How much does it cost to have one anyway? And can I put it on one of my thousand fly-by credit cards? because I don't wanna miss out if it's a dang good deal at corporate Wal-Mart.

Boot Camp Reply from Techno Deafened and Polluted Alf:

Read my pen and read my decibel deafened techno product allergic mind. Because you have an overindulged/spoilt/undisciplined/

self-gratuitous child, with a commercial television promo created screw loose, in your cough, mutter and splutter so-called adult mind. Because I do not see a mature adult operating within any of that material acquisition and must-have commercial spin-doctored consumer reality, socially contagious reality, big greedy business fuelled reality, marketing genius propelled reality, fruit-loop product addicted reality. This material wanting and product buying neurosis, is coming from a marketing genius manipulated subliminal child, embedded within the product deluded so-called adult. Compliments of saturated commercial television in childhood.

Clarification: A saturated product buying program that has been installed in the subliminal mind, from saturated commercial TV indoctrinated product brainwashing in childhood, is preventing adults from ever growing up into the Spiritual System. A commercial media indoctrinated and out-of-control accelerating consumer treadmill of material product acquisition, to satisfy the subliminal wants and needs of the lost child embedded in the adult. That childhood sourced immaturity is exactly what the pea-brain marketing/advertising brigades exploit. Through saturated advertising and image-creating to capture the subliminal workings of the unexpanded adult mind.

Boot camp wake-up call:
You are under their commercial promo spell, as well as shop-until-you-drop Wal-Mart neurosis. Your ding-bat brain has become a commercial wired, product programmed, manipulated curser tool of the sociopath marketing genius and other commercial money-making associates, holding the global economy mouse – got it?

We will never get past St Peter at the gates if we do not bring out that lost child that is directing the adult's all-consuming must-have must-buy $ activity on this product polluted planet. We need to bring that I, I, me, me, have, have, want, want, natural function of the child into a conscious adult view, because it should not be a natural function of a mature adult, that self-gratuitous, undisciplined lost child and its commercial TV indoctrinated/acquired/brainwashed wanting activity is directing the immature desires of the grown adult. It urgently needs to be made free of that commercial television created entrapment, to be able to grow up and act like a responsible adult, not a commercial product manipulated ding-dong adult.

When the subliminal content of the adult mind is made conscious, we will then be functioning with a integrated personality. That consciously expresses that child through the maturity of the adult's thought, and expressions. More, you will be able to laugh and experience the child's spontaneous joy within those mature thoughts of the adult. More, you will once more experience the innocence that is the divine of Nature within a child, and that innocence (openness) is the means to access the, 'field of all possibilities,' within divine Nature and its self-referral Laws. To then move on with our adult evolution, and out of that shop-a-holic, product and promo manipulated, commercial television indoctrinated, going no-where superficial life, as a positive life-supportive result.

We will then have expanded the adult mind so that the conscious thought of the thinker, functions deep within the complex mind. To then communicate with the subliminal child and dissolve its unproductive childhood indoctrinated content that includes the adult's belief-system? Then we will have cleared a path through all its embedded denied childhood acquired clutter, trauma and emotional entanglement and make it a conscious activity for the adult to deal with. Then we will also become free of those who can capture and exploit the subliminal workings of that lost child, namely the saturated marketing/advertising/product/promo spin doctor brigades. Because you have unknowingly, become a slave to them and too big corporate greedy business. The $ agents of ugh and double ugh?

Boot Camp conclusion:

Q: How do we create/restore communication and integration of the conscious thought process, with the denied flotsam and jetsam and repressed content of the subliminal mind?

Q: How do we bring out that subliminal child with its childhood indoctrinated unresolved content, that is trapped within the unexpanded adult mind?

Q: How do we dissolve the retained denial, repressed/suppressed emotions, frustrations, unfulfilled desires, incessant wanting, needing, possessing, pettiness, jealousy and other unresolved childhood acquired immature behaviours. That also equates to being pockets of trapped repressed thought energy, that in turn, sources residual-stress that becomes locked within the subliminal layers of the mind, from out of the trials, tribulations and trauma of childhood?

Note: To also be a cause for psychological disorders, personality problems, neurosis, depression, unhappiness, delusion, denial, paranoia, irrational thoughts, emotional chaos, destructive intent, conflict, ambivalence, obnoxious behaviour and negative expression. Arising in a delinquent sociopath adult and linked, to a dysfunctional unloved childhood, poor parenting and family and social chaos and negative acquired perpetuating karma. That fuels uncontrollable unproductive bad habits

Q: How do we resolve bad habits?
A: We incorporate the short practice of Correct Meditation into our daily routine, to eventually rid the subliminal (sub-conscious) mind of the residue of childhood acquired flotsam and jetsam and the unproductive karma (influence) and habituated denial that goes with it. This achievement, accomplished without the conscious thought process of the adult, becoming overwhelmed and neurotic with all its childhood negative acquired residual trauma and memories. Because much of this childhood acquired and retained emotional flotsam and jetsam in the adult mind, is the childhood created product of unresolved residual stress. That equates to trapped

thought energy, locked-up in the subliminal workings of the unexpanded adult mind.

Note: When we become well practised in its simple technique, then while we are transcending the activity of thought during Correct Meditation, it allows residual stress to dissipate naturally. Therefore, without having to become involved consciously with its process and without, having to copy the method-acting of Hollywood and Co; to act it out and bring it all out in public. Along with being paid millions of bucks and awarded gongs, for its delinquent/adolescent/obnoxious socially destructive behaviour in movies; that is called explosive drama and gripping entertainment and freedom of artistic expression.

When its residual stress is fully dissolved, then will we have freedom from its immaturity interfering and influencing the adult's conscious thoughts and expressions. Then that individual's 'I,' can become a positive interactive integrated 'we.'

Comprehend that everyone has a positive or negative subliminal child functioning within them. Therefore, become aware of it within you and accept it within you, because within the positive child is the power to re-connect to the self-referral Laws of Nature that create, *order out of chaos*, in life. An intuitive spiritual connection that leads to the field of all-possibilities for the mature adult. But not, a product consumed $ and winning-obsessed adult.

When we consciously incorporate that child's positive expression within the grown adult's expression, then we will function in spontaneous happiness and joyful interaction with others without having to pretend and act the part. Therefore, adult expression and creativity structured in positive, harmonious, totally integrated thoughts and feelings in conscious consideration of everything around us and that accomplishment, is the sign of a mature adult, not what is on the top of this page.

The Child within:

Giving, caring
Sharing and complete
This is how we all should meet
Through this interaction
Create a loving action
Then gentle is our sleep
In words and play throughout your day
Dwell not upon yourself
In giving thus
To others trust
You
Will make heaven your way

From every action there is a reaction
The influence of which returns to us
Better by far to compliment the star
That is shining down on you
In the heavens above there are lessons of love
Doubt not that of which you know nothing
But seek instead
To explore that in your head
That which is intuitively given

The spirit within
Knows not of sin or words
To cloud the divine
Simple and sweet effective and neat
To all good intent, it thus listens
For your spirit is the link
That will not let you sink
No chains does it have for us
How soon you will reach

The heavenly seat
Upon which all destiny rides

So give this some thought
And soon you'll import
The rhythms of Nature's grace
For she will return
Without question and form
Pure love in the chamber of your heart

Yet remember again
Suffering and pain
Are not meant to inhibit us
But first, you must lose
Then find and choose
A path more heavenly sent

Alf's Boot Camp Oratory No (6)

About the Laws of Nature ... Spiritually Speaking that is

Cranking up the science boot camp rhetoric:

Oops! Here we go around the human created product mulberry bush, and another visit to the human-created delusional product funny farm again.

Why?

Because no one in science has sourced the self-referral Laws of Nature in their un-manifest state in the 'unified field', that is their transcendent acquired spiritual home. Plus, existing science, is too busy blindly experimenting on all aspects of life and this physical world, using the static Laws of Physics in their electro/magnetic relative fixed fields of physical expression, to comprehend that the physical senses of perception in the human being are just that. They are created and evolved to interact with Physical Creation and not Spiritual Creation, its invisible source.

Therefore, in our existing structure of biological created consciousness, we have no existing scientific created means of entry into that non-physical Creation where everything physical manifests out of, therefore, it does not exist as an experienced reality. That means we must create the means for it to become an experienced, proven reality. Just like science does now with a light bulb theory, they put its theory into practice and examine and quantify the results to prove or disprove the theory. Abstract Intelligence is no different; you apply the means (correct meditation) to be then able to measure the result in society and prove it, not before.

Oh dear, Alf will not be very popular in some rigid unbending science circles or perhaps science squares. Because that last statement, is going to be hard to swallow and print in all their physical science manuals. They will have to revise their scientific logic and denial cry of, *'prove it to me first before we will accept it,'* if they do, and that is not allowed. It will upset the status quo that they currently own in creating and directing all science reality, to become media-saturated indoctrinated reality for us un-scientific lot on the planet to have to live with. Justified out of a human self-given mandate to do what we like on this shared planet, in the name of scientific progress and saving humanity. e.g. weapons of mass destruction, synthetic polluting technology, toxic chemicals galore, the life re-arranging laboratory, ten billion $ plus atom trashing machines, toxic nuclear waste ... to mention but a few.

Surely it is time to democratically put it to a world vote and not, a politician's vote. It is called a people's referendum on world issues, that affect those that come after us to reap what we have created, which currently is pollution galore. That inclusion of a people's referendum could be called creating real progress and democracy functioning on a level playing field. Not an exclusive top end of town, political, science and big corporate business created and media-saturated exclusive playing field.

According to the spiritual boot camp manuals, the spiritual home of the Laws of Nature lies at the un-manifest level of Creation. You cannot take a Disney ride to their home. You cannot take a big greedy business ride to their home. You cannot take a political, acting, the image created, marketed, catwalk or Hollywood ride to their home, but the thought of the thinker resting on the created vibration of a 'mantra', can and most certainly do, take a ride to their home. More, when the thought of the thinker returns to conscious appreciation within the thinking process of the mind, then that thought is imbued with the qualities of all the self-referral Laws of Nature. Laws that create *order out of chaos* and are the manifested active intelligence of the Creator, permeating within all matter and energy in this interactive Universe.

Interjection from a science enthusiast:
"Holy non-scientific Moses!!! do you mean to say, that all the big tax bucks spent on invading and polluting outer space ... as well as this planet. Along with conquering the other planets and Martian Klingnongs that have run out of H2o and on the return journey, blowing up rogue asteroids that are going to bump us off, if we don't land on the asteroid and plant nukes and atomise them first, is never gonna get us to the real heaven?"

Reply from Alf to scientific scriptwriters, techno spin doctors and macho Hollywood and Co; "Yep, you bet your techno bottom product dollar, that's exactly what Alf is saying and a dang lot more to boot. Especially to science, N.A.S.T.A. big greedy corporate techno business, commercial television, Sky News, Fox News and Hollydud and Co."

Clarification: The gross physical aspect of the Laws of Nature that science uses to understand Creation with are but one function of the Laws of Nature. In Spiritual Creation that underlies and underwrites this Physical Creation, those laws of physics have no physical form or structure whatsoever. So, we cannot possibly understand the workings of other non-physical dimensions using the laws of physics or mathematic. Even Albert, eventually came to that intuitive conclusion.

So, and I know it is going to be hard on the intellect and sensibility, of a lot of very intelligent people that keep ignoring Alf's verbal boot camp ego-battering rams. However, we must intuitively understand and accept, that that the laws of physics have limitations just like the human beings functioning out if its present state of dissolvable biological created physical consciousness. Because the science uncovered laws of physics, are the transformed gross functioning physical aspect of the self-referral spiritual Laws of Nature. Sorry about that disappointing revelation to physical science, in their life-altering synthetic laboratories and underground atom trashing bunkers. But that truth is a spiritual fact from out of the Upstairs laboratory, where we and all life have come from. Not from a test tube, syringes and freezers and spiritually blind human creativity, in the unchallenged life and gene re-arranging, germ-free but not human free, scientific spiritless laboratory.

Comprehend the physical Laws of Nature that Science understands and uses, change and function differently in Spiritual Creation that underwrites this Physical Creation. What is more, there is a no-time-continuum operating at the un-manifest level of Creation.

Interjection from science enthusiast: *"Oh no! not another lot of Dr Who intergalactic gobble de gook."*

Reply: Yep, sorry about that, Alf can't help himself. It's a contagious motor mouth disorder, contracted from out of commercial television, radio shock jocks and the marketing media – ugh! What is not gobble-de-gook, is that operating within that no-time-continuum, are all the innumerable planes (dimensions) of Spiritual Creation. Non-physical planes of Creation that our spiritual essence is evolving through on its journey back to its source, and what is that source? It is the Absolute uninvolved transcendent Abstract Intelligence that everything has manifested out of the silent Creator.

The bottom line: Science and religion, will only become compatible with their respective human created physical realities, when they both function out of that silent uninvolved Abstract transcendent Intelligence with their endlessly talking involved biological intelligence. The spiritual means to solve that physical problem have been given, but no one is interested in listening, why?

Conclusion: No wonder Alf has resorted to using boot camp ego denting comments to get the message from Upstairs across to the deaf media, governments, science and big greedy corporate business, that have conveniently ignored his previous polite correspondence.

Kind regards from Alf once again to the top end of town, and the Laws of Nature this time around.

The Laws of Nature

The Laws of Nature Precipitate Time

Precipitate the universe, precipitate the mind
For the Laws of Nature are heavenly and divine
For they permeate Creation as pure intelligence refined
Manifesting thus as the deities of Creation
Then as the physical inception of Man's incarnation
They procreate life through their symmetric interaction
As the creative element of Mother Nature's inception

In their presence and purity
They permeate all life
Permeate the diversity of the changing day and night
This light and shade of Creation glorify God
Interacting with unity
That is little understood
Ever expanding, ever creating in this interaction supreme
Beautiful vibrations of energy
That should constitute our dreams

For nothing is without them and nothing would exist
So it is time to pay them homage and honour their creative bliss

And how do you acknowledge something
That is invisible to you
Yet responds to every action
From every thought and deed you do
For God has given duality
Through his creative Almighty State
To share with life intelligence
The essence of that grace
So, pay tribute to the energies that constitute the mass
Constitute the universe fabricate all life
For such is their intelligence ethereal and supreme
Without them life could not exist
Within the cosmic scheme

By complementing their perfection
With good deed and good intent
Through saying grace at mealtimes
Before partaking of your meal
In this you honour Creation by thought and of its seed
For this penetrates the ethereal
Invisible but very real
Thus, in simple action harmony does result
Through vibration supreme and subtle
To compliment Nature's love

And when you compliment in acknowledgement
Their presence in your life
All harmony is restored to the origins of strife
For all influence you create

Through your thought and of its state
Is manifested thus
And returned in kind post haste
Better that you honour them
With all kindly intent
In mutual understanding
In love pure and meant

Then the blessings of Nature
Will shower down on you
On your families on your loved ones
Invisible but true
For everything is reciprocal
Within the Universe and you
So, returning what they give
Is the natural thing to do

The love borne within a mother
That nurtured you at birth
The tenderness she showed you
Through her ever loving worth
Her thoughtfulness, her givingness
Her concentrated love
Are but reflections of energies
Born within the Universe

For how else does all life share
The expansion of their young
In mutual understanding of caring that is done
By nurturing, by touching
By giving of themselves
Thus, do all parents know of Nature's Laws unfurled.

Alf's Boot Camp Oratory No (7)

The Hecklers of Physical Creation versus the Planes of Spiritual Creation

First interjection from heckler: *The planes of what???*
 Reply: The numerous ethereal strata that constitute the invisible spiritual platform and workings of Creation. Thus, the spiritual domain of Nature that underlies and underwrites this physical Creation. Comprehend that the innumerable strata of consciousness in that Spiritual Domain contains the individual and collective key-signature of every form of life intelligence that is evolving. Along with a karmic created, *cause and effect,*' link sourced to every individual, to every family, to every functioning organism on this planet. Thus, spiritual Creation contains the spiritual blueprint of all that is physically evolving in the universe.

Second interjection from heckler:
What a lot of crap ... we think you've been mixing it with the toadstools again and watching too many Dr Who television re-runs.
 Reply: Frankly, me' dear, Alf don't give a hoot or a dang what you think, because there's none so dumb as those who think they know everything and therefore have nothing else to learn ... except when they pop off the planet. So, this information is for those who do want to see, who do want to learn, who do want to evolve further within Creation, who do want to know silent God, who do want to know the Divinity within Almighty Nature.

Spiritual fact: The Spiritual Planes of Creation contain the afterlife activity of our spiritual essence, along with the afterlife spiritual essence of all other life intelligence, that is also contained within different vibratory fields (layers) of consciousness within Spiritual Creation. A spiritual essence that has nothing whatsoever to do with our physical created, 'I' and 'got it wrong,' belief system and reality, that the hecklers are functioning out of and getting up Alf's and Tinkerbell's nose because of it.

Spiritual fact: So, to all the professional hecklers out there in the big world — grow up and get a life and get that disbelief act together. Otherwise, when we depart this chaotic world, we ain't never coming back ever again to be able to reach heaven as per the divine purpose of human evolution. So, unless we start understanding a further spiritual reality to acquire and function through down here on terra-firma, then St Peter sure ain't gonna let us out of whichever gates we are stuck behind in the afterlife, to return and enjoy heaven on Earth. For that is what this beautiful evolving planet should be and is going to be, which is a physical reflection of the divine heaven that exists within the Spiritual Planes of Creation, the positive end of it that is.

Third interjection from heckler:
Oh Yeah! Well you don't look or sound very Holy or Angelic to me, which end of Creation have you come from?
Reply: Both, that the Laws of Nature function through to process all of Creation from, have you got the negative and positive spiritual message yet, if not digest the following.

The Planes of Creation

So how do we connect to a view

That is invisible to you
A source so powerful that it instigates life
Instigates the cosmos
So gentle is its might

First culture the awareness within
To transcend to that beyond everything
Find in this silence the transcendental mode

The means to explore all uncharted roads
For such is the diversity of creation
Beyond its physical manifestation
New horizons of truth
Become open to proof
Beyond doubt or any speculation

The senses of perception
In their physical form
Have only access to what is considered the norm
Yet in Man's ethereal state
A body exists too
Its function is to connect the universe to you
aligned and assigned
To your physical form
A replica of the matter that constitutes this norm

This consists of atoms whose 'vibrations' are light
That surrounds your physical form
Throughout your life
For everything is in vibration
In the relative state
Each plane of existence resonates at a given rate
That has Quantum proportions
Beyond physical sight
Functioning from laws within ethereal light
That has its basis in a universal field
That is spiritual, magnetic
Tangible and real

This must be transcended by the awareness within
For its proof to become known
Cemented and bring
Its knowledge and content to the physical mind

Created through discipline practice and time
Its frequency is too subtle to contemplate
With the senses of perception
From your physical state

This silence is the norm by which we propagate
This field of potential
That is the cosmic state
Certainly, there are ground rules to observe within
To expand this field of consciousness and begin
A voyage of self discovery
To compliment evolution
Through fusing and using
The celestial constitution

So, rest and set the wheels in motion
No effort is required
For this universal connection
Thus, the contents of the mind
Are not required for this journey
For this evolves through skill
Innocence and pure creativity
The emotions and thought are put to rest
In the process of surrendering the intellect

Thus, the mantra of meditation
Vibratory and fine
Stills the nervous system along with the mind
Thus, better by far
That you develop to who you are
Within the silence and perfection of Creation
By transcending the strata
That contains all the data
Pertaining to earthly consideration

> The coherence this creates
> Compliments and makes
> Vibration conducive to Creation
>
> And how do we know this exists?
> It is simple
> Its expression is bliss
> That introduces the mind
> To all that is kind
> That emanates from the heart of Creation.
>
> Alf's Boot Camp Oratory No (8)

Sexuality, the Laws of Nature, the Primordial Human Being and the Sexual Facts of Life Revisited:

Alf cranks up the uncomplimentary boot camp rhetoric and points the finger, especially at the all-powerful out-of-control media, the internet and the also anything goes entertainment industry.

Q: Sexual interaction, should it always be respectful, dignified, private, personal, mutual, empathic and harmonious?

A: Yes, most definitely, according to the Spiritual Laws of Nature and Upstairs ... and especially, if we want to get past St Peter at the right and not the wrong gates at human closing time.

Have we got that missing spiritual fact of life across, to the saturated do what you like marketing/advertising brigade and Hollysexbug and Co, and the league of actors? Along with the sex warped artist's forum, the fashionable catwalk of fop, bling and sexual image fame, the comedian's house of dead brain sex jokes. Not forgetting the music pied piper top of the pops sexually gyrating video clip guild, the scriptwriters and producers sexual fantasy club and the reveal all, closet gossip dead brain glossy magazine sex library.

Note: Along with other, 'got it wrong,' so-called successful human beings with a social, psychological and sexual screw loose, in the adult maturity department. All are leading the fashionable new-age sexual promiscuity charge to no-where land, for adolescent retarded adults. On a new-age, media and entertainment prescribed and saturated, and ancient Greek endorsed ego and the narcissistic body beautiful sex worshipping tablet. Phew, that sentence should be an ego denting winner, in Alf's self-esteem demoting stakes in the so-called successful top end of town, surely?

Upstairs Fact: Because it is this, 'got it wrong,' human creativity in the sexual expression department and its saturation in the public arena, that has created a total lack of dignity and respect for the sexual act within the consciousness of a sex-hooked and deluded society. A sexual expression that is currently degrading to Life and Nature, irresponsible to our children, crude, lewd, undignified, immature, thoughtless, self-gratuitous, socially destructive, spiritually debilitating and totally out of touch with the Laws of Nature responsible for procreation.

Note: A sexual degradation spell, that spells big, 'as we sow, so do we reap,' trouble for all concerned at the end of the human day in the Real System. A Real System that has the last say on this sexual degradation subject note the entrenched opposition in the top end of town? That has already had their media and entertainment saturated spin doctor sexual say in the public arena and the reason, why it has got out of control in mankind in the first place.

Q: *So what if the karmic influence that we create out of our sexual interaction is not conducive and harmonious to primordial Nature's interactive workings and the Laws of Nature, who cares.*
A: Everyone should care, comprehend that it is Nature's primordial workings that create and orchestrate the sexual drive, create and

orchestrate conception, create and orchestrate orgasm, create and orchestrate life, create and orchestrate the archetypal qualities of our children, all before they come into this world.

Q: So, why are there so many contagious destructive sexual vibes hurtling around this planet's spiritual atmosphere on the Upstairs radar?

A: Those invisible destructive euphoric sexual vibes, are sourced to growing karma created *cause and effect* destructive influence/entity, created out of the product of sexual expression without love and respect for Nature. Because there should only be the positive qualities of mutual love, empathy, respect and tenderness within the human created sexual influence, that enters Nature's duel negative and positive impersonal primordial spiritual workings from out of the sexual union.

Why?

Because out of the interactive, negative and positive, spiritual archetypal primordial intelligence that underwrites and processes life, comes the physical means to conceive, the means to bring children into the world. At this point, we are bringing life into this world saturated with a contagious destructive karmic influence, coming out of media, internet and entertainment eulogised sexual promiscuity to capture the public's attention, sell products and preen the immature ego with a euphoric high. A commercial and entertainment sponsored delusion that is sourced to Darth acquired brownie points and not Upstairs spiritual acquired brownie points.

Note: those in the media spotlight and those that want to be in the public spotlight with their procreation attributes and bodily geometry, to acquire a delusional self-esteem, adulation, fame, big bucks and of course, so-called success.

Spiritual Fact:
We are conceiving our precious children, in the negative influence of growing sexual degradation from the thoughtlessness, opportunism, retarded adolescence, adult immaturity and, 'got it wrong,' creativity

of those mentioned above. Along with the ever-growing contaminating influence of porn, the ever-growing contaminating influence of the sex slave trade and prostitution. Prostitution that has now become legalised to earn money on the stock market, from out of greed and entrepreneurial predatory big business. Big business that is driving the Global Economy and being rubber-stamped by economy obsessed election driven Governments; Governments that are also socially blind and have lost the plot of life in the Leadership Stakes because of it?

Comprehend this euphoric transmitted sexual degradation and its ever-growing contagious influence, is coming out of saturated, 'got it wrong,' communication mediums. That blatantly exploit and eulogise sexual promiscuity within their content. That promotes no respect or dignity, within the function of procreation and the divine of sexual union. That spells big spiritual devolution trouble, for that Darth deluded, 'got it wrong,' going no-where sexually liberated society, in the interactive physical and spiritual workings of primordial Nature.

Clarification: Sexual Union that should not be acted out for others to gawp at and applaud, from immature actors with an 'I love me' ego disorder and a delinquent or irresponsible, do what you like and act how you like, 'got it wrong,' freedom of artistic expression delusion in society. The boot camp message is that all concerned are in big trouble with their Spiritual Evolution at the end of the human day. As a cure, they are to report to Alf's Sin Bin Detention Room for, 'got it wrong,' uncivilised human beings, to address that socially irresponsible and thoughtless ego problem before departing earthly matters ... having upset St Peter with the heavenly keys big time?

Downstairs Fact:
Comprehend that human beings, become lost to their spiritual evolution in this, *anything goes attitude,* in the sexual department delusion that is called freedom of artistic expression, entertainment and sexual liberation in society. It is sourced to an ego created euphoric

delusion, coming out of poor-quality consciousness and, 'got it wrong,' human beings in the top end of town, leading the charge. Those so-call successful human beings in the driving seat, are currently taking this civilisation to a terminating spiritual conclusion, with this greed, fame and ego driven sexual exploitation and its degradation of the divine function of the sexual organs to create life.

Note: Therefore, not to degrade Nature and life and make big reputations, big bucks and preen the immature self-gratuitous ego in the public arena … also called, success, fame and realising our childhood dream for some inexplicable reason. Comprehend if we ever want to reach heaven and claim our harp, then sexual intercourse should only take place in privacy and within the spiritual boundaries of marriage and its worded vows to honour, respect and cherish each other. Vows that contain a positive karmic influence of love and respect for each other, Nature and life, to pass on positively to our offspring through its created harmonious life-supporting sexual karma.

Clarification: Sexual activity outside of this positive life-supporting parameter, draws destructive entities to the unconscious psyche of the human being. Negative influence that becomes attached to the psyche of both partners through a destructive entity. A destructive entity that not only gathers around the spiritual psyche, but becomes attached to it and is passed on to contaminate another casual sex partner through orgasm. Comprehend that big spiritual devolution trouble comes to contaminate the family and society, as a result of sexual infidelity, wife swapping, saturated porn, prostitution and media, actor and scriptwriter promoted sexual promiscuity, called gripping entertainment and adult drama.

The serious bottom line:
Big trouble appears everywhere in a civilisation, from out of promoting undignified wrong to Nature sexual expression and sexual promiscuity and its worship. Namely, sexually transmitted disease (STD)

and psychological disorder in the sexual department. Because we have contaminated the archetypal spiritual intelligence of Primordial Nature that orchestrates life and our human intelligence, with our wrong to Nature sexual expression/activity/creativity. Created from the accumulative, negative, not life-supportive karma, that comes out of that disrespect for Nature and lack of dignity and respect for the sexual act and its creative function. Namely, to bring life into this world.

Clarification: When this uncivilised wrong to Nature sexual activity and its created karma and associated entities, reach critical mass in the interactive primordial workings (archetypal intelligence) of Nature, then the civilisation responsible is unknowingly in big devolution trouble. Because it encourages malevolent entities out of the ancestral past, to be drawn into the spiritual and physical workings of impersonal primordial Nature in the present.

One of those destructive entities is powering the growing sociopath/psychopath driven sex slave trade and saturated porn. That, in turn, is empowering growing paedophilia, prostitution and other sexual abnormalities, in our deluded, 'got it wrong,' in the sexual department civilisation.

Note: A perpetuating destructive malevolent 'life force', that should not be in the primordial system of Nature in the first place. However, has been created out of the wrong sexual activity of past civilisation's and that this also, 'got it wrong,' civilisation, is now adding too. Those that created its destructive entity/influence long ago, have been dissolved within evolution, but they left its perpetuating entities for their lineage to inherit and reap the same dead-end devolution result in the present. Created from out of promiscuous promoting sexually degrading, 'got it wrong,' civilisations in the past.

Comprehend that sexual union, should always be accompanied by the positive karmic influence of love, tenderness and respect for our partner in the confines of privacy, never in public, on the TV or big movie screen or in glossy magazines and the internet. Therefore, sexuality is not to be exploited by the media to grab the public's attention. Not to be exploited to get ratings and the advertising dollar on commercial television. Not to be exploited to make big bucks and big reputations in the top end of town.

Therefore, not to be exploited by marketing geniuses and advertising gurus to corrupt young impressionable minds with. Not to be exploited by the House of Fashion to degrade the human being and family values.

Therefore, sexuality is not to be exploited by artistic degenerates with an ancestral inherited sexual screw loose in society. Not to be exploited to capture the vulnerable, sexually charged, 'I know everything,' adolescent mind. Not to be exploited to capture the sexually immature delinquent adult's attention. Not to be exploited to preen the immature, I love me ego, from parading our procreation attributes in the market place. Not to be exploited in dead brain glossy magazines to sell products and create delusional self-esteem. We are all in big trouble with Upstairs, from this media and entertainment acquired, lack of respect for sexuality and the sexual act and its divine function.

Q: *What is that divine function?*
A: Bringing new life into this physical world: Those responsible for sexual degradation are currently bringing in destructive influence into this world, that unknowingly authors disease and psychological disorder. It is linked to sexual stupidity and the irresponsibility of promiscuous promoting so-called successful human beings in the top end of town.

Comprehend that wrong to Nature sexual practices, create a destructive influence/entity that grows to contaminate the primordial spiritual Intelligence responsible for conception and life. On that fact-finding tour out of the Spiritual System, Alf rests this sexual, 'got it wrong' case, for the need for great positive change on this planet in the sexual education department. Because this adult created perpetuating negative influence is also corrupting our children and potentially their children and their children, through its karmic inheritance perpetuated in the family tree.

Understanding Sexuality ... Spiritually Speaking?

How to begin and place within a verse

The glorious subtlety of this subject
When so many misconceptions
Confuse the perfection
Of its innocence beauty and Grace

The organs of Creation are sacred and blest
To procreate life
In love that is meant
To compliment conception
In union divine
Then this fusing of souls
Is always sublime

Thus sensitivity
Should always accompany the sexual thrust
Then the joy of creation has no boundaries of lust
For the sexual union
As a reflection of the Divine
Is the symbol of Union
In love sublime

So, husband and wife are meant to be
Never have doubt
About this love in thee
For when it is pure and of mutual consent
The sexual union transcends and cements
The spiritual love within husband and wife
That compliments existence
Within other planes of life

Then how beautiful
Is the union of husband and wife
That hours Creation with the flow of sweet life
Where no boundaries exist
Within their experience of love
For each other to give the divine from above

For flowing and natural is Nature's sweet grace
To create with perfection that knows not of haste
For gentle and tender is a woman's soft touch
For the man she loves nothing is too much
As she is to him
So, should he be to her
Giving and taking in natural fervour

For sacred to Nature's Gods
Is the act of human love
Their blessings they bestow from the heavens above
To that which is meant and glorifies Creation
Through the seeds they sow
With Divine inclination.

Alf's Boot Camp Oratory No (9)

About the Unknown Spiritual Creative-Intelligence of Almighty Nature

Creative-intelligence is the invisible spiritual/archetypal substance of primordial Nature. They are spiritual energies, (archetypal intelligence), that create and underwrite physical, biological intelligence and life. Innumerable are these impersonal primordial energies that structure and evolve life, through the self-referral spiritual Laws of Nature. Laws that we could call the Government of primordial Nature. Laws that structure, 'order out of chaos,' in its opposing yet interactive, negative and positive poles.

That interactive process is sourced too and comes under, the authorship of divine Intelligence that we have called Cosmic Law, the ultimate Law in Creation that underwrites all others. It is for that reason; we could call that divine Intelligence the status quo Intelligence of this Creation.

Example from the distant past:

When a dominant species reaches the end of its evolutionary possibilities and its evolution stagnates, it causes the interactive positive and negative archetypal intelligence of primordial Nature, to go out of sync with the self-referral Laws of Nature, laws that structure and process evolution and its divine purpose. It is that ultimate Law of evolution that manifests and dissolves the cause of the chaos and restores equilibrium to the interactive spiritual and physical workings of life and Creation. That event translates as one big cataclysmic upheaval on this planet and life starts again. Ask the dinosaurs for confirmation because it happened to them more than once.

The numbers game:
1. Creative-intelligence is the spiritual component of physical life. It is what physical life and its biology has manifested out of. They are the invisible archetypal intelligence that underlies, underwrites and orchestrates life. We cannot see, and we cannot dissect archetypal intelligence, only in their transformation as the biology and chemistry of life. What we call genes are their physical transformation into biological intelligence. So, we should stop blindly experimenting on them until those in science, have evolved their conscious mind and expanded their awareness; a justifiable comment that applies to those blindly trashing and dissecting the atom also. Because we can only understand and experience their function, through a further spiritual acquired structure of consciousness and its reality.

2. That last statement is the prime logical, common-sense statement of this discourse because the eyes cannot see into spiritual creation.

    Because like the human mind and body, they have evolved to experience and interact with physical Creation. That is why calling existing science, 'blind science,' and 'divorced from Nature,' in its present expression and creativity is the truth of the matter, and not being rude or disrespectful at all, merely blunt. Because after five years (now ten) of ignored sent correspondence, science just like the media and governments, will not listen to knowledge greater than their own and a reason, to become a dreaded I-want-my-say blogger on the internet to dob them into the public for bad manners. Because it is rude and disrespectful, to ignore the repeated genuine concerns of others in society, especially from those in charge and creating our realities and giving all the orders. Nothing democratic about that in the adult playground.
3. The interaction of creative-intelligence is the cause of all creativity within the human being. For example: when a specific archetypal intelligence is found highly concentrated in the brain and/or the physiology, then we have the cause of exceptional intelligence, charisma (animal magnetism) gifts and talents. That other human beings do not have concentrated in their physiological makeup. That is why the average person is way behind the 'A' ball at birth where competition, IQ sport, education, conquering, achieving and winning for big bucks is concerned. This incessant brain numbing media indoctrinated message of competing, achieving and winning, has come to dominate the collective consciousness of this civilization; commencing with its indoctrination at school and progressing on to the market place and workplace, to become all-consuming and unproductive to the Laws of Nature. Along with being unproductive to our winning fuelled overworked adrenaline glands.
4. The need to compete and win is an archetypal trait found in the dominant alpha and is sourced, to a primordial driven survival

instinct for power and control and to win and lead in a social species. However, through its media saturation and over the top motor mouth commercial presentations, we humans become addicted to the euphoria, (karmic influence), that winning generates.

It is this contagious alpha winning and conquering neurosis, that has become adrenaline driven addictive obsession on this planet from out of the glorified and saturated sport. Because through its over-saturation in the affairs of humanity and the constant media adulation and worshipping of its winners, the public unknowingly becomes subliminally hooked on the delusional excitement and euphoria it generates. We then unknowingly further fuel this delusional euphoria in society, through becoming addicted to identifying with winners and worshipping them instead of the Creator. Because the delusional euphoria and self-esteem that comes out of winning and conquering is temporary and not lasting in physical Creation. Whereas, the self-esteem that comes out of identifying with Abstract Intelligence lasts forever, like the Creator.

5. Just to stir things up: It is also a non-delusional spiritually acquired self-esteem, that is not sourced to sport, actors, acquiring big bucks, celebrities and motor mouth commentators. Along with, small statues, big statues, gold medals, gold records, gold guitars, golden vocal cords, golden egos, golden trumpets, golden syringes, golden pills, golden dills and golden ills. Along with, commercial TV promos, commercial product brainwashing or buying and identifying with any material products or the jet setting, trendsetting, mind setting, ego setting, $ setting, human product clones that advertise them. Surely that world breaking spiritual news from Upstairs is worthy of headlines, because we can spiritually grow up now with that priceless information. That is not sourced to commercial gold but Upstairs gold; therefore, eternal gold – Wow! Time to get the Upstairs spiritual skates on or we will not pass the finish line, correction, you will not pass the finish line.

6. Comprehend this dissolvable human karma created influence/entity of 'euphoria', interacts with the creative-intelligence that structures our human intelligence and its expression. It is causing growing psychological disorders in sport worshipping nation's obsessed with winning and fame.

    One of its negative symptoms is surfacing in the dominant alpha in society and it manifests as a destructive bent, for confrontation in the home and workplace and to initiate argument out of nothing. This destructive impulse to win an argument and be victorious, no matter how trivial the subject matter or cause, is a growing trait in winning-obsessed nations. Especially in families where both partners have dominant alpha controlling personalities.

    This growing addictive, 'I'm a winner,' nemesis always to win, is adding to the divorce rate and unhappy children in socially decaying nations. Especially, the Good Ole U.S of A. the land of winning, achieving and worshipping Hollywood, fame, sport, big bucks, celebrities and other human-created dissolvable products, all laid out on top of the plateau of Commercial Corporate Mountain.

7. The karma created entity, from out of the above contagious euphoric winning mania, has become the subliminal tool of the Commercial Television Empire, notably through its domination of sports coverage.

    This television saturated winning euphoria has become a created karmic influence/entity, that unconsciously captures the viewing and listening mind and psyche of the public. Because the commercial media, manipulate and exploit this contagious, addictive euphoria to grab our attention and sell products. We should understand, that personal achievement, (in whatever field of endeavour), has nothing to do with material products, yet winning and its euphoria, is being manipulatively used to identify and associate products with personal achievement. A media created and fuelled delusion that has become a contagious entity, (life force), in this commercial product saturated civilisation.

8. Saturated advertising, promos and image creating, also have a similar effect on the subliminal mind of both the child and the grown adult. To unknowingly, capture the ego self-gratification primordial workings of the sub-conscious mind. That is why the greed driven Commercial Television Empire and its saturated product advertising and image creating, need to take a walk out of the family home in the 21st century.

    Advertising belongs in the market place, not in the home and family environment. Where its superficial products, false values and saturated endless message, to buy, buy, buy, become entrenched in vulnerable young minds. To then fuel consumerism, delusion, unproductive habits, product addiction and psychological disorders in adulthood.

9. The least that could be said, about those that exploit society and young impressionable minds for their greed or winning ends, is that they are immature, thoughtless and uncivilised. The worse has yet to be said, but the label 'sociopath' sums it up and is a growing psychological disorder in this $ driven consumer civilization, along with depression and greed.

    The fact that those exploiting and manipulating society, see nothing wrong or perverse in their predatory power and greed driven commercial actions, is the glaring sign of a socially impaired and greed debilitated human beings functioning out of delusion and narcissism.

    Study the history books, because they are full of them and so is a big corporate global money-making commercial business. That now monopolises the world and its consumer direction and dead-end destiny, from abuse of acquired power and greed.

10. The spiritual point to be made: We must place big global business and making money, in its correct order in society and the shrinking $ polluted consumer world we live in. Currently, it is functioning like an abusing, all-conquering, all-expanding emperor, and

worse, irresponsible socially blind governments are just adding to the unconscionable greed it has created on this corporate owned planet.

Nations must start working towards self-sufficiency again, where their economies are concerned because when this all-consuming out of control Global Economy eventually collapses, as it will do out of greed and abuse of power, all globally dependent nation's economies will collapse like a domino effect. The scale of that collapse will dwarf all others that have occurred and so will the misery that comes out of it. It is time to downsize Global Corporations and the business geniuses running them, and they should not be leading the direction of this world until they grow up and understand themselves as well as they understand how to make money and acquire power. They are no example as leaders to my family.

11. In that primitive/primordial ego-driven system of competition, conquering, achievement and winning to acquire self-esteem, adulation and power, the exceptionally born gifted few, will naturally cross all societies created and worshipped finishing lines first, with those born gifts especially, when they are finely tuned as in sport. That is why this indoctrinated practice of competing to win at everything in society and to acquire deluded self-esteem, praise and big bucks out of its winning, coupled to the equally immature practice of worshipping and idolising the winner, is not psychologically or spiritually productive to the vast majority.

Who were not born with the high IQ or gifted talent to be a winner in the first place? Starting in the classroom and on the sports field, they are unknowingly made to feel inferior and inadequate? From a human created system/ideology, they can never win in but are guaranteed always to lose in.

12. The ramifications: When a child has the additional burden of a chaotic unloved childhood to contend with, that classroom/education/sport imbued inferiority and loss of self-worth, unknowingly fuels unhappiness, inequality, relationship problems and

social immaturity. To then cement subliminal resentment and inadequacy in that child, a psychological debilitation that follows them into adulthood and to the grave.

This immature practice of worshipping winners is the cause of many accelerating social problems. Not least, the delinquent anti-social behaviour, that plagues those inadvertently made to feel inferior and worthless through an immature education system. Forever praising and giving awards and acclamation to winners, but indifference and no thought for the psychological wellbeing of all the losers. Who happens to be the majority in the system and its education indoctrinated race, to achieve and be crowned a winner in the classroom or a winner on the sports field and therefore a winner in society, an ego deluded, 'got it wrong,' immature society that is?

13. We need to comprehend, that this immature ego sourced practice of worshipping winners, does not create unity and harmony in a society but promotes disunity, psychological disorder and unhappiness in a society. It also creates and fuels a, 'them and us,' syndrome sourced to born IQ and talent differential in our species.

A child should never be made to feel inadequate, worthless, segregated and inferior because they cannot keep up and compete with the born winners and high achievers. We should not do it in the family, and therefore, we should not do it at school or in the workplace. Everyone has a valued place in society, not just the worshipped winners and born high achievers and so-called successful, that have come to dominate communication mediums as news and information and as products to sell products. Its greed driven contagious influence creates chaos in the Laws of Nature and a negative destructive entity in primordial Nature, that then returns to society and manifests as social and psychological problems and chaos in human beings.

14. This human-created reality/ideology of winning and achieving and worshipping its winners, is sourced to a primordial survival instinct in the animal kingdom, to establish a pecking order in a

social species and where the born dominant alpha always prevails. It is also this survival instinct that instigates the bullying syndrome in a social species, which is a natural instinctive trait of the dominant alpha, to establish control in the pack.

In the human species, this instinctual expression of the dominant alpha to control others is notable in the school playground. Progressing on in adulthood, to become the ego-driven dog eat dog power plays in politics, the workplace, office and of course, big corporate market share and take over business. We call this incessant media driven winning neurosis acquiring power, influence and success in society. A primordial acquired power, that should never be abused in human society, because it creates chaos in the primordial creative-intelligence underwriting and orchestrating life. It is this Spiritual archetypal primordial intelligence that sources our biological human intelligence, expression and creativity.

More Ground-Breaking News

Abuse of power is a recipe for eventually acquiring and receiving, an invisible eviction-notice out of Creation from Upstairs. Created from out of its accumulating, not life-supportive negative karma. The good news for all the power-addicted dominant alphas that are caught up in the primordial power stakes on the planet, is that it works off a karma points system. According to Alf, it is time to get the karma calculator out and do some serious internal mathematics for some in politics, big corporate business, the money markets and of course, the entertainment and commercial television empires.

Summing up the subject of spiritual Creative Intelligence: Human thought is an impulse of creative-intelligence sourced to primordial Nature and its interactive archetypal workings; archetypal spiritual intelligence that orchestrates our physical chemistry, biology, desire and intent. We cannot experience/cognise those energies through the faculty of thought in our existing structure of physical consciousness. In that structure of physical consciousness, we can only experience them, through the emotional/feeling component of the mind and body; that has an interactive link to the spiritual domain of Nature and its impersonal primordial domain. However, in the acquired structure of Spiritual consciousness, we become aware of their existence on the level of knowledge and then, able to discriminate their activity through the faculty of the adult intellect functioning out of Spiritual consciousness.

More *believe it or not* spiritual information:

The spiritual psyche is attached to the physical body from birth to death. Then the spiritual psyche detaches itself from its physical counterpart to continue with its ordained evolution within non- physical spiritual planes (dimensions) of existence. At least that is what should happen at death, occasionally it does not, which is another story altogether and due to circumstances of death and karma.

It is the non-physical aspect of creative-intelligence operating through the self-referral Laws of Nature, that continue to process the individual's Spiritual essence and its further on-going evolution. It is also the self-referral Laws of Nature, that in a different mode of physical function, are the cause of all the Laws of Physics.

The following verse sums up a description of the. 'Laws of Nature'. The reason for also placing its knowledge in verse, is to reach those who still have sensitive minds and not just techno and scientific one-track minds, commercial television product and promo brainwashed minds and entertainment, celebrity, fame and winning indoctrinated minds.

Boot Camp Oratory No 10.

Understanding Natural Law Nature's Divine Spiritual Laws

Nature's spiritual self-referral Laws that create order out of chaos in Creation, when not usurped and degraded, by the not life-supportive creativity of human beings.

Q: What is Natural Law?
A: It is when the human being and all the invisible energies within Nature, function together in perfect harmony and compatibility. i.e., the primordial archetypal planetary sourced spiritual intelligence, that manifests and structures life and carries out the processes of physical and spiritual evolution. Then both we and Nature, are all humming the same tune in the same key and at the same time. Perfect coherence that compliments Creation and enables access to higher states of consciousness for the still-evolving human being.

It is what is spiritually known as natural unity, functioning automatically within the Laws of Nature processing the evolution of life through the creative tool of karma. Note physicists and those in the laboratory meddling with genes and altering the ordained evolution of life through synthetic cloning, syringes, test tubes and lifeless computers. Energies that you do not see, thus cannot dissect. Because they are beyond the physical aspect of the senses of perception, but not beyond the spiritual aspect of the senses of perception via the awareness when spiritually developed that is.

Note: It is this spiritual located archetypal creative-intelligence, that manifests as the biology and chemistry of life. Therefore, everything living is constructed from out of that spiritually interacting primordial archetypal intelligence that underwrites physical life. Comprehend also, that absolute Creation or God, is beyond intellectual dissection in its transcendent domain. Note those born with gifted high physical IQ in academia, religion and elsewhere. Because it is necessary to fully experience the non-ego word, humility, to be able to surrender our individuality, ego and acquired status, to gain access to higher states of consciousness.

We must intellectually realise, that life and therefore, the human being, is a created product from out of the absolute abstract silent Intelligence that created this Creation. Therefore, Creation and its universal (cosmic) spiritual Intelligence, is not a product out of the human being's dissolvable physical intelligence and creativity. Acknowledging that spiritual acquired logic is the first step to understanding and acquiring that elusive humility and respect for Nature. A spiritual quality of many that grows naturally and effortlessly, from out of the regular twice daily short practice of correct meditation.

Clarification: If we wish to know, what it is not possible to know in our existing structure of unexpanded physical consciousness, then we must live a life of total abstinence from all activity and become, the, 'abstract silence,' that thought is superimposed upon. Then, when we depart this planet, our expanded consciousness will merge into that abstract, absolute Intelligence. To then become that absolute consciousness in unity and totality, beyond physical and spiritual Creation yet containing physical and spiritual Creation. Therefore, our individual spirit will have become Existence itself not merely a manifested minuscule created physical part of it.

However, comprehend, the human being is created for the expansion of physical and spiritual Creation, as is all life-intelligence. Therefore, we have conscious free will to choose which path we wish to take to create our destiny, either in active spiritual Creation or absolute transcendent inactive Creation.

It is an internal found junction point that the human being eventually reaches along the silent path of Transcendent Meditation. To then become aware of this spiritual and absolute crossroads and choice of destiny. However, we must first accept, that there is Intelligence greater than our dissolvable human intelligence and acknowledge it, through the application of Correct Meditation. Then we will have acquired the humility, dignity and respect, to be able to enter its crossroads and choose our spiritual or absolute destiny.

In spiritual fact, much within spiritual and physical Creation is beyond our comprehension, until we develop the spiritual component of the mind and body. Hidden spiritual potential of the human being that evolves from out of the regular twice daily short practice of Transcendent Meditation. Along with acquiring the humility, to accept that at this point of our human evolution, WE ARE BUT AS A

CHILD within the transcendent absolute Intelligence, that has created this Creation. If we do not accept this ego denting fact, then we will not evolve to realise our spiritual and absolute potential as a unique human species.

Comprehend that the human mind is a physical mind within a spiritual mind, a universal mind that forms the totality of physical and spiritual Creation. It is that status quo Intelligence, that is structuring evolution through the government of the self-referral Laws of Nature. It is supreme cosmic divine Intelligence that underlies and underwrites the Laws of Nature; that is why it forms the status quo Intelligence of this duel physical and spiritual Creation. It is the progenitor of this duel Creation. It is also, the personal active divine spiritual Intelligence, of the un-manifest abstract silent transcendent Creator. As are the self-referral divine spiritual Laws of Nature the government of the primordial domain of Nature, that life is sourced too.

Repeated spiritual fact:

It is this spiritual located archetypal creative-intelligence that manifests as the physical biology and chemistry of life. Therefore, everything living is constructed from out of that spiritually interacting primordial archetypal intelligence that underwrites physical life.

Comprehend also, that absolute Creation or God, is beyond intellectual dissection in its transcendent silent domain. Note those born with gifted high physical IQ in academia, religion and elsewhere. Because it is necessary to experience the non-ego word humility, to be able to surrender our individuality and acquired physical status, to gain access to higher states of consciousness. The simple silent path to eventually accomplish this miracle is through the twice-daily short practice of Transcendent Meditation using a correct mantra for our physiology.

Kind regards - Alf. CEO of Spiritual Boot Camp.

Section Four

Ripping Yarns and the Lost Manuscripts

First, a light-hearted story for young minds from Stephen, adopted son of Alf. On leave from the Greek translation department of Ancient tablets and manuscripts. Located in the newly updated fictitious North Wing of the British Museum, that finally has a workable loo, the following colloquial Greek translation of ancient history and modern progress has been renamed, 'An Unknown Version of History.' A spiritual translation and not an academic translation of progress, because academia read too many of their books, funny books. You know, with *no* missing punctuation and *no* spelling or typo mistakes in them. So, this version is a special English colloquial translation with *some* spelling mistakes, typos and missing punctuation.

This, to lighten things up in the literary scrupulous editorial top end of town, where University acquired literary exactitude, rules over the subject matter and mistakes and errors, are punishable by literary exorcism according to Alf.

Note: If the following improper use of the English language is not admissible in professional circles, then take a trip to the dentist and have a dose of laughing gas and then read it, but not in the chair. You might end up minus a few teeth and a whopping big bill instead.

And no, Stephen is not signing up with anyone, least of all Hollydude and Co. They are in deep you know what with God, for pretending to be baddies, nasties and procreation nutcases in so-called adult movies and calling it gripping entertainment. Along with worshipping and praying to Oscar, for a walk on his red carpet to collect his selfie gongs. That evidently, you must place in the fridge because they are too hot to handle where they come from; along with its also chaos creating hot cousin, Commercial Television. For driving us all potty with endless sequels of, 'Days of our dysfunctional Life,' 'The Old and the Breathless,' the, 'Rolled and the Beautiful,' 'Sex in the Metropolis,' and other equally brain-damaged reality shows, products, advertisements, promos and celebrity cluttered newsrooms. That also require exorcism, according to Alf.

Anyway, I've found the missing ancient manuscripts from the book, 'The Celestine Potholes'. You know, the ancient manuscripts that got lost in South America, or maybe it was India? Anyways, it was addressed to J. Redsfields to translate, but I do not know him, I've never met him. But I have read the book about, 'The Celestine Potholes'.

Anyways, the newspapers, boobs and abs magazines and other comic books, would not publish my translation, because I am not famous with my boobs, abs, closet and other selfie information. The Commercial Television stations don't want a bar of it, because it ain't got no products, big buck reality shows, game shows or celebrities in it. The BBC said to send it to the ABC for spelling corrections and acceptable syntax first.

The Guverment said I've got to become a politician before they will read it and the sciences, do not understand the word *spiritual* in it, because it is not in their scientific dictionary. So, according to other top end of town experts, the best place for it is on the *anything goes* internet. Anyway, if someone out there understands the word spiritual, and can read my rotten bottom end of town writing and spelling, then please let me know nicely. Then I will translate more of the same and carry on annoying the top end of town with my colloquial English, rotten spelling and punctuation.

Postscript:

Not sure if it is scientifically important or not, but there's something really weirdo at the bottom of this ancient manuscript, it says, (i times d) plus the square root of (m) plus (LN times CM) equals H this-way-Albert." Must be something to do with Albert Stein –or was it Joe Stein? Maybe it was Eff Stein? Anyway some Stein – have included it in case it helps Science, Academia and Hollywood, not forgetting the Pentagon either. As they know all that is going on in the world first, from the late-night ego product show on commercial television. Plus, it says what's faster than the speed of light? *The speed of thought of course* and that's really weirdo. Because everyone knows, that the speed of light is the fastest thing in the Universe. At least, that is what it says in all the funny punctuated science books that I pinched, sorry, I mean borrowed, from the library. You know, E equals MC squared or somefing, not T equals PP squared to infinity, like what Alf in charge of spiritual boot camp says in his tablets. Anyway, youse have the brains and all the university education and clout in the top end of town, so work it out and post me back the answer so I can get some sleep.

There's a load more here – manuscripts that is. So, I will go and paste a few up on some noticeboards downtown, just to keep the, 'speed of thought,' ball rolling. While you sort it all out and I can translate the rest of the manuscripts into good colloquial English, and good American for the Pentagon. Plus, the manuscript I'm currently translating, don't make sense at all – so, I'll have to go and see the boss Upstairs about it on the way – after my tea break that is.

Signed - The Thinker.
You know, that unemployed Greek bloke on the dole? Countersigned by concerned citizen, no, confused citizen Stephen, son of Alf.

Ripping B.C. Yarns from the Colloquial Pen of Stephen

Part (1)
Past, Present and Future

Right here we go:

Once upon a time, long, long, ago, during the, 'golden age,' of the ancient world and before money, politicians, celebrities, glossy magazines, techno goodies, selfie phones, the internet and Hollybug were invented and things went rapidly to pot. Because long ago, mankind once lived in harmony, (in some spiritually civilised parts of the world), with Nature, the animals and themselves. Very hard to believe in the 21st century eh? So too, a special ceremony was always performed at the equinoxes, i.e., the four seasons junction points. A spiritual ceremony to acknowledge the divinity of the Spiritual Laws of Nature, that structure and evolve everything in Creation and create *order out of chaos* in life.

In addition, when the females of Royal lineage of the rulers of those days, who were very nice people by the way, (not like in selfie anything goes Hollynud and Co☺), became fertile and ready for motherhood, it was considered an honour to seek the initial act of copulation from the deities, this is where it gets interesting.

Q: *Who were the deities?*
A: They were the physical manifestation of the spiritual gods of Heaven.

Q: *Wow! So how did they get here then? Because this ain't heaven, except for all the media created winners and celebrities living it up in the top end of town. You know, that live in television newsrooms, movies, newspapers and I-love-me glossy magazines, full of saturated products, boobs and abs and semi-undressed models, on a catwalk trip to fashion, bling and selfie no, no, delusional ego land. Also called fame.*

A: Well they didn't get here in spaceships, flying saucers, techno time machines, the SS Enterprise, test tubes, teacups or the pen of science fiction writers on Prozac, or somefing chemical like that – sorry about that dig, I couldn't resist it.

No, they manifested through the spiritual workings of the divinity of the Laws of Nature. Spiritual laws that were in total harmony with a human being, not all human beings, but evolved spiritual human beings, who had reached the age of 21 and were functioning out of their spiritual bodies as well as their physical ones. Anyway, in this sacrifice of a maiden's virtue and innocence for pro-creational purposes and not, rec-creational purposes? Like on TV the internet, Hollydude movies and in human-worshipping boobs, abs, bottoms and whatnots glossy product magazines, harmony was said to result within all the spiritual planes of Creation, that underwrite our physical seen world that we live in.

Yes, almighty Nature was very much pleased to be honoured with such dignity of her divine procreation gifts to the human being. Thus, that human respect and its harmonious karmic influence structured not only procreation and conception, but also positively influenced the Yin and the Yang or negative and positive, permeating within the duel primordial archetypal spiritual intelligence that orchestrates physical life. You know, the subtle vibrations of creative-intelligence, emanating from the spiritual platform of the planets in our solar system; invisible planetary archetypal intelligence that physical life and its biology and chemistry has manifested from and evolved out of.

It is this spiritual primordial archetypal intelligence, that is sourced to other Cosmic intelligence responsible for the equilibrium of the changing seasons and a lot more besides. According to Alf anyway, but not the experimental laborotorium and atom trashing scientists, changing everything on the planet without Upstair's permission, will agree with Alf that's for sure.

Q: *What is this Cosmic spiritual intelligence you might ask?*
A: The four Deities, (well five in Alf's book), of this Universe, you know, Earth, Air, Fire and Water and all that hard to believe metaphysical jazz

that Alf is spouting on about in his tablets. Because that's fairy stories, according to the learned academics swotting away downstairs in their books, and writing and not making any spelling mistakes, along with other downstairs knockers of Upstairs and Alf, that cannot accept any other *reality* exists outside of their own human created and lived physical one. Because we humans, create reality and then live it, believe it and teach many of them in schools; even though all human created realities are dissolvable, just like human beings.

This lasting unknown spiritual reality that Alf is talking about is not an unscientific fairy story says, God. Because those deities of Nature, are my manifested intelligence within spiritual and physical Creation but, most definitely not the life re-arranging, techno polluting and pharmaceutical scientists. All doing what they like with chemicals, animals, plants and all my wiggly's and atoms on the planet and calling it, conquering new frontiers and creating scientific progress. But, and a big but, without proper consultation with my spiritual self-referral Laws of Nature government, because those divine Laws of Nature, are responsible for creating, 'order out of chaos,' in life and Creation and therefore, in human beings also. But evidently, not at the moment according to Upstairs.

To continue:
The spiritual elders, who were very wise men in those ancient days, guided the well-being and happiness of their people with spiritual acquired knowledge, i.e., eternal knowledge. A spiritual Laws of Nature knowledge and most definitely not, the laws of physics knowledge. You know, decimating the atom and altering physical genes, cloning, IVF and synthetic chemicals polluting this planet to high heaven. Big klingnong trouble for the future, from all this spiritually blind, I-can-do-what-I-like, polluting science and techno-progress in the present, according to Alf's tealeaves that is.

Anyways, via Cosmic knowledge and special spiritual ceremony, mankind honoured that invisible spiritual intelligence of Creation and not trashed it. Plus, they also knew the exact time for planting, harvesting, Thanksgiving and the appropriate ceremony to conduct on all auspicious occasions throughout the year, and in that ceremonial spiritual process, correctly honouring the blessings and providence of this beautiful Earth and Universe in its totality of interactive function.

Because everyfing is connected to everyfing in the Universe through the spiritual component of everyfing. You know, the invisible stuff that underwrites physical matter and that science, knows nuffing about or wants to know about.

Just like others in the top end of town in charge of our so-called progress, their created progress that is. That becomes everyone's progress, whether they like it or not, through education and the saturated non-stop talking media. Because they have no say in creating that progress in the bottom end of town, that happens to be the vast majority on the planet.

Q: *Is everything spiritually connected?*
A: Yes, everyfing, but excluding spiritless Hollydud and Commercial Television, because they live in media created, I-love-me, stretched ego celebrity la, la, land. Along with other big-buck entrepreneurs and other commercial prime-movers and shakers in the winning top end of town, that create and power our greed driven consumer, techno, media and entertainment realities. Particularly within the minds of our vulnerable impressionable children on this planet.

Anyways, more about this new-age media-saturated acted out violence, punch-ups, emotional hysteria and undress and closet entertainment called gripping drama, at world court martial time from Alf – soon. . At this moment, he is busy verbally dishing it out to the so-called successful top end of town. Who are creating the 21st-century media delivered and saturated script, for all our *anyfing goes* and *do what you like behaviour* on this shared planet and calling it progress? Because where they lead, the public is compelled to follow through a primordial sourced survival instinct in our highly social animal species.

This natural primordial sourced phenomenon in the animal kingdom is called, *follow the dominant alpha leader.* As the commercial media know well and endlessly exploit, through the medium of celebrity pied pipers and other worshipped winners in the top end of town, according to Alf that is.

Coming back to the original plot:
If a child were born out of that physical union with the deities in human spiritual form, then the spiritual attributes of that deity would reside within the bloodline of that Royal family, i.e., spiritual family. Because the original definition of the word Royal means spirituality or divinity. From which came the lineage of the astrologers, the wise men, the healers (doctors) and genuine psychics, but not commercial television or Hollydude and Co. Thus, from divine attributes perpetuated genetically, spiritually and astrologically. To then guide, council, heal and direct the spiritual well-being of that ancient society, in its on-going positive evolution to reach the real stars, and not our human-created dissolvable selfie stars. You know, that fill the media, television and Hollywood created heavens and are on the no, no, ego blink with their, *anything-goes*, celebrity twink downstairs according to Upstairs.

Anyway, as us dissolvable human beings possess a collective unconscious that has a karmic key-signature in spiritual Creation, so this knowledge spreads around the world as similar forms of worship and expression, but not as closet entertainment. Just like the wheel, the pyramids and now, the media, Hollybug and Commercial Television scripts. Because we are all invisibly connected by the universal computer, structuring the evolution of Creation and life. You know, the invisible spiritual computer of our Universe, that underwrites and orchestrates Nature, life-intelligence and evolution; that our human mind and it's biological computer, (called the brain), is a minute physical, biological and dissolvable creation and reflection of.

"But that's a load of Dr Who intergalactic twaddle with spelling and punctuation mistakes," say all the academics, scientists and other downstairs knockers of anyfing they do not want to understand. *"Because we have it on higher education authority from our famous*

books, (written by us lot downstairs with lots of gongs), that Alf is telling a lot of porkies in his tablets with no gongs." But not so says Upstairs, I was around then when it was created, you weren't so there, put that in your funny human books without spelling mistakes and electronic gizmos and techno robots on the binary blink, and stop overdosing on café latte and researching those dancing pole nightclubs downstairs. Because you've got the wrong, 'out of order,' books with no mention of Upstairs in them, or you are reading them upside down or somefing.

To continue:

The centuries passed and the deities headed back home for a well-earned rest. They returned to heaven, spiritual heaven, that is. But not in spaceships, sorry about that revelation to all the lost in space science-fiction junkies, stranded up in space on Babble'on 5 on Prozac and other laborotorium hubble-bubble toil and trouble chemical compositions. No, they returned via their spiritual bodies when they had passed on from their physical ones, and guess what, things went to pot again downstairs. Much human trashing, conquering, winning and other self-esteem ego authorised wrongdoings to Nature, saturated the spiritual atmosphere of this planet. As a contagious result, the born untalented normal people eventually became very unhappy, because they could never win at anything and be famous and have their picture in the paper.

While all the media-saturated worshipped winners, got lost in, I-love-me, in the mirror selfie-space, fame and big bucks. Like on the commercial television, movies, newsrooms, newspapers, glossy magazines and the fashion catwalk to no-where land.

Anyway, the long and the bad of it all was that the divine spiritual component of Nature was no longer revered and respected. Not acknowledged for her dignity, for her beauty, for her creativity. Spiritual decadence crept into the all-consuming ego-driven self-esteem progress affairs of humankind and the male; became so insecure within his bonce you know his head, that he began to denigrate the female in all her procreation aspects. She lost the right to choose her mate when the seeds of fertility flowed within her and female derogatory jokes and images, were carved on tree trunks anywhere and everywhere.

Crude remarks about the female anatomy began to be shouted in the forests. Rude drawings on stones and cave walls turned up everywhere, and from clever males, in the local temples and taverns, she copped the lot. However, no internet, television, videos or those other things people like you know, glossy product magazines with boobs, bottoms, abs and whatnots.

Note: At least I don't think so, because they hadn't heard of commercial television, promos, reality shows, big bucks, commercial pied pipers, spin-doctors, marketing geniuses, media moguls, catwalks, saturated advertising, glossy magazines and newspaper body beautiful ego-preening in those far off days. We had to have commercial product progress, and democracy first from all the media worshipped winners. That had got made into commercial created status products, spin doctors and pied pipers from out of saturated promos, advertisements, glossy magazines and newsrooms. However, you try telling this to the top end of town, and you will really cop the cold shoulder and worse, get sent to writers coventry for elocution and spelling lessons as payback, for telling them they, 'got it wrong,' with their idea of progress and how to acquire self-esteem.

Anyway, it came to be on this human trashed planet, that the female was no longer revered for her creativity, her beauty, her tenderness, her lovingness, her softness, her feminine intelligence and they have never been the same since. Because the female started to copy and emulate the dominant alpha hairy male and go conquering everyfing, having punch-ups, wrestling matches, massacring an oval ball, ripping off their tee-shirts, showing off their abs and other things and acting as macho males on the adolescent winning blink, on sports fields and fighting wars and all that Hollydud movie invented trashing jazz. *"If you can't beat em you might as well join 'em,"* became the female war cry in guverments, on sports fields, the television and in movies.

We are not staying at home doing the ironing and changing nappies, we are going out to work in the market place and on commercial television and sports fields, and at dancing pole nightclubs and topless casinos, to earn our own money and give the noisy kids to some other mug to look after. *"We are entitled to be macho alpha males, with gold chains around our necks, tattoos and use male aftershave just like them,"* echoed down the corridors of female *me too* acquired power in movies, politics, high scientific places, universities, newsrooms, sports fields and glossy magazines. *"We'll sort youse out, because we've got female brains, plus a lot more you haven't,"* and guess what, the male and the female have never been the same since.

What a top end of town created and media, entertainment and newsroom delivered mix up. As in, women as men and men as women and the kids stuck in the middle and lost in consumer, techno, product, movie, computer, mobile phone and commercial television, spiritless space forever. What a crazy world, I wonder if there is something drastically wrong, in our new-age progressive social system, of, say-what-you-like, do-what-you-like, show-what-you-like, create-what-you-like and act-how-you-like in public and for the education of our kids of course. As in, I've got my democratic rights and freedom of expression and *no one* can tell me what to do as an adult; unless youse got big bucks and a stretched limo and can get my picture in a newspaper or a glossy product magazine, or on a commercial television, big buck reality show and make me famous and a worshipped celebrity. However, unknowingly, on the superficial ego-preening deluded blink to spiritless no-where land, according to St Peter with the keys to the other nice place Upstairs.

Because evidently, no-one believes in that fairy story about real heaven anymore. Because all the worshipped winner's downstairs with the help of the saturated media, big business, Hollydud, commercial television and big bucks, have created their big buck image created heaven in the top end of town that everyone in the bottom end of town, now wants to go to even though its dissolvable, unlike the real heaven.

Evidently, they can view that media-saturated deluded heaven in glossy magazines, movies and on the television, but not the real one anymore. At least, that's what Alf and the Tea Lady reckon has happened downstairs. You know, down here on this human progress trashed planet.

Time for my tea break and go to the loo. Be back soon with part two.

This Add-on Extra from Alf. CEO of Spiritual Boot Camp

We need to spiritually understand that we are very special to Upstairs as human beings. We are a one-off never to be repeated, and we are fast losing spiritual connection with the Laws of Nature, creating *order out of chaos* in life. Those spiritual acquired Laws should function harmoniously within our minds, bodies and primordial survival and sexual instincts but not in commercial television and entertainment created human products. Comprehend a woman is a woman, and a man is a man. One is the nurturing reflection of the female creative womb of Nature, the other is the reflection of the silent Cosmic male component of Nature, and we have different biological energies working within males and females because of it.

When we are not dysfunctional and lost in commercial television and entertainment image created selfie space, then those male and female archetypal energies should operate in perfect harmony in a relationship, any relationship. That spiritual acquired harmony comes from the spiritual Laws of Nature, to evolve and support everything physical and spiritual that is evolving in Creation. Along with creating, *order out of chaos*, in life and Nature, but not the commercial product, entertainment and body beautiful indoctrinated human being in the 21st century. According to Upstairs that is, but obviously not downstairs.

Comprehend, within the spiritual function of the self-referral Laws of Nature, it is very abnormal for a mother with young children to work full time in the marketplace. If you wish to work in the marketplace and devote your life to it, that's fine. Freewill and equality of the sexes on this planet should always prevail, but NOT when we have the responsibility of young children. They need the close nurturing loving bond of their mother above all else, NOT substitutes and not part-time. Otherwise big trouble within the Laws of Nature, therefore big unhappiness and chaos trouble for you and the kids sooner or later and society.

Understand a young child's life, is one of total dependence on interactive parental nurturing, love and bonding. Without it, they do not complete each necessary stage of their mental/psychological/emotional development. Comprehend they do not grow and mature properly into adulthood, without that unconditional parental love, harmonious interaction and commitment.

Clarification: Infants/children, need our constant, harmonious interaction, commitment and mature duel parental love and its security, to allow them to grow in accordance with Nature's Laws that structure a child's complex mental/emotional and physical growth. Along with a gentle, but firmly administered teaching of respect and consideration for others. All copied learning by adult parental example, *and not media, internet and entertainment example,* that allows our children to form lasting happy relationships and respect in adulthood for themselves, others and society, or do not bring them into this world. Understand a mother, (when not dysfunctional and lost in delusional product, promo, advertising, glossy magazine, entertainment and television image creating space), is naturally the nurturing love of Creation. They are the tenderness of Creation, the beauty of Creation, and your children need those female maternal spiritual qualities that come from divine Nature, to enable them to reach twenty-one maturely and happily - got it? Then and only then, are they able to access their spiritual essence to further their on-going evolution, from out of your combined *mature* love and close parental attention throughout childhood. Just like marriage, they are a full-time commitment; in other words, no ifs or buts or clever, *'you can have it all,'* delusional top end of town, very poor advice about it.

Single mums, without abusing the welfare system but respecting the welfare system, ask your Governments for understanding and support, to enable you to do your nurturing maternal loving job properly, especially in their formative years. Because very few men can do it for you, they are not biologically equipped to do so. The male is biologically equipped to support you in all circumstances in all situations, when they are not dysfunctional and lost in the delusional, do-what-you-like top end of town indoctrinated space that is. Therefore, learn to meditate correctly and consistently and restore balance and harmony within the functioning integrity of Nature's Laws. Otherwise, we will never ever get to heaven to collect our harp, but the other place to collect our shovel instead.

Kind regards, – Alf. CEO of spiritual boot camp.

Ripping Spiritual Yarns Continued from Stephen

Part (2)
The Goodies, the Baddies and the Selfie Syndrome.

Anyways, to pick up from where we left off from Ripping Yarns (1). Plus, I'm not happy either. The boss Upstairs does not like being disturbed on trivial matters, and I got a right earbashing for disturbing his tranquillity on minor, inconsequential problems. Sorry, can't remember or spell the long words.

Evidently, Upstairs has sent someone down here to sort all the trashing and selfie ego problems out; only he can't be heard above the noisy commercial television and its entertainment, product, promo and big buck rackets – no, racket going on down here. Anyway, youse all got to pay attention and stop making so much noise and worshipping movie stars and other media created celebrities, sports stars and other winners on this trashed planet and go back to drinking tea for a change, so that Alf, can do his spiritual boot camp job properly. Also, it takes a long time to see the boss Upstairs. So in the future, it's gotta be something very important for me to be on the receiving end of his gout again. It should be youse out-of-control café latte lot, living the jet setting, commercial television, entertainment, selfie and the techno product scientific good life copping it, not me.

Well, the reason that the ancient manuscript that I was stuck on, with its translation into proper good English, (and American for the Pentagon), was so hard to decipher, is because I thought the problem had gone out the back door a few thousand years ago. Like all us learned men did – you know, fairy stories of Lucifer and all that House of Hollydude marketed scary jazz. However, evidently, its Beelzebub inheritance keeps cropping up into human affairs, from the karma created entities of those who created it. You know, our ancestral lineage and their dirty laundry or somefing? Because we are all related to those who lived thousands of years ago – otherwise no one would be here on this planet now. At least I don't think so, and no, I ain't gonna ask the boss again, my ears are still ringing from the last time.

Anyway, it's just like that Greek mythology thingo about Jason and the Hardnuts and those seeds that turn into monsters, when youse plant them in the wrong place and don't nurture them properly like kids. Alternatively, what quality of karmic influence we have sown with our thoughts and deeds on this planet, remains down here as a perpetuated influence in the spiritual workings of Nature. Eventually, future generations inherit its returning ancestral created influence in the form of *entities* down the track of time. Because, as creative human beings, what we sow is what we reap in the spiritual system that underwrites and orchestrates physical life and its evolution. Plus, humankind has a collective unconscious operating in the spiritual workings of primordial Nature and its invisible creativity. What humankind sows individually and collectively with their karma, is what humankind reaps generation into generation, through the *law of karma* that underwrites our evolution.

So scientifically speaking, that fairy story about, '*as we sow, so do we reap,*' and '*what goes around, comes around,*' is how the, 'Real System' works and not a fairy story at all, but a hidden karma sourced spiritual fact of life contained in our on-going evolution. Because even though we are very clever as a species and award ourselves gongs, adulation, gold medals and big bucks for winning, conquering and knowing everyfing, we don't understand the spiritual workings of Nature and we can't stop unstoppable evolution, only temporarily stuff it up. Anyway, that ego-denting hard to understand spiritual fact is what universities, scientists, academics, big business and politicians know nuffing about or want to know about. Because they can't see it or experiment on it or make big bucks out of it, and that aggravation gives them chronic indigestion to even think about it. So, they don't think about it and put it in the too hard basket and go back to doing their own thingo and drinking café lattes, after rejecting Alf's boot camp oratories and shredding them.

Anyway, the inside and the outside of the shredded matter is that we must all do the right life-supportive thing to Nature and its Laws on this shared planet, if we wish to evolve and claim our heavenly spiritual harp. Then, when we leave on our cosmic travels after we have popped off, we haven't sown the wrong negative karma out of our creativity and mucked the downstairs system up, for others to inherit its returning destructive karmic influence through the Law of Karma.

However, we don't leave this planet in techno spaceships and flying saucers, of course they are just not reliable enough to reach heaven because they are synthetic and manufactured by us clever lot downstairs and subject to rust, decomposition and too much-marketed techno warping in media hyper-space, movies and comic books. Like from those loony science fiction writers on the intergalactic blink with their creative twink. Whom Alf says, are stoned out on chemical junk and live in the land of the techno warped Klingnongs. Plus, forever dreaming up weirdo stories for scientists, politicians and Star Trek fans to read in bed at night and in the loo, instead of Alf's spiritual articles.

If we do the right life-supportive to Nature thing down here on the planet and not, the new-age media and entertainment saturated *anything goes* progress thing, then we don't upset the primordial system of unstoppable evolution for others to cop its grotty returning karma afterwards, because that's what's happening right now, even as I write this cross-my-heart-and-hope-to-doie true story to youse from the

Bronx. Because, unofficially, I'm over here to return a retranslated, untranslatable tablet to their museum, that they sent to our museum when they stopped drinking cups of tea ages ago, and started importing mugs of café latte instead, no wonder they can't translate tablets. Anyways, it's a long story that happened a couple of centuries ago, but I will try and explain over a cup of tea that is.

Well, it all started at the Boston Tea Party in America. Evidently, your big wigs had invited our English big wigs for one of those official overseas dignitaries' scoffs. That they always have in high places to make sure everyone who's not having a good time, knows that they are having a good time for them. However, it all went wrong and turned into a right political punch-up and gunpowder kerfuffle, when our big wigs said to your big wigs, that they hadn't paid the Tea Ladies Tax retrospectively since the last overseas dignitary scoff. Anyways, that hard nose declaration from our English big wigs, really upset your American big wigs constitution big time. Because they didn't see why they should have to pay a tea tax in-between official scoffs, especially when they weren't over in England to drink it. Quite right too, when youse think about it?

Evidently, your big wigs spat the political dummy over that unfair tea tax and stirred all the local Natives up and said by constitutional law, that everyone could carry blunderbusses and flintlocks to protect them from the overseas English Red Coat Tea Tax Collectors. Then your big wigs, dressed up like Indians on the warpath, went and dumped all the imported tea bags into the Boston Harbor and said to our big wigs, *"tax that lot, if you can."* Well, it was all very beneficial to the constitution of the fish swimming around in the harbour, because they read tablets good now through drinking tea. But evidently, it wasn't very beneficial to those two nation's constitutions. Because they had a big war over it, that emptied their tax coffers, and both nations went broke and had to go on the dole.

Anyway, its unproductive returning influence has been floating around in Boston Harbor and the American System ever since. So that now, everyone carries guns and goes around shooting at things that go bump in the night, and other human things they do not like. So officially, that's what I'm over here to try and fix for Upstairs. Because its antiquated law that says everyone can have a gun under their pillow, has gone past the use by date in its worded Constitution and needs to be amended in the 21st century. Otherwise, the American people will never get to heaven to collect their harp and that's a shame, according to Upstairs. Because they mean-well in their Constitutions but have got it wrong where the words progress, entertainment, democracy, big corporate business and guns are concerned. Just like a lot of other so-called civilised nations in the world, that don't understand themselves or Upstairs. They only think they do.

Well, as I was saying before I got verbally shredded by the opposition in the top end of town. According to Upstairs, it's time to settle the karma books and start again downstairs. Not only with the Tea Ladies Tax, but also in Hollybug and Co; and everywhere they are stoned out on café latte, products, entertainment, movies and commercial television in this civilisation. That now worships big bucks and human beings called celebrities, winners and stars, instead of the Creator. The primordial spiritual system that underwrites physical life and its evolution, just can't take any more, 'got it wrong,' human beings doing what they like with their creativity downstairs. Like in that, 'critical mass' thingo, that the scientists have created and are always talking about over cups of café latte and biscuits in their laborotoriums and underground atom trashing bunkers and can't stop talking about it, can't help themselves even when they go on holidays with mum and the kids and auntie Mabel to Afghanistan and Iraq or somefing.

No, they are always getting into trouble from Upstairs, for all that funny science dude language and mathematical mumbo jumbo they've invented, to explain to us untalented lot how everyfing works. Sorry, I got that wrong, how it doesn't work, I mean. At least not according to Alf, and he's knowledgeable about how the 'Real System' works. Not like in the top end of town and Hollydud, but that's another potty selfie story called ego self- aggrandisement or somefing. So, I'd better get on with this one, otherwise I will be getting into trouble from all directions and not only from the big wigs in the British Museum, the White House, the media circus, science fiction writers, the book club, commercial television and hollybug and Co.

Now coming back to what I was saying before I got interrupted again:

Every two thousand years, give or take, a few science, techno, mathematical and astrofizzics University acquired wobbles, the Solar System goes around one spititual cycle, and somefing very nice happens. Then guess what, and I didn't know this, every ten thousand years the Universe goes around too spiritually speaking of course. Then the cycle starts again within the hapless happenings of human beings and especially, the innovative big wigs in the driving seat running it all out of their human created realities. Anyways, according to the tea lady, it is something to do with that fairy story about, *'what goes around, comes around* and *what goes up must come down again,* like karma. You know, that other fairy story that isn't a fairy story in the, 'Real System', only in our human-created realities and their marketed, entertainment and media-saturated systems downstairs.

Anyways, it's all a bit above my head, but I will try and explain it again in scientific dude language this time, that I haven't quite got the hang of because I can't write articles without making spelling and punctuation mistakes yet. Plus, I don't drink café latte, watch commercial television, dance with the stars, take mobile phone selfies or read glossy magazines and science fiction books in bed at night or on the loo. The unknown Upstairs fact of the karmic matter is that all destructive karma - created influence from the human being, is returned to the human being - sooner or later. If youse don't cop it personally because you are not downstairs anymore, then those you have left behind cop it. You know, the family tree and all that. Its perpetuated karmic influence is also spiritually contained in our genes. So, it's really two invisible channels of negative or positive influence that we inherit from our ancestors. One is in our bloodline and the other is, 'written in the stars,' so to speak.

Because believe it or not, it is the interactive spiritual intelligence of our solar system and its planets, that is also the invisible primordial archetypal intelligence of our physical minds and bodies and personalities. You know, it manifests as our biology, genes and chemistry and all that hard to understand scientific physical stuff. Because according to the spiritual book of Alf, life has gotta have come from somewhere, because nuffing comes from nuffing. That means whether we like to admit it or not, there must be somefing greater and more intelligent than us dissolvable human beings that created the means for everyfing and of course, that is where the word God comes into human affairs, to explain its paradox through religion and its human written books and on-going religious punch-ups. Because each religion, thinks their specific worshipped God is the real God and that other religions have got it wrong with their worshipped God. Therefore, other religions need to be trashed for telling porkies and for not worshipping the real God or somefing like that.

Anyway, when youse think about that statement of, 'nuffing comes from nuffing,' and work it out by replacing the double f with t and h, then Socrates logic says, that everyfing down here and in the Universe, must have come from somewhere or somefing to be here in the first place. Otherwise, there wouldn't be anyfing anywhere, or any place and nuffing would exist to experiment on and re-arrange in those science laborotoriums. However, youse try telling the scientists and other clever mathematical people, that nuffing comes from nuffing and they will send you to elocution, spelling and mathematical lessons, as well the funny farm for thought rehabilitation. Because in questioning the activity of science and talking about spirituality and God, you've obviously lost your marbles and become a bad influence in society. Called a nutcase by some in the media and a science and astro-fizzics heretic, in all those knowledgeable Universities. Because as well as being top of the class at writing, spelling and passing exams, they are not allowed to be wrong in anyfing in Universities. Otherwise, our University educated world would collapse, and we would all go back to living in the dark ages again. You know, like in commercial television programs and all that.

Just like what happened in the Middle Ages, when the then resident Pope in Rome, blew his top and confiscated all the telescopes and science fiction books in Universities. Because some nutcases called astronomers who are now called astro-fizzizists or somefing, had been peering into them and telling the people, that our Earth wasn't the center of the Universe and that it was sort of round, like an orange. When of course, everyone in the Vatican and the bottom end of town, knew that it is was flat and that you would fall off it if you went for a long walk with the dog.

Anyway, for telling big porkies to the people, they got branded a heretic by the Pope and roasted over the coals and sent to science and astrological purgatory. Anyway, in this century, it's Alf's turn to be a heretic and get roasted by the new-age scientists, Star Trek fans and astro-fizzizists, and not the Pope, for telling big porkies to the people. At least that's what tea lady at the British Museum where I work reckons, and I don't argue with the tea lady about anyfing, because she controls the biscuits as well as the tea trolley.

Anyway, according to the heretic book of Alf, it's from another spiritual dimension of Creation, that the primordial archetypal intelligence of Nature materialises to structure our physical bodies and evolution as well as containing all our human-created karmic influence in its spiritual domain that underwrites life, our Universe, our planets and their solar cycles, but not in push-bikes. Because they haven't got them Upstairs yet, only techno space junk from NASTA and the Pentagon and plastic bottles, tins and fast food wrappers from you know who? (not allowed to advertise on official business). However, youse try telling the scientists that and they will lock you up or worse still, experiment on you and re-arrange you in those laborotoriums to see what makes you tick funny. Like they do with everything else that walks, talks, moves or wriggles on this living planet. Well on second thoughts, not all scientists. Some are very nice people indeed and talk the talk and know what is up and what is down. If youse get my *negative v positive* human creativity drift in those laborotoriums, underground atom trashing bunkers, polluting techno spaceships and the movie and entertainment script writing brigade, the book club and commercial television.

Anyway, if you want to avoid men in white coats carting you away to the funny farm, best to keep this new heretical spiritual information top secret for the time being, until the good scientists, (the nice positive ones), that don't mind my rotten spelling, gain control of things down here once more and start pressing the right and not the wrong polluting buttons in science. Because some of the, 'got it wrong,' super clever ones, that look like butter wouldn't melt in their mouth and can talk the hind-leg off a donkey, are cuckoo and on power pills with their brilliant scientific creativity. While others have got lost in Dr Strangelove chemical pill space in their money-making pharmaceutical laborotoriums. Plus, all they have to say is those magic clincher words to make it happen, as in creating progress, irrefutable science info, techno innovation, big bucks, the economy, Nobel and new frontiers to conquer.

Along with that other clincher of an argument from the non-scientific politicians to the public. As in, we must have science and techno-progress to save mankind from its own created problems and for those politicians, to get re-elected again by a grateful public. So that guverments, just cave into those super brilliant ideas from incomplete science and cough up the official licence, for them to do what they like in their life-re-arranging animal laborotoriums, underground atom trashing bunkers, military weapons of mass destruction, techno space ships and science fiction books on conquering the planets and outer space.

Just like socially blind Guverments, give the official nod to greedy Big Corporate Bizo and the global Piggy Banks to own the World and gobble it up, from out of Multi-National Corporations and all their, got-it-in-the-bag, I'm-alright jump-in-jack, affluent global shareholders. All living the jet setting, money-making, stocks and shares good life, at the expense of the planet and its future and us marketed product, commercial television, entertainment and newsroom brainwashed mugs in the bottom end of town, and that's really weirdo when youse think about it. Because we let them do it and say thank you very much afterwards and can I have some more please, sir. On top of allowing all-consuming corporate global expansion, takeovers, monopolisation and the control of nation's economies and lots of other out of control entrepreneurial big buck activity. All being justified in the name of the global economy, creating progress, democracy, free enterprise and affluence on a level playing field they have made, not us. Because we ain't allowed on it, not even to bring the tea and biscuits to the private enterprise boardroom where it all happens. Because they even made the tea lady profession redundant, to make more money for their shareholders and big bonuses for themselves, who only drink café latte on walkways and pavements.

What a 'orrible, unfair, corporate, media, commercial television and marketing genius created product mess indeed. It's full of wrong selfie brownie points and unmenchinable things that go bump in the night in the boardroom, as well on commercial television and in Hollybug. According to Alf that is, who only drinks tea and doesn't read glossy magazines or science fiction books, or go dancing with the stars on commercial television, or at those dancing pole nightclubs and topless casinos in the desert. However, no one else see it Alf's way, of course, because they are all stoned out on commercial television visual magic mushrooms, the global economy, reality shows, anything goes entertainment, techno cooking programs, caffeine overdose and into big bucks, techno products and celebrity selfie mania.

Anyways, my friend, the tea lady, reckons we have been television, newsroom and Hollydude brainwashed into the ego authorised selfie syndrome. From watching and copying, the I-love-me and look-how-successful-I-am ego antics of saturated winners, stars, celebrities and undressed body beautiful males and females. Who have all become media created attention-grabbing commercial *pied pipers*, that are taking adults and especially our children, to the newsroom, commercial television and glossy magazine created no-where land. The land of spiritually lost human beings on the selfie ego blink. You know, *"look at me, look at me, I have the biggest ego on the media, entertainment and commercial television created selfie tree."*

Evidently, through its 24/7 saturation, we have unknowingly become selfie and fame indoctrinated from its media delivered contagious celebrity *pied piper* spell. This, through watching too much commercial television, movies, advertisements and promos, the body beautiful and *anything goes* entertainment. Along with dead-brain reality shows, game shows, sex, boobs and abs programs and verbal political punch-ups in Question Time in the House, and of course, Hollydud invented, 'birds and the bees,' closet info. At least that's what Alf and the tea lady reckon and Alf is usually right about the shenanigans of the celebrities and the politicians. With their big buck, living-the-good-life, ego-preening selfie doings, and he doesn't get his info out of, I-love-me glossy magazines and newsrooms, and its look how successful, brilliant and beautiful I am, media promo selfie spiel either. No, he uses them for mulching in his garden and in another place we all use every day, for economy purposes that is.

Anyway, the last time we had a chat on her trolley rounds, the tea lady got stuck into the selfie shenanigans of the attention-grabbing, non-stop talking, 24/7 commercial news media. She reckons, they've got too big for their news and product boots and are barging into other people's lives without politely asking them first. Along with running after others and sticking their cameras and microphones up their noses and throwing their commercial weight around everywhere in society and calling it, freedom of the press, free speech and news. Along with digging up endless celebrity closet information and undressed females, as headline news and ground-breaking selfie info in newsrooms, newspapers and glossy magazines.

Note: Along with big noting themselves interviewing and endlessly sycophantly praising or slagging, all the saturated winners, celebrities, sports stars, pop stars and politicians in the top end of town. She reckons the media, Commercial Television and Hollydude, have gone off the rails of evolution and taken us newsroom and entertainment desensitised lot along with them. Just like sexually potty Caligula and Nero did in Roman times. You know, those Roman emperor dudes, that had acquired the power to do and change anything they like in the top end of town, just like the media, commercial television, the entertainment fraternity, greedy big corporate business and piggy banks. She won't be making tea and biscuits for that selfie lot anymore, that's for sure.

Anyway, coming back to what I was saying before about the Devil and all that spooky jazz, that no one believes in anymore. Evidently, there are these other bad dudes' downstairs, (you know, the opposition to Upstairs), and these not very nice dudes, that are called sociopaths and psychopaths in translated Greek *and often, appear as nice dudes to others to get what they want,* are doing what they like in society with their born gifts, magnetic alpha charisma and acquired power. Evidently, it was their conquering, bashing, trashing and winning alpha ancestors, that created the perpetuating karmic influence/entity of megalomania, violence and greed, that plagues every civilisation and every nation. That's why these dominant alpha bad dudes, are stuck with its conquering and winning ancestral inherited nemesis in this life. That causes them to trash Nature's Laws and society and its positive spiritual values and commercially exploit and rip other people off, and want to win at everyfing and rule the world. You know, be King of the Castle and all that ancestral inherited megalomania selfie stuff.

Note: Because spiritually speaking, its ancestral negative created karma accumulated over the generations. To then became powerful destructive *entities* in the spiritual system of life and primordial Nature; that is passed on from one generation to another in their procreation gene line. You know, their ancestral family inheritance and all that. That's why these ancestral created destructive life-forces (entities) are still in the spiritual and physical biological system of life and the family tree of these bad dudes and that Alf calls, the Faust enigma. You know, always doing sociopath wheelie-dealies with the opposition to Upstairs, to have anything they want in life downstairs. Along with jetting around the world and having a good time at Fred's casino, posh ala-carte restaurants and those dancing pole nightclubs and making 24/7 headline selfie winning news, for everyone to talk about and copy.

Anyway, recently the bad dudes have been trying to bring their ancestral big boss back, by doing a load of chanting and geriatric theatricals and dressing up as fruit loops, but not in Hollyrude of course. No, they dress-down instead, like in the movies and television and glossy magazines full of products and the body beautiful. Evidently, like artists and pop stars, they make more money by having no clothes on when they are doing their marketed promo attention-grabbing thingo downstairs. You know, showing off their abs and boobs and whatnots and singing, dancing and chanting nursery rhymes and clapping each other afterwards like in adult pantomimes and all that. Just like at Oscar's Place, where they even collect statues for doing it with no clothes on, after hours that is.

So evidently, being a baddy instead of a goody in society is all to do with having an ancestral inherited entity on the blink in their family tree, and doing what they like on the planet because of it. Along with others copying them and calling it acting, entertainment, stardom, fame, artistic freedom of expression and becoming a worshipped celebrity or artist or pop star on the stretched ego selfie blink. Sort of like being in kindergarten as a kid, only worse. No, they just haven't grown up yet and learnt to respect Nature and the gift of life. Alternatively, how to act socially responsible and with dignity, humility and thought for others in society and not just themselves, and their all-consuming ambition to be rich and famous. At least that's what Upstairs says, and they should know, because they made 'em. But not anymore.

Upstairs has had enough of them doing what they like downstairs and calling it success, achievement, fame and being a big buck paid worshipped winner in the top end of town and that other people have been brainwashed to go potty over, through their saturation in the news media, movies and especially, on commercial television; where they make even more big bucks selling products and themselves. Plus, the real nasty baddies and the other acting nasty baddies, are also earning millions of bucks for stuffing everything positive up on the planet, with their *anything-goes* creativity, born talents and magnetic pied piper alpha charisma. That other fruit-loops in the media chasing them, call being sexy and alluring for some strange reason; as well as making them into famous public pin-ups and celebrities through their media saturation or somefing just as potty. Because we are not supposed to worship other human beings, especially if they have not got an Upstairs issued Spiritual licence, through helping those born less fortunate in life. You know, like J.C.? Because worshipping individual achievements like winning at everyfing or being top dog and collecting big bucks, don't mean nuffing Upstairs. It just means we have lost the spiritual plot of life, in the delusional plot of big business greed and a stretched selfie ego on the fame, ambition or megalomania blink.

In fact, just like other sociopath baddies in entreprenudial big corporate greedy business, piggy banks and big business economy mesmerised political systems, also plagued with the ancestral inherited megalomania enigma. You know, like that age-old selfie authorised and now media and movie delivered directive, *"I am this, and I am that, I am the cat that sits on the mat, tread on my patch and then its splat, just ask the mice they know about that, because I am this and I am that, so everyone should know that important fact."* That for some weirdo reason downstairs is called having self-confidence and a belief in yourself, as the best thing since teabags were invented, but not Upstairs. Where according to Alf, it is called ego authorised, ancestral inherited, delusional narcissism or somefing like that. Because Alf reckons, it means they ain't got no spiritual connection with the, *order out of chaos*, function of the Laws of Nature in their creative and talented brainbox. You know, through being worshipped by others, they've become a law unto themselves and their super-duper ego and all that human gone-wrong psycho megalomania stuff, just like Adolf, Mussolini and Stalin and Co; in our all-conquering history books. Anyway, the new-age ones are on the same ancestral inherited megalomania ego blink. As in conquering and trashing the world with their innovative creativity, only in a commercial media delivered acceptable way, that we are calling progress – but, got it wrong progress where our spiritual evolution is concerned – got it?

Well, as I was saying before I got carried away with my verbals. What's really got up the noses of these powerful bad dudes lately, is that they've just found out that our boss has beat 'em to it – he's already here. Just like Dr Who and the Tardis on the BBC, he's been here for ages, which means of course, that they just can't win at playing gods and goddesses or dialeks and klingnongs anymore, like there used to doing in the successful top end of town. No, they muffed it good and proper last year at their annual picnic day, from all their weirdo chanting and Hollybug antics of worshiping statues, selfies, products, big bucks and the body beautiful and its whatnots. Anyway, according to the Delphi Oracle and not Alf this time, it's down the cosmic tubes they all go in the finger pointing departure lounge.

Unless they get their, 'got it wrong,' selfie act together and grow up and start being goodies and not baddies anymore. Because according to Alf, it's like winning a family race. Because the elder son, is always going to beat his younger brothers and sisters to the finishing line, simply because he's been around longer, and he knows how the Upstairs brownie point system works, i.e., first come, first served and I'm Dad's favourite in the finger - pointing departure lounge. If you get my Hobsons Choice drift?

Anyway, from now on, all that selfie klingnong big buck paid activity for the media saturated winners, has got to change. So that everyone can pass the spiritual finish line together, all grown up as equals in the spiritual department assuming they want too? Then everyone can get a pat on the back and a gong, for being successful and happy with their lot downstairs–and, not just the born gifted, talented, privileged, wealthy and so-called successful. All living the top end of town image-created good life on extra serotonin, from being saturated by the media and from telling others what to do and how to do it in newsrooms, advertisements and glossy magazines, to then be called successful and a winner in society. Because Alf reckons, they are not winners Upstairs, only downstairs.

Note: Where it don't count in the departure lounge when we trash the Laws of Nature with our creativity and go around being baddies or playing at being baddies in movies and on commercial television; along with worshipping fame, big bucks and winning to acquire self-esteem, power, adulation, big bucks and so-called success. So, according to Upstairs, that 'orrible spiritless system and its top end of town indoctrinated *reality* called success, has got to change if we want to go to heaven. Because that top end of town created *reality* of inequality and greed and I'm all right jack and the exploitation of the majority, by the born gifted and powerful so-called successful minority, are in for the high jump. You know, straight out of Creation in the departure lounge, with no return ticket and all that hard cheese jazz because we cannot fool the Boss at the end of the day. Although, some baddies think they can, by pretending to be goodies while they are alive. You know, by convincing other people that, *they are a jolly good fellow*, and all that, *pat on the back* spiel, for being successful and a winner in society.

Anyway, according to the Boss, the so-called successful top end of town, have gotta understand that the, *big fish eat little fish and the dog eat dog primordial instinct to be a winner,* is not allowed in the human species, only other less evolved animal species. Because most human beings are born less fortunate in their IQ, winning and artistic talent and this makes them easy to exploit and manipulate, by those of higher IQ and those with magnetic alpha leadership charisma and other born talents, that newsrooms and newspapers rave about. Also, any exploitation of the public makes those responsible baddies, only pretending to be goodies, in the top end of town. Where that other primordial survival instinct of, *'follow the leader,'* has become much abused and misused in our greed driven, media and entertainment saturated, commercial product indoctrinated consumer civilisation, that is well and truly on the media and entertainment promoted, *anything goes*, progress blink to no-where land according to Upstairs.

Returning to the other fairy story as some might say.

The eldest son is always in charge of family matters whenever dad's gone away on big bizo, after he reaches twenty-one that is. It has something to do with the natural, *order out of chaos,* function of the Spiritual Laws of Nature in the family structure. Unfortunately, not many people realise these spiritual Laws or have intuitive access to them anymore, in their commercial television, entertainment and marketing genius brainwashed minds. No, they are far too busy doing their commercial television instructed and entertainment copied thingo downstairs. Along with having a jolly good time at Fred's gambling casino in the desert, or was it a bad time? (dunno, can't remember), to intuitively realise God's intelligence in Creation. For that's what the Laws of Nature are, in their spiritual manifestation within the human mind. To prevent us from going off the spiritual rails of evolution and into consumer and human worshipped superficial celebrity no, no, land, like we are now.

All life-intelligence functions through the spiritual self-referral Laws of Nature. The instinct driven animals are naturally in sync with them, because they do not have *conscious freewill and an ego* to do what they like. Therefore, positive progress for them with their evolution is automatic. We, unfortunately, have become media, entertainment and commercial television saturated and have lost spiritual connection with those self-referral laws as no, no, indoctrinated psychological result. Because human beings, have the conscious free-will and creativity, to ignore those intuitive spiritual Natural Laws and their, 'order out of chaos,' function in our brain, also called, having a conscience. Especially, when we become lost in making big bucks and worshiping winners, celebrities and media created selfie status, to acquire self-esteem. You know, having our body beautiful or ego-preening mugshot in television newsrooms, newspapers, advertisements and glossy magazines. That is called, *'realising our childhood dream of being famous and a media acclaimed winner,'* downstairs, but not Upstairs.

Explanation: The problem being according to Upstairs, it don't do nuffing for our spiritual evolution in its superficiality, sycophancy, self-aggrandisement, adulation and selfie fame and big bucks of course. In fact, its top end of town ego created delusional path called success, leads to ignominy in the departure lounge. So that St Peter, won't let us in through the gates and gives us the finger instead. You know, like in that famous painting on the ceiling in the Vatican of the Boss and some bloke called Adam, that the Pope likes and that religious visitors, go potty over and have crook necks afterwards. Evidently, and not many visitors know this true version, Adam got caught pinching, (you know, scrumping) apples in the Boss's orchard in his garden of Eden and blamed it on someone called Eve. When in fact, she wanted to put it back on the apple tree, not eat it. Because she had the brains to know she was not allowed to take what did not belong to her without asking first. Whereas Adam, functioned from everywhere else but the brain when he wanted somefing and just did it, whatever?

Anyway, the Boss gave Adam the finger and sent him packing out of the garden, but not for pinching apples, but for telling big porkies to him about Eve. Because even though she still got the blame *for doing it* downstairs by the Vatican and visitors with crook necks, Eve had nuffing to do with it and it was all Adam's fault, because he couldn't behave himself and did just what he liked. You know, like in Commercial Television, Fox News, Sky News, Fred's Casino, Hollybug and Co and other commercial big buck winners in the successful top end of town. Anyways, got-it-wrong Adam, really blotted his downstairs karma book, when he gave the finger back to the Boss and evidently, other baddies have been copying him ever since. Because in doing what they like downstairs and becoming media famous for doing it, they all think they are invincible. Just like media moguls and their shareholders. When of course they are not, only the Boss is invincible because he cannot be dissolved like us physical human beings.

Alf reckons, it's the out-of-control commercial media, media moguls and *anyfing goes* entertainment, that have created that no, no, to our collective spiritual evolution and nuffing to do with Eve either. Because the only thing they are interested in is in grabbing our attention and making big bucks and big noting themselves in the media-saturated ego-preening selfie process. You know, just like in newspapers, glossy magazines, commercial television and Hollydud and Co; because they will show, say and do anyfing to shock us and make us look at them. You know, good or bad, true or false, obscene or violent, crude or obnoxious. You know, foul mouths and other not allowed in boot camp bleep bleep stuff. Just like actors, celebrities and body-beautiful undressed sirens and other attention seekers in glossy magazines, the internet, promos, newsrooms, reality shows and other so-called entertainment on the television.

Note: That all want to become famous as baddies downstairs, (and infamous Upstairs), and endlessly talked about and be paid big bucks for doing, showing and saying, whatever they like in public to grab our attention. You know, any publicity is good publicity to big-note yourself. Because it makes you famous and chased after by the news media. To then become a saturated big buck paid commercial product clone and of course, a worshipped celebrity on the look-at-me selfie blink in television commercials, newsrooms, glossy magazines, product promos and newspapers. But Alf reckons, with no spiritual connection in their creative brainbox to the intuitive Laws of Nature; that are responsible for creating order out of chaos in the human mind. That evidently, is very bad news in the departure lounge, for a so-called successful human being on the fame and big buck attention-grabbing sociopath or delinquent ego blink.

Anyway, (*and not even all-knowing Universities know this un-mathematical fact*), it is the spiritual self-referral Laws of Nature, that should silently complement the human mind and its creativity, to function with integrity, dignity, humility and a conscience, and live in perfect harmony and happiness with everything in Creation. Not go around wheeling and dealing with Faust to be famous, or bumping people off, or conquering others, or exploiting others and winning at everyfing for big bucks; you know, like in the top end of town? Alternatively, scientifically treating it like a kids mecano game and lego, from all its bits and pieces and calling it scientific progress, saving humankind, technological innovation and conquering new frontiers. Because evidently, we are polluting everything to high heaven and gobbling up the planet's irreplaceable resources, in that so-called techno and science laborotorium created progress for humankind, and that's very weirdo. According to the book of Alf and the knowledgeable tea lady at the British Museum; where I work translating too hard to translate tablets, like this one?

That brings us back to some of those big-wig genius scientists again, who are not in Upstair's good books one little bit. Simply because, they are always experimenting on everything willy-nilly and swapping bits and pieces and parts around, to see what happens afterwards, you know, like in Frankenstein and the Island of Dr Moreou or Professor Morriarti or somefing, sorry, can't spell names. Then patting themselves on the back and collecting gongs, because they THINK they've passed the finish line and can get the media trumpets out to blast us all with its techno dude information. When of course they haven't. No, the boss says they haven't got a spiritual clue, but are very good at convincing our lot, that they know everyfing because they have been to University and are very clever ... or was it not so clever, dunno can't remember all the words now. Anyway, Alf reckons they are very clever and gifted in Universities, but have lost the spiritual plot of life and taken the rest of us science and techno brainwashed lot along with them. Because they and the astro-fizzizists and other spaced-out Star Trek fans are going the wrong way to reach heaven. You know, the real heaven and not the downstairs science, entertainment, media, fame and celebrity created one, that is dissolvable like human beings.

The long and the shredded of it all, is that Upstairs wants those experimenting ad hoc with other life-intelligence, re-arranging chemicals, the atom and conquering the planets and doing what they like with anything and everything, to 'down tools' until we have reached the end of Alf's spiritual boot camp talking journey. If they do not listen and understand a different spiritual reality than their physical human created dissolvable one, then they are in for the high jump, good and proper. You know, down the cosmic tubes in the departure lounge with their spiritual evolution. We must all understand, that we cannot do just what we like on this delicate biological living planet with our human intelligence and creativity. No, a conscience, wisdom, ethics, foresight, social responsibility, dignity, humility, empathy and spiritually understanding our-selves and Nature, must come into it too. Those silently acquired spiritual qualities are currently missing in our science, techno and entertainment and consumer consumed selfie civilisation. In Nature's dictionary, it is called acquiring the maturity of spiritual consciousness and the consideration of Creation, as a very intelligent interacting system, yet very delicate and vulnerable, to the spiritually blind, *anything-goes*, creativity of dissolvable human beings.

Anyways, it's as the tea lady says, *"We all live on this shared planet, not just those blindly experimenting on everything in the name of progress and like-minded others, wanting to conquer outer space and the planets and create weapons of mass destruction and rule the world."* Because once they create anyfing in their synthetic laborotoriums and techno-science factories and put it into the system of Nature and life, we are all influenced by it for good or for bad, and a lot of it is polluting the physical and spiritual Intelligence of Nature in the form of synthetic toxic pollution, especially for those who come after us. Upstairs reckons, we are spiritually blind with our scientific twiddling of the atom and experimenting willy-nilly on life and scientifically re-arranging chemicals and conquering everything in Creation. Because this spiritually blind activity, is unknowingly destroying the means for life to exist on this living planet.

So, we must understand where life comes from and the Intelligence that created it, before continuing any more of that so-called scientific, techno and conquering the planets progress for humankind. Otherwise, according to Alf and his tea leaves, we will physically self-destruct as a species with our existing so-called progress.

I've gotta go now and book an urgent ticket with Upstairs to get home quick. Because I've just been summoned by the British Museum big wigs on my intergalactic cell phone, to get myself back in the office to explain what I'm doing over here with their tablets in the opposition's museum. Anyway, I've asked Alf to post this story to the top end of town, because I aint allowed, owing to my rotten spelling and diction. Then I'll go and post some other translations of the Celestine Potholes on notice boards in the bottom end of town, then youse can all start working it out. Then after I've had a cup of tea and sorted out that tea lady's tax problem in America, I'll be back with some important leaflets from Alf, explaining how to neutralise the baddies and get to spiritual heaven. Simply through understanding how the 'Spiritual System' works and practicing correct meditation with the correct mantra.

p.s. Just got home.

I forgot to mention, that Upstairs says if we keep worshipping I-love-me Hollybug and Co; and Oscar and watching dead-brain soap operas, closet info, reality shows, celebrities, winners and other body-beautiful created human products on the television and in newspapers, then we won't go to heaven but the opposition because he's got gout, the Boss that is. He reckons it's us product, newsroom, entertainment and celebrity addicted selfie lot down here, that have given him his painful gout problem. Evidently, we will get the finger in the departure lounge like Adam, if we keep on that media created path of glorifying and idolising winners, celebrities and other born gifted and talented human beings for their pied piper animal charisma, creative brains, acting skills, looks, artistic talent, boobs, abs and what-nots. Because we cannot spiritually evolve and reach heaven, going down that delusional euphoric selfie path of superficial and dissolvable ego accomplishment with no spiritual accomplishment to go with it.

The boss reckons that media saturated celebrity and winning adulation does not belong in heaven, so it should not belong downstairs especially when we turn twenty-one. So those lost in its, I-love-me and look-how-successful and beautiful-I-am selfie space, have got to spiritually grow up and cross off the word's self-aggrandisement, conceit and ego-preening and write the words, *humility, dignity and social responsibility*, ten thousand times instead. Because evidently, that is what is missing in the so-called successful top end of town in the driving seat of progress. Anyway, more about this abuse of acquired power from Alf, because its nuffing to do with me. I only translate too hard to translate tablets, like this one. Anyway, I'm going for my tea break before the big wigs in the office upstairs, scoff all the biscuits again. Like that lot upstairs at the BBC, but that's another long story.

Oops! Nearly forgot to include the following updated downstairs quote. Especially for those perpetuating garbage-creativity on this shared planet from their ancestors. So, here's a capital letter sticker for the stretched limo bumper bar, to all the baddies and so-called successful winners' downstairs.

THERE ARE MORE THINGS IN HEAVEN AND EARTH, THAN EVER DREAMED OF IN OUR HUMAN CREATED REALITIES.

Anyway, I reckon that bloke Shakespeare the Bard, got it right, in one of his famous plays about, 'got it wrong,' powerful human beings on the blink with their ancestral inheritance, what do youse think? You can answer that question if you want to, but only for a little while because I'm going on my archaeological digging holidays soon and don't know when I'll be back. It's up to the boss Upstairs, because he's got the annual leave and return dates, I haven't.

Kind regards – Stephen. On behalf of Upstairs.

Read All About It

A Stephen translation and Alf narration, of the twelve missing manuscripts from the mind-boggling blockbuster, 'The Celestine Potholes.' This new spiritual information on the origins of life, evolution, religion, God and humankind, will help negotiate the pearly gates in the positive end of the departure lounge and not, the other no, no, ignominy gates at the other end for a change.

The following translated manuscripts pasted by Stephen on other public notice boards. All rights reserved on Upstairs authority. License No: AD 1999 issued from Upstairs, not downstairs, and not to be confused with the Dead Sea Scrolls. These are the Live Sea Scrolls and pre-date and post-date them by several millenniums.

1) WHAT IS A HUMAN BEING?
2) WHAT IS GOD?

3) IS IT RIGHT TO WORSHIP CELEBRITIES AND OTHER IDOLS?
4) THE SEEDS OF THE GENERATIVE STATE?
5) PSYCHE - WHAT'S THAT?
6) WHAT'S THIS?
(I times D) plus the square root of (M) times (LN plus CM) equals H. (extra Brownie points for Universities if you solve it before the Christmas Hols).
7) BULLSEYE TIME?
8) QUESTIONNAIRE TIME? (by Stephen Gripes)
9) THE UNEMPLOYED?
10) IS THERE SUCH A THING AS THE "DEVIL?"
Or is it the Anti-matter of the other Universe ... ask Albert he knows?
11) WHO WAS JESUS?
12) DAY OF RECKONING - ALL NATIONS?

Manuscript 1.

What is a Human Being?

FOR HERE LIES CREATIVITY WITH ENDLESS POSSIBILITY PRIMORDIAL AND BALANCED BY NATURE

The human being creates both physically and spiritually. The creative power (karma) of human thought shakes other invisible worlds, that science would call dimensions. We also shape the afterlife spiritual planes of Creation and all that is in them. For those spiritual worlds are created by the human being – not God. Those human constructed spiritual planes of the afterlife, are the karma (spiritual) construct of the created lived realities of humankind, imprinted in the creative spiritual fabric of Creation. Karma and its creative vibratory influence, that is a created spiritual product out of our human physical thought and desire, that enters the interactive spiritual domain of primordial Nature. Thus, what human - created reality we prescribe too and live on this planet, is where our spiritual essence ends up when we pass on from physical to non-physical existence at death. Because, what we have sown with our creativity, is what we reap in Nature's interactive primordial intelligence.

About humankind as an individual and as a collective:

When the primordial negative and positive spiritual archetypal intelligence structuring our physical biology and thought process, goes out of sync with the, *order out of chaos*, function of the Laws of Nature, our ordained spiritual evolution stagnates on the physical plane of life. This means our afterlife evolution, also spirals out of sync with the self-referral Laws of Nature and chaos, manifests in both the physical and spiritual aspects of our human evolution. The cause of this spiritual located malfunction is from human-created destructive karma and associated destructive entities; that accumulate and contaminate Nature's primordial archetypal intelligence and usurp the function of the self-referral Laws of Nature; laws that are responsible for, '*order out of chaos,*' in both physical and spiritual Creation. Divine laws that are also responsible for gaining higher states of consciousness in life and at death. This human created malfunction of evolution means humankind's ordained spiritual evolution has stagnated.

Clarification: This malfunction of humankind's spiritual evolution, is from accumulating destructive karma and associated entities, sourced to humankind's not-life supportive actions and creativity. It is a destructive cause and effect karmic influence/entity that corrupts humankind's spiritual evolution and is alien to the divine workings of Nature that sources life and its evolution. A divine Intelligence that underwrites the self-referral Laws of Nature and forms the status quo Intelligence of this Creation. When these destructive entities reach, *critical mass,* in the spiritual domain of primordial Nature, accelerating atrophy/chaos sets in within the interactive primordial archetypal intelligence of Nature that orchestrates physical life and its biology and chemistry. This, *critical mass,* equation will eventually cause the divine status quo intelligence of Creation to manifest and restore, '*order out of chaos,*' to the primordial processes of life and Nature.

Unfortunately, many in the top end of town cannot believe there is divine Intelligence greater than their human intelligence. Because that understanding would mean having to accept something greater than themselves and their human-created realities. A concept that is very difficult to accept in a spiritless mind divorced from the Laws of Nature.

The accumulative karma created effect of this humankind created premature entropy (atrophy) in the primordial workings of Nature, creates irrationality within the discriminating aspect of the thought process of human beings. Correspondingly, human judgement and logic are impaired, and delusion becomes rife in the affairs of humankind. Disorder grows in the activity and expression of the accentuated negative human being. Bloodshed, disharmony, destructive behaviour, psychological disorder, sexual disorder, negative creativity, intolerance, polarisation and ambivalence, gain dominance in a spiritually decaying civilisation. But it is not seen as such, by those contaminated with its destructive karmic influence and associated entities.

In spiritual understanding, it means the dissolving negative archetypal intelligence of primordial Nature, has become dominant in the humankind's expression, creativity and logic.

Clarification: Chaos, in the form of the collapse of positive life-supportive family and social values and loss of integrity and human dignity, is the collective unrealised negative outcome in humankind. It is sourced to destructive life-forces, becoming dominant in primordial Nature's negative and positive archetypal intelligence orchestrating life. When trapped in its destructive influence, it is not possible for the individual to realise the negative effect it has on human thought, actions, desires, deeds and creativity. It is contagious, karma created, accumulative negative influence, that invisibly retards the positive creativity of humankind but accelerates the negative creativity in humankind. Those afflicted, become blind to the consequences of their actions, become blind to common sense and rational reasoning, becoming indifferent to wrongdoing and positive life-supportive values. In its place comes denial, clever semantics, narcissism, ambivalence, divisiveness, procrastination, an endless argument that we call debate, and social chaos where once there was dominant order and harmony in nations.

In spiritual terms of understanding, we could call this rectification of human-created chaos, a Cosmic authored re-birth cycle, sourced to the status quo divine Intelligence of this Creation. A cataclysmic upheaval of physical Nature that has been triggered by humankind's accumulating destructive activity. A human created fate that has befallen other chaos creating civilisations before ours. The Greek philosopher Plato put this two and two together in his day and gave the reasons, in a dialogue about the fate of mythical Atlantis. No one has put two and two together since, except perhaps in the much translated, misinterpreted and misunderstood Bible.

Scientists should stop their blind experiments on everything on this planet. Place them on temporary hold, until we have completed our spiritual journey and understood in depth, what is being spiritually explained. Then science will have truly saved the human species from physical self-destruction. This current indiscriminate blind science activity, especially its synthetic chemical pollution and cloning is adding to the problem, albeit unknowingly. Comprehend existing science only understands the physical component of life. They will become aware of the spiritual component if they temporarily down tools and correlate, what is being explained along our spiritual fact-finding tour.

Religions should refer to their scriptures to comprehend what is being explained. Then it is back to 21st-century language, for a further spiritual understanding of those scriptures. We live in the 21st century now, and a different epoch of consciousness prevails in this century for humankind. Therefore, we must understand God, and we must discuss God, we must acknowledge God, we must teach our children about God, from a transcendent acquired spiritual level of God. If you remain in the past, the Laws of Nature cannot help your specific religion evolve further. The means to acquire that spiritual structure of consciousness is through the twice-daily practice of Transcendent Meditation and the use of an intoned mantra.

Manuscript 2.

What is God?

God! Or the idea of God! comes from God!
Because the idea of God is Creation

About the uninvolved abstract silent Creator and words for thought and not denial.

Paradox: God is both Absolute and Relative and the transcendent uninvolved architect of Creation.

Paradox: The abstract inactive Intelligence of God is beyond Physical and Spiritual Creation, yet contains Physical and Spiritual Creation.

Paradox: The manifestation of God is Creation and the totality of existence, eternity and the cause of everything.

Paradox: There is both a personal never-changing inactive silent aspect of God and an ever-changing impersonal active aspect of God.

Paradox: The transcendent personal never-changing aspect of God, is pure absolute abstract silence. As the activity and content of Creation is the ever-changing impersonal manifested aspect of God.

Conclusion: God does not talk. The abstract silent transcendent Intelligence of God is beyond talk and all activity. Only the creations of God talk. For example, human beings.

Conclusion: No human being can be said to speak for uninvolved transcendent God, only speak through the manifested active Divine spiritual intelligence of God.

Conclusion: That active personal intelligence of impersonal transcendent God is not human, but Divine.

Conclusion: Therefore, the active Divine intelligence of God is not religious ideology, because that religious ideology is of the human being's creativity.

Conclusion: Therefore, no human created existing Religion has automatic entry to Divine intelligence or exclusive access to transcendent silent God.

The solution to finding uninvolved God:
Comprehend that transcendent located God is everything, including infinity. When we have fused the physical and the spiritual aspects of God, through the consistent practice of transcendent meditation, then will we have become a spiritually evolved human being and where, no more paradox or delusion exists. It is called enlightenment. It is also called self-referral spiritual consciousness or Cosmic consciousness, that finds the fulfillment of evolution in a further evolved structure of consciousness called God consciousness. Because that acquired spiritual structure of consciousness has a personal link with the active self-referral Divine Laws of God. The spiritual domain of which has been called the 'Veda' in the Sanskrit language of ancient India and the birthplace, of spiritual enlightenment. We can also understand the 'Veda', as the cosmic computer of Creation. That is the nucleus of divine intelligence and the status quo spiritual intelligence of this Creation. Comprehend it is not God as such, but is from the pure creativity of the silent uninvolved abstract transcendent Intelligence of God. As is everything in Creation.

Comprehend this physical evolving Universe, is underwritten by spiritual Creation and from where our physical Universe was born the big bang? The human being, with its evolving biological created primordial physical intelligence, is currently trapped in physical Creation on the level of physical thought. The human being must leave that concept of thought and understand the concept of abstract silence. Fuse these two components, (Absolute and Relative), through the long-term practice of correct meditation, then we will eventually become free of that physical entrapment and move on with our spiritual evolution and its infinite possibilities. The never-ending debate of God vs no God and life after death finally solved if we wish it to be. Because as human beings, we create our reality along with our destiny in Creation, not God.

IT IS SO SIMPLE - IT IS SO BEAUTIFUL. THE ESSENCE OF CREATION IS YOU.
Thus, are we the manifested seed of the eternal Creator – as is everything that exists.

Manuscript 3.

Is it Right to Worship Celebrities, Winners and Other Human Created Idols?

Wisdom from the past

WHEN I WAS A CHILD, I WORSHIPED AS A CHILD
I LOOKED UP AS A CHILD
I SPOKE AS A CHILD
I ACTED AS A CHILD

About media-fuelled celebrity obsession:

To those identifying with media-saturated celebrities, artists and winners to acquire their self-esteem. Along with those in the media spotlight, on the receiving end of its human adulation to fuel their self-esteem. Know your silent inner temple to acquire that all important self-esteem, otherwise we will never reach heaven to collect our harp. That transcendent located temple at the source of thought is the positive life-supportive place to silently worship the Creator as the mature adult. For it is the centre of Creation and the temple of all temples in Creation. All have access to its transcendent unifying source of absolute intelligence, the Creator, through the simple short practice of Correct Meditation.

It is time to start a spiritual journey out of that ego identification entrapment, of worshipping celebrities and winners. Its media saturated euphoric influence has become a powerful delusion-creating contagious entity in humankind. As an adult, its entrapment is retarding our individual spiritual evolution and preventing those afflicted, from spiritually growing up. Comprehend the idolising of human beings with acquired status, gongs, influence and power in society, is sourced to a primordial survival instinct that we have called, *follow the leader.*

    This natural phenomenon in the animal kingdom has become a media and marketing genius exploited instinct, for grabbing our attention and acquiring self-esteem, from out of identifying with media saturated celebrities, artists, winners and commercial products. That has nothing to do with respecting and appreciating others or acquiring dignity, spiritual maturity and self-respect. This media saturated and contagious euphoric influence, (celebrity worship), is retarding the spiritual development of humankind.

About Hollywood and Co:
    We are all actors upon the stage of life – did not Shakespeare the noted playwright on human 'got it wrong' affairs say so? However, some born gifted human beings through a quirk of primordial Nature, are exceptionally talented at acting, i.e., at attention seeking, pretence and superficiality called acting and drama. Then immaturely showered with gongs and accolades and media saturated, to create news, closet information and attention-grabbing gutter headlines out of. To then invariably become commercial product pied pipers and paid vast amounts of advertiser's money, in the spiritually unproductive devolution process. An obscene big business greed authored practice, for others to see and puzzle over, in our spiritless world of created inequality and worshipping winners, fame and big bucks, called success. A spiritless big business created reality, that has become divorced from Nature and its self-referral Laws. Notably, from out of worshipping all things monetary, human and dissolvable and nothing spiritual, absolute or lasting. Such is celebrity worship.

    A, 'got it wrong,' world of unconscionable business greed and the exploitation of the majority, by the born gifted and media-saturated so-called successful small minority. A human created reality of eulogising humankind's pathological disorders as entertainment and praising those that act them out the best in movies and plays. This ego sourced, immature adult practice, of worshipping celebrities and winners and paying them obscene amounts of money for their exceptional talent, physical attributes, material accomplishments and acquired status, has no place in a mature civilisation. Only in an immature, self-absorbed, self-gratuitous thoughtless one, that has fallen off the rails of spiritual evolution and is psychologically self-destructing in its commercial media-fuelled delusion. Such is celebrity worship.

Clarification: The saturation of celebrity worship out of the media, is unknowingly creating psychological disorder in society and retarding its spiritual evolution. This immature idolising of winners and celebrities is the culmination of human self-aggrandisement and self-worship. Created from the misuse of acquired power in the commercial media, to grab the public's attention and hip pocket and big note themselves in the superficial sycophantic process. Comprehend the adulation of gifted human beings and paying them vast amounts of money, is a psychological recipe for creating narcissism, over-inflated ego disorder, megalomania and self-aggrandisement in those being worshiped as well as creating inequality in society. It is a human created ego practice for acquiring self-esteem from adulation that destroys the spiritual qualities of humility and dignity in society. It is a, 'got it wrong,' inequality creating media practice, that when saturated in society, becomes a contagious euphoric entity in the interactive primordial workings of Nature. It becomes a contagious euphoric life-force that usurps the Laws of Nature structuring, 'order out of chaos,' in human consciousness. Such is celebrity worship.

Repeat: Comprehend the worshipping and idolising of human beings and not the Creator, fuels sycophancy, hubris, conceit, self-aggrandisement, self-importance, narcissism and ego sourced delusion in society. The fact that celebrity worship has become saturated in society through the media is the sign of a spiritually decaying civilisation. Both Socrates and Plato of ancient Greece, came to understand this perpetuated human ego driven failing and its sycophancy, but could do nothing about its contagious euphoric influence/entity, that grew to saturate the Greek civilisation and corrupt its spiritual evolution. We can do something about its recurring nemeses in our civilisation. The means to dissolve its human ego created contagious delusion is through the collective practice of Transcendent Meditation in society.

Note: A simple inner practice, that evolves human consciousness up the ladder of spiritual evolution and out of its acquired pathological disorders and ego created delusion. Comprehend we become spiritually debilitated, by the euphoric karmic influence generated out of worshipping, glorifying and idolising human beings. Therefore, once we know something is wrong, harmful and unproductive to our spiritual and social evolution, do not do it. Do something about it instead and grow up out of its celebrity pied piper spell, that the commercial media exploit to capture our attention and sell products. The means have been given, to dissolve its human created delusion in society and spiritually compliment life, the Creator and ourselves in the unifying process. Because the constant worshipping, glorifying and sycophantic adulation of celebrities and winners through the media, is a spiritually unproductive, past the use-by-date, immature ego-preening practice in the 21st Century.

Manuscript 4.

The Creative Seeds that Sow Human Reality and its Destiny

Therefore, the unrealised power of thought, desire and intent, from the creative processes of human thought and desire. Thought, that interacts with Nature's primordial archetypal spiritual intelligence that orchestrates life, through the creative spiritual product of karma.

At the spiritual located level of Creation where human thought manifests from, the reverberation from a physical thought, is like the blow from a woodcutter's axe echoing within the silence of a great forest. That 'silence,' is the absolute abstract intelligence of the Creator. Thus, also know the spiritual value of trees on this living evolving planet. For they, like everything else in Creation, are a seed manifestation of God's pure creativity. Because everything in existence, is from the creative seed of the diversifying never-changing absolute transcendent Creator, but in different individualised forms of self-perpetuating manifestation where life and its seed is concerned. The age-old conundrum, of whether the tree came before the seed is resolved in that spiritual understanding. Because they are one and the same at their Absolute source, as with everything in Creation. It is only appearing differently as seed and tree, in the different stages of its physical evolution and self-regenerative cycle.

We must comprehend at the spiritual level of life, the creative karma from the product of thought has power and influence beyond our present comprehension. Ask those mathematically dabbling in quantum physics, for their interpretation of its no-where but everywhere domain and multi-dimensional activity, that can vanish into nothing, or so it would seem from a physical perspective. Those that start their spiritual journey out of our human-created mess on this planet will understand that incomplete science knowledge, in a different context than physical mathematics on the path of spiritual knowledge. Those that do not come, will not comprehend its significance or potential, consequently left far behind with their spiritual evolution.

As a physical reflection and creation of the Creator's pure creativity, human thought possesses the potential of the Creator to create with also. Thus, we should understand, it is the human being's thought, desire and intent, that creates physical reality and the interpretation of that reality. It is human thought, that has created all ideology, (created realities), that have been and will continue to be created and lived out of on this planet, not God. The human species unknowingly also creates the afterlife spiritual planes of Creation ad-infinitum with their unique creativity. They are a negative or positive, *cause and effect* karma created product, from out of the created realities (ideologies) we all live. Therefore, from the creative seed of human thought and its regenerative fertility, sourced to the transcendent Creator. They are transient worlds, sown into the spiritual fabric of Creation out of human thoughts, deeds and actions and the creative spiritual product of karma.

Therefore, what we sow in this life with our creative karma, is what we reap in those Negative or Positive planes of transitory afterlife existence and where our spirit ends up at death, for we have created that plus or minus afterlife destiny while we are alive, nothing to do with uninvolved God. Did not Jesus say so in the language of his time at the end of his life? He went to create his spiritual Heaven for others and verbally said as such, just as enlightened Mohammed did for others when he passed on from physical to non-physical existence at death.

Further to the misunderstood and often misinterpreted or misunderstood Koran and Bible.

Killing, maiming, destroying, murdering, conquering, subjugating, intimidating, manipulating and exploiting other human beings in the name of God, means those responsible and those inciting it, have no connection to God. Understand categorically, absolutely and definitively, they are under the influence of destructive ancestral inherited karma, linked to a human created destructive entity out of the past. Entities that evolve out of a lived ideology and the creative seed of human thought and desire. Therefore, avoid like the plague those inciting and perpetuating this religious mayhem out of the past in the present. Do not give them power or status of any description in society and no access to our vulnerable children, under the delusion of religious instruction. No matter how gifted, eloquent, articulate, educated, charismatic or brilliant they may be.

Understand uninvolved abstract silent God, has nothing to do with killing and maiming. Only the unbalanced and deluded negative accentuated primordial human being; that has lost intuitive connection with the self-referral Laws of Nature structuring order out of chaos in Creation. It is also time to understand the ancestral inherited pathological disorder of megalomania. Sourced to the immature human ego and acquired power in society and not sourced, to divine power or God. A human perpetuated inherited nemesis (megalomania), that is also behind the centuries-old religious fanaticism and killing in the name of God, to own the religious status quo in the world. Consult our history books for further unequivocal confirmation?

Comprehend the human created spiritual planes of transitory afterlife existence, can be positive, or they can be negative, in the context of furthering our spiritual evolution at our physical re-birth cycle. Because we inherit the Negative and Positive karma of past lives to either support our on-going spiritual evolution, or retard our evolution to higher states of consciousness while we are alive. There also comes a ten thousand years divinely authored spiritual re-birth cycle, to deal with continuously born negative accentuated human beings, that have become permanently lost to positive evolution. In that re-generative solar cycle, positive human spiritual essence automatically evolves further, but the negative accentuated human spirit is removed from the system of life for eternity.

Comprehend as human beings; we have conscious free will to choose the direction of our personal evolution, thus our afterlife destiny also. That unique conscious freewill, is the Creator's gift to the human species to evolve itself up the ladder of spiritual evolution through its own life-supportive actions. Thus, do we create and choose our up or down destiny – no one else. Therefore, let it always be positive and in accordance with evolution and Nature's Laws and in harmony with others on this shared planet. The transcendent acquired effortless means to create that universal harmony has been given. It is the same means, for a negative accentuated human being, (a lost soul), to come out of its ancestral inherited destructive karma and evolve further or be dissolved. Because that divinely orchestrated spiritual regenerative cycle has arrived in our solar system. Therefore, on this life-sustaining shared planet that we call Earth.

Manuscript 5.

THE EVOLVING SPIRITUAL PSYCHE

Not to be confused with the dissolvable created psyche, a physical created persona/personality that we call the individual I or self.

Every individual, every family, every tribe, every nation, the whole human race, every form of life-intelligence, has an individual and collective spiritual psyche. The spiritual psyche functions as a vibrational karmic key-signature within the interactive archetypal spiritual intelligence of primordial Nature processing life. The evolving spiritual psyche of the human being ... but not its dissolvable physical created psyche, contains a divine potential to be eternal in spiritual Creation. A divine potential that is subject to our continuing positive spiritual evolution as human beings during life. That is where the equation of, 'evolve or perish,' comes into human affairs, in the divine plan of evolution and the spiritual evolution of the human species.

Clarification: In the interactive spiritual and physical workings of primordial Nature, brain structured life functions as individual intelligence being processed and evolved, through the, *cause and effect*, influence of its created karma. Karma that is a creative spiritual vibration, that comes out of the activity of thought and desire. To then enter the spiritual domain of primordial Nature and interact with its primordial archetypal intelligence underwriting and orchestrating life. Therefore, orchestrating the biology and chemistry of life, orchestrating the genetic structure of life, orchestrating the evolution of life. Comprehend all the branches of brain structured life, are spiritually linked to the archetypal primordial intelligence of Nature, that processes its individual karma for the purpose of evolution.

Karma, the creative tool of evolution and the cause of the continuing physical re-birth cycle of the human being. A perpetual re-birth of the individual spirit of the human being that is linked to the karma of unrequited desires from a previous life.

This spiritual knowledge of Nature is missing in our existing physical-only understanding of life, ourselves and Nature. That is why those indiscriminately experimenting on Creation and its components can be said to be spiritually blind and divorced from Nature with their science and technological creativity. Because in blindly re-arranging, changing and meddling with life and the atom, incomplete science is unknowingly usurping Laws that underwrite, 'order out of chaos,' in life and Creation. That means science, is creating and accumulating, a *cause and effect*, karma created destructive entity, that interferes with the self-referral function of spiritual Laws of Nature. Self-referral laws, (spiritual energies), that are processing, 'order out of chaos,' in the primordial archetypal spiritual intelligence that underwrites life. Spiritual Laws that are the divinely structured government, of the duel (negative and positive) archetypal spiritual intelligence of impersonal primordial Nature.

When the collective negative karma out of our human creativity reaches, 'critical mass,' in primordial Nature's workings, its karma created destructive entities, will trigger the status quo Intelligence of this Creation to manifest and restore the divine function of the Laws of Nature. In that automatic status quo authored process of the restoration of spiritual evolution, life starts again, (as it has in the past on this planet), when the duel physical and spiritual evolution of life has stagnated. However, obviously, not through our human *cause and effect* karma, as our species had yet to come into existence. This pending avoidable cataclysmic restoration of spiritual evolution will be down to our human species and its accumulating, 'got it wrong,' creativity, causing the devolution problem.

To dissolve that humankind created devolution problem and evolve further with our spiritual evolution, we need to acquire the transcendent means, to stay in sync with the spiritual intelligence that underwrites life. We need to come out of our existing primordial structure of physical consciousness and acquire a spiritual one. We need to comprehend that all life, is being processed for the purpose of evolution, by higher intelligence of greater magnitude than human intelligence. We need to acquire that spiritual structure of consciousness and operate intuitively out of its universal intelligence with our creativity and karma as human beings.

We can identify that Divine intelligence as the, 'Cosmic Mind,' the progenitor of physical Creation and life; this divine intelligence is the manifested active spiritual intelligence of the uninvolved Creator or God. We could also call that composite Divine intelligence, the Cosmic Spirit, or perhaps the Holy Spirit in religious terminology. That is authored and underwritten by transcendent, abstract Absolute Intelligence, the intrinsic manifested substance of Creation and that Religion, has called God.

Comprehend that spiritual intelligence and absolute intelligence are eternal intelligence; unlike biological created human intelligence and its obvious physical dissolvable limitations. A spiritual logic that some very intelligent human beings are going to have to come to grips with in our current, *make it up as you go along*, incomplete understanding of Creation. Because existing science, for all its painstakingly acquired physical knowledge, has not got a clue as to what makes life and Creation tick in the spiritual department. Therefore, they do understand what not to do with their gifted human physical intelligence in the life and chemical re-arranging laboratory.

Alternatively, that ten-billion-dollar atom trashing machine, in the, 'got it wrong,' scientific quest to find the God particle. Because God is not a physical particle, but a transcendent Intelligence that seeds Creation and all that is in it. That seeds all the different strata (dimensions) of Creation of which 'physical creation', is but a part of its interactive whole. Creation that was not created to be trashed by the human being, in the ego sourced delusion of creating progress and blindly conquering new frontiers spiritually speaking.

Governments also come in for special mention in this spiritless department. They also have no intuitive connection to the Spiritual Laws of Nature in their political activity, legislation and governance, only the human ego and the created ideology of big corporate money-making business. That, under the glorious banner of the unstoppable global economy, is destroying the future of this civilisation with unconscionable greed. Because money and what it buys, has become the all-consuming holy grail of our, got it wrong, consumer civilisation. In that human-authored delusion, we are blindly polluting everything on this living planet out of human conceit and irreverence for life and calling it progress. Greed propelled progress that the powerless majority have no say in. Only the gifted minority, creating and/or fuelling those realities we are all compelled to live, have a say in that progress. Because they are creating it in the top end of town but, without an Upstairs issued spiritual licence.

This delusion we are calling progress is unknowingly stagnating our spiritual evolution and destroying the future of our civilisation from out of unchecked greed, consumerism, overpopulation and synthetic toxic pollution. It is devolution progress, fuelled by destructive influence we have no comprehension of in our existing structure of physical consciousness. Paradoxically, those who are creating and contributing to its growing destructive karma, are made spiritually blind by its karma created entities. It is those destructive entities that instigate irrational all-consuming behaviour in our species, along with fuelling greed and an insatiable ego authored desire to conquer and acquire power. It is also the accumulating power of destructive entities, that instigates self-destruction and terminates the positive evolution of the spiritual psyche of the human being.

Manuscript 6.

Science - What's This?

(I times D) plus the square root of (M) times (LN plus CM) equals H.

Clue - each letter represents a word.
Warning for the problem-solver: The content contains a spoiler to the equation.
Its product (H) is the logic out of a word equation sourced to spirituality, not a number equation sourced to physical mathematics. It

could be equally expressed by mathematical logic. Thus, the logic to be found in words is the same logic to be found in a math's equation, merely expressed differently from different locations in the human brain.

Pure logic can also be expressed through harmonious, uplifting musical notation, art and architecture when linked to a positive accentuated psyche. That coherence of expression out of positive human creativity is the subtle appeal of the master's works to the physical senses of perception of their audience. Thus, as pure logic transposed through human creative expression, its expression is appealing to the mind of human beings in all its many diverse expressions, including mathematics, architecture and music. These expressions of human creativity all originate from the source of thought and its reflection, as an impulse of creative-intelligence emanating from the spiritual source of life and the transcendent absolute Intelligence that seeds it.

It could be said that, *pure logic* (perfect coherence), reflects the, 'order out of chaos,' function of the self-referral Laws of Nature. These Spiritual laws are the government of the negative and positive primordial archetypal intelligence that underwrites the biology and expression of life. The coherence of expression and creativity of which, should come naturally to a human being, when its conscious thought process is intuitively connected to those self-referral spiritual Laws through the unconscious mind; that forms the spiritual psyche of the human being. When the human mind goes out of sync with primordial Nature, then conscious thought and creativity has no anchor to those intuitive self-referral spiritual laws, that are structuring, *order out of chaos* and *coherence* in life. In that negative karma sourced debilitation of thought and desire, the mind loses the natural ability to intuitively know what is supportive of Life and Nature and what is not supportive of Life and Nature. In its place comes delusion, denial, negative structured creativity and logic and the inability, to understand right from wrong. Therefore, what compliments the individual, society, life, Nature and evolution, and what does not compliment the individual, society, life, Nature and evolution.

For example, the negative structured logic of ...
   The self-destructive suicide bomber and fanatical terrorist.
   Those decimating the atom to see what makes it tick.
   Those creating and selling weapons of mass destruction.
   Those indiscriminately re-arranging chemicals and life in the science laboratory.
   Those saturating life with synthetic chemical pills and its toxic pollution.
   Those socially blind governments selling off publicly owned infrastructure, to generate immense wealth for the few and fuel greed and inequality in society.
   Those allowing all-consuming Global Big Business to dominate, own and trash the world, to fuel the global economy and unconscionable greed.
   Those that are allowing trans-national corporations to buy and own another nation's natural resources, to generate money and immense wealth for those with a piece of the big buck exploiting action.
   Those saturating society with humankind's pathological not life-supportive behaviour and calling it entertainment, art and freedom of expression.
   All the above human created realities (ideologies) are being driven by human logic and reason, that has no connection to the coherent value of the self-referral Laws of Nature. Because the not understood common denominator of those human lived ideologies, is that they are all unknowingly self-destructive to life and Nature and the spiritual purpose of evolution. Not seen as being destructive by those in the driving seat of those human-created ideologies. Comprehend when divorced from the Spiritual Laws of Nature with our human thought and creativity, we become blind to the consequences of our human actions. In that karmic sourced debilitation, we delude ourselves with our misplaced logic and reason and therefore, in what we are calling progress.
   When trapped in that human-created delusion, then megalomania, narcissism, self-aggrandisement, greed and acquisition go into overdrive

in civilisation. Activity that is illogically called success, accomplishment and progress on a level playing field.

The human-created cause of the delusion:
   When the negative archetypal intelligence of primordial Nature, gains dominance in the collective consciousness of a civilisation, then abuse of power, ruthlessness, manipulation, exploitation, corruption, degradation of sexuality, crudeness, loss of dignified expression and irrational behaviour dominates human affairs, along with intolerance, belligerence towards law and order, a couldn't care less attitude towards social responsibility, lack of manners, dignity and respect for others. Coupled with growing behavioural and psychological disorder and a, *do what you like,* anything goes mentality flourishes in mankind. It is sanctified under a very abused freedom-of-expression edict, with a no morals code tagged on for good measure in our media and entertainment saturated civilisation. All those human-created devolution karmic influences and their entities become dominant, in a dysfunctional civilisation divorced from its spiritual roots and the Laws of Nature. A human created negative karma sourced debilitation, that prevents the self-referral function of the Laws of Nature from maintaining, *'order out of chaos,'* in our human logic, reason, expression, creativity and consciousness and therefore, in what we are calling progress.

Clarification: When our human consciousness becomes lost from the coherent value of the Laws of Nature, harmony and positive life supporting values go out the back door in human society. Negativity, disunity, ambivalence, depression, psychological disorder, social disorder, health disorder and dissent become dominant, especially in the born disadvantaged of nations. Violent, self-destructive illogical behaviour gains ascendancy in humankind, and it begins to self-destruct with its social and spiritual evolution unknowingly.
   This growing unrealised premature entropy in our Civilisation is directly linked to what we are calling progress and the greed, corruption and negative creativity that is propelling it. It is time to understand

what has caused this civilisation to become self-destructive without realising it. Because there is no escaping the invisible karmic influence/entity behind it; this contagious influence unconsciously debilitates everyone trapped in the primordial structure of physical consciousness. It is a human created devolution influence, that prevents us realising or agreeing, on the destructive damage we are unwittingly inflicting on this planet out of our so-called unstoppable progress.

The evolve or perish bottom line spiritually speaking.

It is time to dissolve this euphoric delusion we are calling progress and create a coherent, unified, harmonious world in the process. The first step is to incorporate the twice-daily practice of transcendent meditation into our daily routine and acquire some humility for a change and not; ego brownie points out of worshipping ourselves for our material accomplishments and so-called success. The solutions to all our human-created problems will come to us if we do just that, as well as acquiring Upstair's brownie points, to replace those Darth acquired brownie points for a change. It is that simple a solution, to dissolving the contagious delusion we are calling progress and have become lost in as a global civilisation. Because progress divorced from the spiritual roots of life in its material content is progress divorced from the Spiritual Laws of Nature structuring, *order out of chaos*, in Creation.

The spoiler: Individuality times diversity, plus the square root of the mass, times the Laws of Nature, plus collective meditation in society equals, automatic coherence in our human creativity and consciousness. Therefore, the means to evolve further with our spiritual evolution and collect our spiritual harp at the end of the human day with our progress, also known as heaven, in Upstairs circles.

Manuscript 7.

Bullseye Time

About the unknown spiritual system of Nature that underwrites physical life, and about the unknown cause and effect, our human creativity has on its negative and positive primordial archetypal intelligence. A report to the Boot Camp detention room memo, for all those in the driving seat of so-called progress. Location www.alfsbootcampblog.com and don't forget to put the ego into neutral and bring your earplugs with volume control?

About human terminating malignant disorders, percolating in the interacting primordial archetypal intelligence of Nature that physical life and its biology has manifested out ... of the cause?

Was it a Monkey?
Was it a Pig?
Was it a Rat?
Was it a Mouse?
Was it a Bat?
Was it a Sheep?
Was it a Cow?
Was it Human?

Q: *Was it related to the exploitation and mistreatment of animals and disrespect for Nature and Life by, 'got it wrong,' powerful creative human beings saturated with greed?*
    A: BULLSEYE.

Because what plus or minus quality of karma comes out of human thoughts, creativity, deeds and actions, enters the interactive spiritual workings of primordial Nature that underwrites and orchestrates the biology and chemistry of all life. When it is accumulating negative destructive, not life-supportive karma, then impersonal primordial Nature responds accordingly via the Law of Karma. As in, '*as we sow, so do we reap,*' with our human creativity in its physical and spiritual interactive workings. By cranking up its negative archetypal intelligence, to dissolve the dysfunctional species responsible. Aids is a classic example, as are all sexually transmitted diseases. Diseases created and triggered, from out of the wrong to Nature sexual activity of the human species.

Comprehend, we have not solved the cause of Aids with viral drugs either. Its terminating bug has merely hibernated from those chemically synthesised drugs and is invisibly re-grouping and re-creating itself. Because we have not dissolved the perpetuating human karma-created destructive entity, that created its malfunction in Nature's archetypal spiritual intelligence. We have only arrested its manifested physical aberration with synthetic chemical drugs, not dissolved its spiritual located destructive entity. We have become even more conceited in our, 'do what you like,' sexual and procreation re-arranging scientific laboratory affairs. Especially in the cloning, genetic reconstruction, life re-arranging, test tube meddling, harvesting of eggs and sperm and IVF departments of an incomplete science. We must understand that existing incomplete science, is not infallible or invincible in the spiritual Intelligence that underwrites physical life and its evolution.

Science means well and has done much for humankind ... of course it has. However, it only has half the information of life up on the science blackboard, the physical part, not the spiritual part, that underwrites it. Yes, medical science has and can create miracles with its acquired physical knowledge and dedication, but it is doing so with a blindfold on. It is time to remove that blindfold before creating any more miracles. Because some of these science-created miracles are short term gain for long term loss, not only for the human species, but all of life.

Comprehend that humankind is co-creator in this physical Creation. We are also king of the animal kingdom on the ladder of evolution with our human intelligence, conscious free will and creativity. That human power is a humungous responsibility in the primordial workings of Nature and the Laws, that underwrite, *'order out of chaos,'* in its interactive physical and spiritual domain. That human power is a double-edged sword in the, *'as we sow, so do we reap,'* primordial workings of Nature and evolution. That human power can turn into the sword of Damocles when we abuse it and degrade Creation and Life with our human creativity, especially in the sexual and procreation department.

Comprehend when we lose intuitive spiritual connection with the Laws of Nature with our human consciousness, we go off the rails of spiritual evolution and into devolution self-destruct mode with our logic and creativity. In boot camp terminology, we stuff up the system of life and evolution and create disorder and chaos, in the spiritual Intelligence that underwrites it.

Comprehend all disorder in Nature, is created by the human being and the human being alone. Thus, are terminating life-destroying bugs, created from the human being's accumulative destructive, *cause and effect*, karma and sourced, to our total lack of respect for life and the thoughtless subjugation and exploitation of animals. e.g. Unnatural to Nature farming practices and indiscriminate blind experimentation on animals, in the divorced from Nature spiritless science laboratory.

Q: *Are we in big trouble on this living evolving planet, through human conceit and spiritual ignorance and no understanding, of what makes life tick in all departments, including the mind?*

A: You bet your spiritual boot camp boots we are.

Comprehend we cannot abuse, exploit, subjugate, degrade, change, re-arrange and experiment blindly on life, under the human ego dictum of creating scientific progress and conquering new frontiers. We are the personification of delusion and conceit when we go around doing what we like on this living planet in the name of progress. When we go around denying the existence of Intelligence greater than our dissolvable intelligence, we deny the glaringly obvious. Because where has everything come from, if not from Intelligence greater than our dissolvable human intelligence.

Comprehend, when we go around denying the logic that, *'nothing comes from nothing,'* we are the personification of delusion. We are now in big devolution trouble with our spiritual evolution from out of its human ego sourced delusion, and the bard had nothing to do with it. He knew what he was talking about, unlike most in the top end of town, blindly creating our progress as well as our collective destiny. Thus, there are more things not only inside, but also outside of heaven and Earth than ever dreamed of in our existing human created understanding of life.

Serious boot camp stuff.

Comprehend it is chaos that we are currently creating on this planet from out of our so-called progress. Comprehend that we cannot over-populate this planet without self-destructing. It has finite resources that are not renewable, resources that we are re-synthesising and gobbling up at an ever-accelerating rate of consumption. Progress sourced to greed and spiritual ignorance and, 'got it wrong,' human beings in the driving seat of that all-consuming greed. We must stop blindly polluting Nature with synthetic toxic pollution and indiscriminately, re-arranging and experimenting on everything, without understanding where that everything has come from.

Clarification: If we do not come out of our human immaturity and start understanding, respecting and working with the Intelligence that created Life, then there is no future for our human species, and a lot of other species on this shared planet. In boot camp detention room terminology, we will eventually self-destruct as a dysfunctional species and go out the back door of Creation. It is time to acquire the spiritual knowledge and means, to avoid that human-created dead-end destiny because human beings create their destiny on the ladder of spiritual evolution, not God.

Manuscript 8.

Questionnaire Time

Compiled by Alf and completed by Stephen
for other learned men (and women).
Please fill your own in and post it back post-haste.
Part (1)

About contagious adult acquired unproductive habits and behaviour in our children ad-infinitum.

Q: Are, smoking cigarettes and pot, taking chemical pills and sniffing grot and being lost in thrills and kicks as well as mental fits and blips from other promo saturated movie, television, entertainment copied behaviour in society, predominant in the 70% of the 100% of young age groups due to the following:

1) Unable to read the, 'for adult entertainment, and adult use only,' directions on advertisements, promos, glossy magazines, billboards, junk mail, CD and DVD covers, computer games, bongs, beverages, bottles, fast food wrappers and fizzy drink cans.
Yes/No?
2) Too much pocket money to spend on the above and other must-have status techno goodies, with all mod cons and trendy twiddly bits.
Yes/No?
3) Not enough school excursions to Hollywood and visits to Disneyland, Parliament House and Commercial Television Stations to dance with the stars?
Yes/No?
4) Unable to express themselves any other way, but through copying, scriptwriter and marketing genius instructed celebrities, film stars, sports stars, rock and roll stars, and all the other human-created stars. That litter the communication highways but not the heavens?
Yes/No?
5) Too much adult pressure exerted on them to achieve and be crowned a winner and therefore, an easily recognised up-market product educated successful citizen in society.
Yes/No?
6) You must be top at everything at school, or you do not receive enough education brownie points and accolades, to climb up the childhood ladder and claim lasting happiness and the jet-setting money-making top end of town created adult good life?
Yes/No?

7) Poor home/social/education/communication environment, lack of mature parental love, life-supportive adult example, positive interaction, and nurturing within childhood?
Yes/No?

8) Unable to reach 21 fast enough to escape childhood forever and become a successful commercial media, entertainment and product educated adult and a corresponding media-accredited winner in society, to create news and closet information out of?
Yes/No?

9) Cannot stop habitually worrying about all the above growing negatives. That has somehow been miraculously re-created into positives, to acquire self-esteem and status recognition in society?
Yes/No?

10) Placating their acquired feelings of inadequacy, emptiness and unhappiness, at not being able to measure up to media, education and adult expectations. Expectations coming out of a top end of town created playing field, that does not understand the born disadvantaged players in the bottom end of town one little bit?
Yes/No?

11) Unhappiness compounded by being written-off as losers and left behind, in a top end of town created success, winning, product-consumed, human celebrity worshipping society on the scriptwriter, movie, commercial television and marketing genius deluded blink?
Yes/No?

Q: Does the last statement, mean that Alf is advocating doom and gloom in the departure lounge for scriptwriters, marketing geniuses, commercial television and the born gifted high achievers and so-called successful in life?

A: No, but Upstairs is. Because the gifted top end of town, has created a playing field for creating unhappiness and inequality, in those who cannot possibly compete or keep up with them. Who were not born with the *concentrated* archetypal intelligence in their physiology that powers the activity, desires, intelligence, motivation and self-esteem of the successful top end of town? Who become lost, used, exploited, manipulated and psychologically damaged, in ego and material driven ideologies to acquire self-esteem? Ideologies, (created realities), that have no lasting spiritual foundation, only dissolvable material foundation, to underwrite that all-important self-esteem.

So, no, Alf is not recommending purgatory for the born gifted, worshiped, followed and so-called successful in the top end of town, but a trip to spiritual Boot Camp to acquire the Upstairs means to dissolve their delusion, earn their harp by helping others born less fortunate and thus, avoid purgatory in the finger pointing departure lounge. It is doubtful if anyone in the so-called successful top end of town is going to collect their harp, least of all those in the driving seat of our so-called progress. Because the media-acclaimed gifted and successful winning minority, are leading the unsuccessful losing majority, in the wrong direction with their acquired mandate to create and direct progress. All-Consuming material progress that has become lost from the spiritual roots of life and the coherent value of the Laws of Nature. That should underwrite the human thought process, its creativity and progress, and not the primordial ego, greed, pollution, big bucks, worshipping winners and material values and creating inequality and unhappiness in society.

Part (2)

Q: Are most adult personality disorders, bad habits, (subliminal thought patterns), and growing depression and unhappiness in society due to the following:

1) Unable to understand Sigmund Freud and contemporaries?
   Yes/No?
2) Unable to find a dictionary to translate the, make it up as you go along, technical terminology used by the above. Affectionately called psycho-babble in the bottom end of town on the receiving end?
   Yes/No?

3) Watching too many saturated baddies and not enough saturated goodies, on the television and in movies in childhood?
Yes/No?
4) Pursuing unrealistic childhood dreams recommended by the, cough, mutter and splutter, successful top end of town?
Yes/No?
5) Unable to acquire a piece of the 24/7 media-saturated top end of town winning the action and therefore, the big bucks, adulation, fame and worshipped status that go with it?
Yes/No?
6) The psychological residue from an unhappy desire, frustrated inadequate childhood. Made worse, by the media bombarded negatives that have been created into eulogised positives to acquire self-esteem and happiness? As listed in parts 1 and 2 of the Questionnaire?
Yes/No?

Wow! this will cause an uproar and loss of earnings in the top end of town. It cannot be as simple as unhappiness at the root of the growing social devolution problem. Created from a decaying chaotic civilisation, that has fallen off the rails of spiritual evolution and is in self-destruct mode with its all-consuming material, entertainment and technological polluting progress. After all, we have all our books, expensive clinics, expert advice in glossy magazines, promos and advertisements to prove otherwise. Even though we, the psychology profession and errant marketing geniuses and politicians, have not solved the unhappiness problem in society yet, we are certainly making a very good living. So, keep coming, reading glossy magazines, buying products, taking chemical pills, watching commercial television and promos and dancing with the stars. We will save you from finger-pointing St Peter in the departure lounge, if you have money that is.

A signed complaint from 70% of the 100%, to the 30% of the 100%. It ain't working, at least not according to the tea lady where I work. Plus, we ain't got the money youse got it all in the top end of town.

Endorsed by Stephen on behalf of Upstairs for those left behind downstairs.

Manuscript 9.

The Unemployed and the Unemployable

A report to boot camp memo for the re-occurring, swept under the carpet, alienated, forgotten, techno and science deficit, rag and taggle, uneconomical brigade. Location www.alfsbootcampblog.com

Right you lot, nothing comes from nothing except nothing. On that understanding, it is time to put your shoes back on and go out into the marketplace and see what is cooking and become active in the work department. Because as well as becoming increasingly unemployable downstairs, you are in imminent danger of becoming unemployable Upstairs in the divine plan of evolution. As an aged and ailing, Albert Einstein said to his nurse, when she scolded him for not resting with his mathematical pen, *'what is the point of living if I cannot work?'* or something similar. Either way, like the Romans, he got it right. We are all born to action; it is a self-referral Law of Nature. So back to work you go if you want to earn your harp.

The crux of your problem, (that you have become a victim of), is not necessarily of your making, but the circumstance of birth and genes and the out-of-control techno and science revolution. Along with a top end of town created myth, that we are all born equal and can all aspire to be a worshipped winner residing in the top end of town because the bottom end of town cannot keep up, in our all-consuming education, science, technology and big buck driven civilisation.

For starters, your misfortune in not possessing the born artistic talent, business acumen, high IQ academic exactitude and gifted techno skills of others, that the polluting new-age spiritless technological and science revolution requires. Your misfortune in not being able to dance with the stars on commercial television, look like James Dean or Marylyn Monroe and endorse products and the body beautiful.

Your misfortune to be labelled as inconsequential in the sacred temple of profit and loss and economic rationalisation, that has sold out to obscene salaries, bonuses, sumptuous lifestyles and big corporate money-making global business. That in turn, has lost the spiritual plot of life in the plot of material greed and not in analogous St Peters good books because of it.

It is time for the top end of town to come out of the primordial jungle and put people and society and its well-being and further evolution first and not, acquiring power, self-gratification, self-aggrandisement, money, gongs, titles and other ego awards, the seven-star good life and big corporate money-making business first. That keep creating redundancies, unemployment and inequality in the workplace, in the name of economic rationalisation and creating progress. Because that big corporate business progress is driven by greed, profit, opportunism, exploitation, manipulation, takeovers, and abuse of power. That can only lead to creating chaos for the many, who then return that chaos to those that caused it in the top end of town. Because, 'as we sow, so do we reap,' in the interactive primordial workings of Nature.

It is also time for poll quaking re-election driven economy obsessed governments, to have a little more compassionate understanding for the born disadvantaged in nations. Because those in charge in the top end of town and creating our destiny, are leading *us all* in the wrong spiritless direction, not just the jobless. Because those without power in society, are instinctively compelled to follow those that do have power in society. This, 'follow the leader,' phenomenon is a primordial survival instinct at work in a highly social species. However, unfortunately, always becomes abused in human society, through the human ego affliction of megalomania. A megalomania and self-aggrandisement neurosis, that corrupts the ego and just about everything else in the affairs of mankind. Megalomania, (the karmic mark of Cain), is a 'power corrupts' affliction, that comes in all shades and configurations in human society and always rampant, in the top end of town where the power is.

So, you are to band together and make your plight acknowledged and seriously understood by governments, the clever top end of town and big business alike. Not placed in the too hard basket and blamed on you or its problem disguised, and its employment figures manipulated by clever minds and treated with lip service only double speak mentality; as has become the norm in politics and bureaucracy gone to seed and denial in a lot of so-called civilised nations. Those in charge, have not got a clue as to what it is like to be on the bottom rung of society; because those who live in the top end of town, live in a different world. A world of created privilege for the highly intelligent and exceptionally gifted and talented minority; a world of self-indulgence and the money to do anything and go anywhere; a world of dog eat dog in the corridors of power, functioning for self-interest and the good of the part and not the whole; a superficial world that has lost the spiritual plot of life in the plot of greed and is self-destructing, with its all-consuming polluting material progress because of it.

The positive boot camp directive is to let us hear from your positive vocal cords and not your negative vocal cords. Alternatively, from the loutish antics of other anti-social behaviour, that sends the 24/7 media into a frenzy of adversarial reporting, scribbling, pointing the finger and wooden spoon stirring, otherwise big devolution trouble in the departure lounge to go with all your other troubles. Be positive and constructive always and *you* will eventually cross the finishing line.

Q: *What line is that?*

A: Work. That is essential for a human being as is self-respect, laughter, happiness, equality and a truly caring, cohesive, positively functioning society, operating on all levels of its expression. Not merely operating for the benefit of the idolised gifted, the born talented, the winners and the rich and famous. Who comprise a very small percentage of the population and are unwittingly, going backwards with their spiritual evolution; that has lost out to worshipping material values, big bucks, gross excess, self-aggrandisement, power, acquired status, self-interest and delusion in the top end of town. Therefore, do not go with them, find yourself instead through the regular twice daily silent practice of transcendent meditation.

Comprehend the spiritual path of transcendent meditation, finds a lasting contentment, happiness and self-esteem and solves all delusion and misery along the silent way, no matter what your born circumstances, because it gives the mind access to the spiritual problem-solving self-referral field of Creation, and a lasting spiritual acquired self-esteem and self-worth. That does not require material values, only spiritual values to compliment work and life and acquire happiness. So, forget about wanting to be something you are not in the workplace or in the top end of town, to find that lasting happiness and self-esteem. In the meantime, use the internet forum to bring public pressure on your governments, to communicate with the T.M. Organisation that is based around the world in many nations, and ask to have its teaching made available through government subsidisation. Then you and the government will enlist the support of Nature's Intelligence and its Laws to get you off that bottom rung and lot more besides, and don't knock back manual work cause it aint cool and does not fit into your past the use by date childhood dreams when looking for work. We start at the bottom and then work up – got it?

Comprehend that hard is work is very healthy mentally, physically and spiritually productive to boot. As in, 'wash on and wash off,' and all that Zen self-development jazz. So, forget about wanting to be something you are not, wear your own work boots in the marketplace to acquire that elusive lasting self-esteem and self-worth. Not someone else's boots from the top end of town that do not fit and never will fit. Moreover, while we are on the Zen philosophy bandwagon, don't rub the boss up the wrong way, because you can't take orders without having a tantrum and reverting to childhood acquired resentment of authority. It's his/her job to give the orders, not yours. If you give 100% to the boss's interest, as in running the business and making sure it does not go broke and that you get paid, then a good boss with their head screwed on will always give you 100% of their interest to make sure you stay happy, because you will have become a very valuable asset to the business and treated with respect accordingly, instead of a pain in the butt and treated with disrespect accordingly. As we sow, so do we reap - got it?

Summing up: If you do not want Upstairs peering over your shoulder, then do not abuse the welfare system. It is there to support those in desperate circumstances, not of their choosing or making. It is not there as a way of living life at others expense. You will not get to heaven with that got it wrong philosophy. You will only get up society's nose and worse, St Peter's nose in the departure lounge. To then become even more unhappy, disenfranchised and miserable. Remember, the human being was born to action in the scheme of evolution. Positive action that is?

PS. Positive action means an action that supports life, Nature, evolution, society and yourself and not devolves it. If you go down the silent path of correct meditation twice daily, you will acquire the spiritual intelligence to be able to tell the difference. As the socially blind top end of town needs to do, to get you off that bottom rung.

Manuscript 10.

Is There Such A Thing as the Devil?

No, not according to the spiritual boot camp notice board at www.alfsbootcampblog.com. It's all in the creative mind, the unexpanded human mind that is. As are all the other dissolvable human created realities, that we identify with and live our lives out in.

The unknown karma facts of life:

What humankind creates is what humankind becomes and nothing to do with uninvolved abstract silent God. Because humankind is co-creator in this Creation, with its creativity and the perpetuating, *cause and effect*, creative karma that comes out of it. So, if there is a Devil, then it has come out of the human being's creative mind and not the creativity of the Creator. Therefore, just like the human being, it is dissolvable when it has no positive contribution to make to the Divine plan of evolution underwriting life. Note those in the driving seat of so-called progress in the top end of town, creating the direction, destiny and reality for others, from out of their born gifted intelligence, creativity and acquired power. An acquired primordial, *follow the leader*, power that comes with great responsibility, not to abuse it in human society if we want to collect our harp in the departure lounge.

However, while Alf has not come across the Devil, (or flying saucers and little green men), on his spiritual travels, he has certainly come across and clashed with, perpetuating human created malevolent karma and associated destructive entities. Specifically, from karma created out of an occult worshipped reality lived long ago, the created and lived destructive reality of a past early civilisation. A karmic influence created long before Christianity or any other one God religion for that matter. A destructive entity (life-force) that is still permeating in the creative affairs of humankind and its evolution, as on-going ancestral karma returned result. A human created malevolent influence that has taken up permanent residence in the negative archetypal intelligence of primordial Nature responsible for dissolving life. Along with other destructive entities, that have come out of humankind's, 'got it wrong,' creativity and lived ideologies over the last ten thousand years.

Clarification: Entities are a negative or positive (benign or destructive) karma created product, from out of the past and present lived ideologies/created realities of humankind. They are also a perpetuating life-force, (karmic influence), drawn out of the negative and positive archetypal intelligence of primordial Nature, through ancestral karma affinity to the present lineage of those who created them. Comprehend human created entities, become a residual life-force, locked into primordial Nature's negative and positive archetypal spiritual intelligence that underwrites the physical biology and chemistry of life. Therefore, its reproductive biology also. As in, mankind reaps what it sows with its karma created entities. Therefore, garbage procreation creativity into primordial Nature from mankind, equals garbage procreation creativity and its associated negative created entity, coming out of primordial Nature.

Explanation: It is an occult created negative entity out of the ancestral past, that has a primordial located affinity, with the family tree of those who created them. Therefore, drawn through inherited ancestral karma to a negative accentuated human being in the present. A lost soul forever trapped in Nature's primordial negative archetypal intelligence with their spiritual essence and its physical re-birth cycle. A fairy story that is not a fairy story in the spiritual system that underwrites and orchestrates life. Only a fairy story in the physical human created dissolvable realities, (ideologies), that we live our lives out of and worship in the present; note sceptics and other dedicated knockers of anything they do not want to understand?

It is time to come out our existing primordial structure of physical consciousness. Along with some of the realities/ideologies and their entities, that we have become lost in and do not support life and the spiritual evolution of humankind, but unknowingly decays it. An entrapment that prevents us from reaching our spiritual potential and its knowledge and further evolution as human beings. Comprehend that negative is drawn to negative, as positive is drawn to positive in the impersonal negative and positive spiritual workings of Nature. As in relationships, ideas, interactions, procreations and the physical rebirth cycle of the spiritual essence of the human being, initiated through sexual union.

That is why sexual bonding and conception should always take place in a positively charged environment. As in a harmonious, loving relationship, marriage and its commitment and the positive created karma, that comes out of that love and respect for each other, and creates a positively charged environment. Then we are giving our precious offspring a good start in life, because their spiritual essence, will be drawn out of the positive component and not the negative component of the spiritual planes of Creation. A spiritual factor that also dictates the positive or negative quality of the human being's consciousness and its creativity on the ladder of spiritual evolution.

It is also negative inherited ancestral karma that manifests as black depression, or 'night of the soul,' in religious terminology. A negative karmic influence and its entity that most will have to pass through on their spiritual journey out of primordial Nature's impersonal domain. Because as human beings, we share a collective consciousness and karma in the impersonal workings of primordial Nature, that returns all karma we humans create. We have also called that existing structure of physical consciousness in humankind, ego propelled biological structured physical consciousness. To differentiate it from spiritual acquired consciousness. Thus, this experience of negative karmic influence, is a trial to endure and pass through, on the spiritual path of expanding the physical mind into a further spiritual structure of consciousness. It is inconsequential to a positive psyche that does not add to its negative influence, with their naturally positive orientated thoughts and deeds. Like a bad dream, it is a merely transient experience to a positive accentuated psyche, nothing more.

Clarification: Comprehend malevolent karmic influence just like instinctual fear, only has power if we give it power through destructive thoughts, actions and deeds. Evil to him/her, that evil does, as the saying goes? Once understood and accepted that it is merely transient experience and nothing else, it eventually disappears off the conscious radar of a positive accentuated human being. It has no substance in higher states of consciousness, does not exist in those higher planes of consciousness. It is purely human created destructive karmic influence trapped in Nature's primordial domain. A primordial domain that we have yet to evolve out of, in our existing structure of primordial structured physical consciousness.

Transcendent meditation and the silent product that comes out of its regular twice daily practice, will dissolve the karmic power of destructive entities, to influence the archetypal intelligence of primordial Nature and therefore, the human species that created them. With the infusion of abstract silent Intelligence into our physiology out of correct meditation, we also acquire the spiritual means, to know intuitively what is positive and what is destructive to Nature with our human creativity. Then all human actions and desires, automatically become positive actions and desires that support life and the divine purpose of evolution with its created karma.

Clarification: When the mind and spirit becomes anchored to the silent product, (Intelligence), that comes out of transcendent meditation, then it is not possible to become lost in the experience of destructive entities or become their unknowing tool. As a growing number of negative debilitated human beings are, in this spiritually decaying civilisation. Because greed, exploitation, manipulation, deviousness, Machiavellian plotting and scheming, organised crime, brutality, corruption, sexual degradation, megalomania and abuse of acquired power, has become rampant in our dysfunctional greed corrupted civilisation. This accelerating sociopath activity stagnates spiritual evolution and corrupts a civilisation with its growing contagious karma. To then become the magnet that draws destructive entities to the spiritual psyche of a negative accentuated human being, to then influence the unconscious and subliminal workings of the human mind and its creativity. This entity sourced debilitation means those afflicted, have no connection to the Laws of Nature responsible for creating, *order out of chaos*, in life. They become lost souls in religious terminology and a pain in the butt to life, civilisation and spiritual evolution. But of course, not seen as such by those afflicted with its destructive ancestral inherited nemesis.

Clarification: Perpetuating destructive karma and associated entities, are locked into the creative processes of primordial archetypal intelligence that in turn, processes human intelligence and its creativity. Destructive entities are toxic to the self-referral spiritual Laws of Nature, responsible for, 'order out of chaos,' in life. The growing effects of that human created malfunction of evolution is also manifesting as the destabilisation of the primordial forces of Nature; that leads to cataclysmic upheaval and natural disasters and the destruction of life on this planet. It is also manifesting as increasing irrational behaviour, in the form of growing psychological and sexual disorder in humankind and the acceleration of disease in all life. Thus, human negative (not life supportive) creativity and the destructive karma that comes out of it, has the power to adversely affect everything evolving in Creation, ultimately destroying humankind as a returned consequence.

Comprehend, 'as we sow, so do we reap,' is a Law of Nature contained in the spiritual evolution of a human being. We become a very destructive species when we go off the spiritual rails of evolution with our all-consuming, all-conquering, ego-driven creativity and euphoric winning megalomania. Re-study our history books for its recorded ever-repeating narrative, in the dysfunctional primordial sourced conquering and winning affairs of mankind.

The means to dissolve that destructive perpetuating influence/entity and restore, the coherent value of the Laws of Nature to our collective human consciousness has been given. Comprehend, if we respect life and Nature and not debase and degrade it with our human creativity and sexual expression, then the mighty forces underwriting Nature, life and evolution, will respect us and help further our spiritual evolution, but not otherwise.

The double bottom line:

When the divinely orchestrated spiritual re-birth cycle of this planet is complete, destructive karmic influence and associated destructive entities will be dissolved. Along with the spiritual evolution of those human beings perpetuating it. In that restoration process of stagnated human spiritual evolution, the functioning integrity of the Spiritual Laws of Nature is restored to the negative archetypal intelligence of primordial Nature. The spiritual equilibrium of this planet and its divinely ordained trajectory is once more restored to positive evolution in Creation. Thus, harmonious interaction between the negative and positive primordial archetypal intelligence of Creation returns, to ensure spiritual evolution in accordance with the transcendent silent architect of life and Creation and that we have called God?

The uncomplicated means to accomplish this spiritual transition without the cataclysmic upheaval of primordial Nature is through the simple collective practice of Transcendent Meditation in nations. If we do not follow its spiritual path as a global civilisation, then that spiritual transition will be accomplished through accelerating cataclysmic upheaval, chaos and disease on this living planet and life as we know it, will start again as it has done in the past. A fact that has also been made available through the gifted brains and accumulating knowledge of science. It is time for science, governments and this global civilisation to understand why it happens. Not go into the, 'state of denial,' or counter accusation and derision, because our existing incomplete understanding of Creation and human-created realities and lifestyles have been challenged for spiritual logic and direction. Because spiritual evolution is a divine potential and birthright of the unique human species that we have yet to understand or develop.

Kind regards from Alf. CEO of spiritual boot camp.

Manuscript 11

Who Was Jesus?

According to Alf's research, a spiritually evolved divinely gifted human being for all seasons, all ages, all people, all religions, spiritual teacher par-excellence.

Jesus, a fully evolved spiritually enlightened human being and not the incarnation of God. As is taught in some make it up as you go along versions of scriptural religion. Versions that have become lost in words, ritual and the perpetuating karmic influence of a religion created *entity* out of the past. Jesus prayed to God and not to himself in the much-misunderstood Bible, did he not? Jesus, whose spiritual essence came from the divine planes of consciousness in spiritual creation; also referred to as Heaven on the boot camp detention room blackboard and elsewhere. Once reached through evolution, there is no more primordial structured physical re-birth on this planet of the spiritual essence of a human being. Only through the silent will of the transcendent Creator is this miracle possible. A miracle processed through the active divine status quo intelligence of the Creator (the Cosmic Mind) structuring the divine plan of evolution. An Upstairs augmented process repeated down through the ages, whenever spiritual evolution has gone into decay in mankind through the, 'got it wrong,' primordial driven affairs of humankind. Abraham, Moses, Jesus, Mohammed, Krishna, Buddha to name a few, were all instruments of that divine process, sourced to the Absolute Intelligence of Creation or God.

Clarification: A divine restoration process that has come alive in our spiritually decaying civilisation, through the tireless dedication of Maharishi Mahesh Yogi and the silent blessings of Guru Dev, his Vedic Master and a divine incarnation of the Hindu god Vishnu in human form. Guru Dev, a divine manifestation (one of many) of the transcendent Creator eternally active in spiritual Creation that underwrites this physical Creation and its evolution. Having set the spiritual restoration wheels in motion through his devoted Holy disciple Maharishi Mahesh, Guru Dev returned to his eternal spiritual status in the divine active workings of God. Whereas, on completing his holy task of restoring Vedic knowledge to our civilisation, Maharishi Mahesh Yogi has moved on with his spirit to the Absolute realms of existence and become as one with God and the whole and not the part. As was his life's wish, having completed his spiritual evolution through many past lives on this planet. That freely given timeless Vedic knowledge, included the teaching of Transcendent Meditation as the silent means, to restore the wheels of spiritual evolution and the Laws of Nature to the consciousness of our civilisation. A Vedic sourced knowledge now contained in its entirety, in the teaching curriculum of the Universities that Maharishi founded around the world to preserve that Vedic knowledge.

The point to be made:

Governments are in the driving seat of progress and in charge of the destiny of a nation's people with their quality of consciousness, gifted intelligence, governance, political ideologies, direction and legislative power. It is time for governments around the world, to come out of their existing structure of physical consciousness and make use of its Vedic knowledge for their people. Therefore, adopt the teaching of Transcendent Meditation in its education policies, public schools and universities. To then create the spiritual means for themselves and the public, to understand its Vedic knowledge and move on in the scheme of evolution with our consciousness, direction and destiny and avert calamity. Because it is human beings that create their destiny in evolution, from out of their lived ideologies and creativity, not God. Therefore, It is us human beings with our gift of conscious freewill and unique creativity, that must acquire humility and respect for Nature and its Laws and implement the transcendent acquired means, to avoid our own created catastrophe, not uninvolved God.

Jesus, like Mohammed, had a divine purpose for being born back on this planet in physical form through natural birth. He had one purpose, and one purpose only for being born, to fulfil the earlier Prophet's declarations and, like Abraham, Moses and Mohammed given divine guidance to restore the spiritual path of evolution for humankind. A divine mandate that came from the silent will of the uninvolved transcendent Creator. Jesus, a spiritual teacher with the divine power to create miracles and divine spiritual worlds, which he did for humankind. Those who have followed his teachings without hypocrisy or delusion, but with the loving heart, know that when you move on from this world, step into the light of Creation and out again then you will truly know the Heaven of Jesus. For that spiritual realm is of his creation, from out of the pure creativity of the Divine Laws of Nature; thus, it is perfect.

The Divine Laws of Nature, the spiritual government of Nature. That, in innumerable modes of self-referral function, create, structure and process the evolution of everything in Creation. The fullness of that process is beyond full comprehension in our existing primordial structured physical consciousness. That is where the words humility and respect for Nature and its Laws, should come into the equation of the activity and creativity of the human being on this planet. Few are those that understand the reverence, dignity, humility and respect for the spiritual divine component Nature, that is necessary to evolve to higher planes of consciousness in life. Those spiritual qualities are acquired naturally, from out of the sustained regular twice daily practice of correct meditation. Eventually, a crossroads is reached along its path of inner silence. Then is required the cemented silence of the Creator, not to become lost along the path of expanding the mind further, to acquire the divine potential of spiritual consciousness.

Why?

Because human beings, when experiencing spiritual phenomena or miracles, without the acquired silent anchor of Abstract Intelligence, invariably go bombing off into delusional creative la la land with their thought. Often with make it up as you go along versions of the Scriptures, to understand and explain their spiritual experience to others. Scriptural interpretations out of the past that often appear illogical to the reasoning processes of an educated human being in the modern world. Its rejection as a plausible reality in the here and now is inevitably brought to question, from such diverse interpretation of the Scriptures from its innumerable self-appointed preachers, ambassadors, administrators and translators down through the ages. Along with a collection of new age self-appointed interpreters, preachers, evangelical super salespeople and other commercial entrepreneurs, cashing in on religion and Jesus.

Comprehend that acquired physical knowledge of a subject, is not acquired spiritual experience of a subject. They are two separate paths that must merge into one silent path in religion, (and science), if they are to be free of the human being's creativity, ego, delusion and unresolved unproductive ancestral karma out of the past. Then there is no making it up as we go along, from out of our human creativity about Jesus or God or Creation. As in, God's permission to get rich quick at another people's expense. God's permission to conquer and run the world out of a human created religious ideology or a, 'divorced from Nature,' science ideology. God's permission to do what you like in a society in the pursuit of fame, big bucks and the good life, also-called happiness and realising our dreams. God's permission to re-create and re-arrange life in the spiritually blind science laboratory to save humankind. God's permission to fly to the moon and conquer the planets at taxpayer's expense. God's permission to trash the atom to find his particle and collect a few gongs in the science obsessed process. God's permission to babble in tongues and turn harps into electric guitars and hand waving human beings into singing minstrels. Along with the laying of evangelical hands to be transported to human-created la la land certainly not the heaven of Jesus.

Note: That has never heard of born again, (so buy my CD), twang bang dang sex, drugs and rock and roll Jesus converts. Alternatively, warbling pied pipers stuck on the big buck stairway to pop star heaven. Alternatively, I love me, fashion models, parading God's blessings on the catwalk and in glossy product magazines. Alternatively, a collection of other God sanctified sports stars, entertainers, celebrities, politicians and entrepreneurs from a galaxy far away. All are adding their two-pennyworth into the religious melting pot, however well-meaning some may be.

According to the spiritual boot camp detention room blackboard, uninvolved silent God and the heaven of Jesus knows not of self-aggrandisement and hypocrisy, big bucks, lavish lifestyles and gross excess. Religious pomp and circumstance. Sumptuous marbled buildings and priceless art. Luxury holiday resorts and seven-star hotels. Fred's casino in the desert with extra-curricular un-religious activity on the house. Marketing geniuses promoting God's cookbook and keep fit manual for dietary Christians. Commercial television stations doing God's big advertising business. Intelligent design enthusiasts re-writing evolution and upsetting Darwin's afterlife peace and quiet. Alternatively, the killing of human beings in the name of Allah, for a one-way ticket to no-where land certainly not heaven, or a paradise stocked with promiscuous maidens.

Note: As from the hacking and whacking holy crusades and jihad of past centuries to keep the population down. Because that is what its human created religious mayhem, delusion and bloodshed accomplished along with the bubonic plague. Created out of the, 'as we sow, so do we reap,' negative primordial workings of Nature, to dissolve the dysfunctional species responsible. The ancestral sourced destructive entity of which is still causing mayhem in deluded religion brainwashed minds in the present. The delusion that has nothing to do with Jesus, Mohammed or God, but everything to do with the ancestral inherited destructive karma of, 'got it wrong,' deluded human beings.

Comprehend the human being is born in pure innocence, not so the inherited ancestral karma that accompanies the re-birth cycle of the human being. When it is destructive ancestral inherited karma, it is the unknown cause of the perpetuated pathological and psychological disorder, mayhem, misery and unhappiness in human beings. It is time to acquire the silent means, to dissolve its negative ancestral inheritance and start a journey into a spiritual understanding of Creation and the means to experience it. Cherish dearly but move on from the old Scriptures in their past understanding of God. Keep the mind and spirit firmly in the 21st century, where it belongs but not, on acquiring fame, power, big bucks and a stretched limo to go with a stretched ego. Understand the reason it is easier for a camel to pass through the eye of a needle than it is for a rich man to pass through the gates of heaven, is not because of their wealth, but because of the inevitable greed and its unproductive karma that accompanies that wealth and the human worship and power attributed to it. Comprehend it is what the human being does with wealth that does not compliment Nature, evolution and life, that creates the inevitable truth of that parable.

Manuscript 12.

Day of Reckoning

Where past, present and future and our human mortality, all catch up with us in the karmic accounting section of the departure lounge if not before.

The unknown spiritual facts of life:

In the primordial spiritual intelligence that underwrites life, the unstoppable spiritual pulse of evolution alternates between the negative and positive poles of Creation, to ignite and propel the activity and re-generation of life. A pulse that could also be called the Cosmic heartbeat of life and evolution. A pulse (vibration) that is processed governed and balanced, by the spiritual self-referral Laws of Nature and underwritten by Cosmic Law the ultimate Law of Creation. It is that ultimate Law of Creation (the Cosmic Mind) that does the math's calculation and presses the ejection button on life when evolution stagnates. Therefore, life must continue to evolve up the duel ladder of physical and spiritual evolution or lose its status for life in the divine scheme of evolution. That which is created must stay in sync with that which created it, or be dissolved.

The only species that has the creative power to disrupt the rhythm and pulse of life and evolution with its unique conscious freewill and creativity is the human species. It is only our highly physically evolved primordially sourced species as co-creator in Creation, that creates destructive karmic influence and entities, from out of negative, destructive thoughts, deeds, actions and creativity. Human created karma that enters the spiritual domain of Nature and interacts with the duel negative and positive primordial intelligence, that life and its biology has manifested out of. Human created karmic influence that when destructive and not life-supportive to Nature, accumulates to become destructive entities that usurp the, *'order out of chaos,'* function of the self-referral Laws of Nature. Laws that are the balance line of Creation. Laws that are also responsible, for maintaining coherence between the opposing negative and positive primordial archetypal intelligence processing life. A delicate balance that becomes compromised, by destructive human created entities that do not support life and evolution but undermine and create chaos.

Explanation: Karmic influence is a creative spiritual by-product of thought and desire, the influence that enters the spiritual domain of

Nature and interacts with the negative and positive archetypal intelligence that orchestrates the biology and chemistry of life. Destructive human created karma is a *negative cause and effect* karmic influence, that undermines the divine workings of evolution and sets up the equation for a 'day of reckoning'. A human created destructive influence that is drawn through affinity, to the negative archetypal intelligence of primordial Nature responsible for dissolving matter. This humankind created karmic equation, forces the alternating balance line of Creation to remain in the Negative pole of Creation. To then accelerate the dissolving function of the negative archetypal intelligence of primordial Nature, as a human created cause and effect karma created result. As we sow, so do we reap, sums up the end-product of its devolution equation, in the interactive spiritual and physical workings of primordial Nature.

Clarification: When the balance line of evolution remains in the negative pole of Creation, spiritual evolution spirals into decay and stagnates. As a *cause and effect* result, the pulse of evolution and the Laws of Nature, go out of sync and cause chaos in the negative and positive primordial intelligence orchestrating life and its evolution. Chaos that reflects through all life, in the form of growing malfunction, social chaos and disease and reflects through Nature, as the upheaval of its physical elements and the destruction of life. We are currently locked into in this devolution cycle and, it is our dysfunctional civilisation, that has ignited its 'day of reckoning' fuse with our polluting toxic creativity in all departments of human creativity. A slow-burning fuse that also contains that destructive perpetuating karma of other dysfunctional civilisations out of the past.

It is this combination of past and present destructive karma and associated destructive entities, that has reached 'critical mass' in the spiritual system that underwrites life. To then create a, 'day of reckoning,' equation to arise on this planet. A fairy story that is not a fairy story in the eternal intelligence that created life and its evolution. It is only a fairy story in our dissolvable human intelligence, unknowingly destroying life and its evolution with its not life-supportive creativity and progress.

About the Perpetuating Destructive Ancestral Karma out of the Past Activity of Humankind:

When one nation/culture conquers another nation and commits terrible atrocities and subservience on its people, then big perpetuating karmic trouble becomes locked into the spiritual evolution of both nations, not just the aggressor. It is this karmic equation, that is at the root of centuries-old perpetuating conflicts in hotspots around the world, especially in the chaotic religion torn Middle East. A re-occurring nemesis that because it remains unresolved, adds to the long list that triggers a, 'day of reckoning,' for humankind down the track of time.

Comprehend all our endless political talking and signing of peace treaties, will never resolve the re-occurring conflicts of humanity, sourced to the past destructive activity of humankind and its perpetuating ancestral returning karma. The only way to dissolve this human created nemesis, is to come out of the primordial physical structure of consciousness that perpetuates its destructive karma. That is where the teaching and collective practice of Transcendent Meditation in this civilisation comes into the spiritual storyline. According to Alf's research, it is the only effective way to neutralise and ultimately, dissolve this looming, 'day of reckoning,' that has come to our now global spiritually decaying civilisation.

The bottom line:

It is time to acquire the transcendent silent absolute Intelligence that can and will, dissolve/absorb the human created destructive karma out of the present, and the human-created destructive karma out of the ancestral past and therefore, extinguish the karmic fuse of the 'day of reckoning'. However, only if we cultivate its silent transcendent Intelligence into our dissolvable human intelligence. Because that absolute Intelligence, lies in the transcendent, abstract field of Creation beyond the human mind. It requires the physical thought of the human being to rest on a vibration called a mantra, to then be able to leave the entrapment of physical thought and gain access, to the transcendent field of absolute consciousness with our undeveloped awareness not thought.

Note: An inward spiritual journey that requires no conscious effort of the mind, only the implementation of an intoned mantra to culture abstract intelligence into the human physiology. A simple, uncomplicated silent process, that captures the conscious thought of the thinker and automatically, takes that thought to the source of thought and beyond, *without being aware of the process.* An inward journey that unknowingly, traverses all the different strata (dimensions) of Creation that human thought has an affinity. Because all the buildings blocks of physical and spiritual Creation are contained in the human mind, as a physical creation and reflection of the Cosmic Mind the spiritual progenitor of life.

Kind regards from Alf. CEO of spiritual boot camp.

Section Five

Introduction

Firstly, a special letter for those that have not yet reached adulthood — followed by a fictional collection of tongue in cheek translated B.C. tablets for young minds to wade through.

Now, about the following special letter from the author of this book to you, that I translated from the fictitious Gleek Department of Translations where I work. Along with a message about *words* from Alf in charge of Spiritual Boot Camp. Because he says that words, come from out of thoughts and create influence in the invisible spiritual workings of Nature and that some words are more potent than others with their creative influence. Evidently, the reason all words, when spoken or written, are important, is because they create a lasting invisible influence called *karma*. It is that human karma created out of the spiritual substance of thought energy, that eventually returns as a positive or negative karmic influence on the person who wrote them or spoke them. So now you know how the spiritual system of Nature works with our thoughts and words, always try to be positive and helpful in what you say to other people. Because then, it is the only positive life-supportive karmic influence that always returns to you, from your interaction and play with them.

Now for the big secret:

That means, even if something or someone hurts you and makes you cry or upset, you will always naturally return to being happy afterwards. Simply because you will only have created happy karmic influence in Nature's Invisible Workings from your positive words, to always come back to you from Nature. That invisible interactive process between *you* and *Nature* and that even adults do not understand is also called, 'As We Sow, So Do We Reap,' with our thoughts, words, actions and deeds in life. However, at this point of our human evolution, we do not understand this spiritual Law of Nature. Because if we did, the world would be free of wars, violence, conflict, greed, corruption and unhappiness. If you are not sure what some of the words mean in this special letter to you, then ask your mum and dad or your helpful teachers at school, to explain them to you. Now, this is a long letter, so it is going to take a long time to read it and understand it. The reason I know that, is because it took me a long time to translate it for you from the author.

Kind regards – Stephen. Chief translator of too hard to translate tablets in the upstairs fictitious Gleek section of the North Wing of the British Museum. That now at long last, has a workable loo and made me happy. Because I do not have to do the long, excruciating walk to the South Wing anymore.

A Special Letter to the Future Adults of this World

Dear children, teenagers and young adults - greetings to you all from the author.

Firstly, you may not fully understand the words in other sections of this book. So, this is a very special section to include you.

Secondly, I am sorry that I have had to take some of your parents to task in its content. Unfortunately, there was no other option. They are lost and cannot hear you properly above all the growing media, television, advertising and entertainment transmitted visual images and noise, that has overloaded and desensitised the human brain as well as being toxic to Nature and its Laws through its 24/7 saturation. Along with commercial television and glossy product, magazine instructed consumerism and big business propelled greed in the world and that this media and technology-saturated civilisation, is calling glorious economic progress, affluence and the global economy. Well, successful politicians and other powerful money-making individuals and private enterprise global organisations in charge of our progress are. However, they are all missing spiritual located logic, in that all-consuming polluting global consumer progress underwritten by greed. Because anything negative or synthetic that is saturated into Nature and Life from out of humankind's creativity is potentially a toxic disaster waiting to happen to Life and Nature. Because along with the media, science and our incomplete education systems, they fail to comprehend that the word *saturation* is not in Nature's non-dissolvable spiritual dictionary, only in humanity's dissolvable physical dictionary. Short term gain in the present, for long term loss in the future, is the potential outcome for polluting Nature and its Laws and the planet.

In simple non-political and non-scientific understanding, we are gobbling up everything on this beautiful planet and synthetically polluting it to high heaven and calling it progress. We are also, on an accelerating consumer treadmill called the unstoppable global economy. That is out of control and about to implode and cause much misery, from out of the unconscionable thoughtless greed propelling it. So, this letter is to ask for your help to sort this devolution problem out, before it destroys the future for those who come after us, and we all end up **not going** to heaven because of it.

Unknowingly, it is our civilisation that has created all the greed, media, entertainment, science, technology and consumer polluting toxic problems on this shared planet, from out of its saturation. Because there are two ways to pollute Nature and this planet with our unique human creativity, one seen and physical and the other unseen and spiritual. I know many adults, will not believe this spiritual fact, especially in science and our existing education systems.

Nevertheless, I can assure you, that this spiritual fact, along with many others, has yet to be discovered in the invisible intelligence of Nature. Because it is the spiritual intelligence of Nature, that underwrites, orchestrates and propels all life on this shared planet. Unknowingly, our civilisation is blindly polluting Nature and life with that all-consuming toxic to Nature material progress.

So, I need your junior help, to dissolve this growing duel pollution problem before it dissolves us. Because *you* are very important to the Boss Upstairs as future adults. Because one day soon, *you* will be in-charge of yourselves and this shared world, armed with the spiritual knowledge to change its dead end future. Especially for your children and their children. Right now, your uncomplicated innocent love is very important to your parents, because many adults have lost that innocent natural love and trust that very young children possess. Your parents may also become confused by the content of this letter, as well as Alf's Boot Camp Oratories if they do not understand them; because they are like you were on your very first day of school. Therefore, lost and bewildered in a new reality they have no experience of. So, you remember this difficulty and you help them all you can, from out of your uncomplicated love and concern for them.

Your parents love you very much, but many adults have become commercial media and entertainment saturated and desensitised and lost to spiritual located feelings and emotions, as well as simple love. Especially from image creating commercial television and its saturated product and promo brainwashing, superficial values and anything goes entertainment. Along with promoting consumerism and self-gratuitous behaviour, as a false means of finding happiness.

Those saturated unproductive superficial commercial values, have created too much taking, wanting, self-gratuitous behaviour and euphoric greed in society and not enough emotional giving and all-important quality parental time for you. So, you must help me in my job by helping them in your job.

Therefore, to be helpful, kind, thoughtful and giving. When the world settles down again after its big upheaval soon that is due, to the constant trashing of it by powerful, clever human beings creating and in charge of our progress, then we will all be much happier, contented and peaceful and that's a promise.

Now changing the system of how we currently behave on this planet, will take time and patience. That all-important patience is something we all must learn if we wish to be happy and reach maturity. Spiritual acquired maturity and its happiness is not something we learn by doing what you like, behaving how you like, creating what you like and having what you like all-of-the-time. Some of the time – yes. Because it is good to let your hair down and do your own thing now and then, but not, if your creativity, behaviour and actions, upset everyone around you and Nature in the silly process. In addition to upsetting the Laws of Nature, that create *order out of chaos* in life. That silly behaviour is called being immature, thoughtless, precocious, obnoxious and inconsiderate of others and society and leads, to eventually being disliked and ostracised (unwanted) by everyone around you, including Nature. So, this is the first lesson to understand and grasp, the meaning of maturity and its positive life-supporting behaviour, when interacting with other people and the invisible intelligence of Nature that orchestrates life.

That acquired self-control and maturity is a very important lesson in life to learn and acquire when we are young, because it is much more difficult to learn when we are older. An immature behavioural problem acquired in childhood, from out of not teaching positive family and social life-supporting spiritual values, only superficial dissolvable material values in childhood. Those commercial media and entertainment saturated spiritless material values become a very bad habit, that prevents us ever finding lasting happiness and the spiritual plot of life in adulthood.

Anyway, the message in this letter to you is that I am here to help you spiritually grow up and not down in Nature. So that you, can then collect your behaviour earned spiritual harp down the track of adulthood, through respecting Nature and its Laws and positive family values. Along with acquiring lasting happiness as a positive end-result.

If you always trust these words, then between us, we will pull off a miracle of positive change in the way we currently behave on this precious planet. Firstly, you are to talk to your parents with honesty and respect. Forget about how so-called grown-ups conduct themselves on adult entertainment and television programs and especially, in movies and on the internet. Because many of them are in big trouble with Upstairs, through their act-how-you-like and do-what-you-like and say-what-you-like immature behaviour and life-styles on the big movie screen and in public, that they think is clever, because other adults and children clap, follow and worship them for doing it. It is the accumulating influence (karma) created out of worshipping celebrities, and other media-saturated so-called successful people, that is unproductive and damaging to the spiritual evolution of everyone. This contagious karmic influence becomes a human-created *entity* that creates a euphoric delusion in the human mind, that has no connection with the spiritual Laws of Nature structuring our spiritual evolution. Moreover, believe it or not, our spiritual evolution is the whole purpose of being born a human being. Because the spirit of a human being contains an unknown divine potential, to spiritually evolve and create miracles in life and afterlife. But not, when we are destructive to Nature and its Laws and other human beings with our creativity and behaviour.

Thus, as media-saturated and worshipped actors, celebrities and artists, they must learn how to say, *'no thank you,'* sometimes, to what they are being asked to do on the big movie screen, in glossy magazines and on television and in public, by other silly immature creative adults promoting its stupidity in society. Who makes up fantasy, write socially damaging scripts and direct others to also be silly, sexually irresponsible, violent and emotionally immature in society, a delusion that is called harmless entertainment? Sort of like, *'Simon Says* do this' and we will pay you lots of money and make you famous and a media worshipped celebrity and a winner in society. Because impressionable children and many adults, think it is clever to copy what actors, winners, artists and celebrities act out on the television, in movies and in public. When of course it is not clever, if it is socially destructive, violent, delinquent or silly obnoxious behaviour, because it means they will never grow-up either.

Note: In the end, everyone ends up acting silly and irresponsible in society, as an entertainment copied result of its saturation in the movies, in the media and on television. The media-saturated content of silly, immature and obnoxious behaviour called acting and entertainment, also means that we will never ever get to heaven either, through applauding it, and copying it, and worshiping those that do it best. Those that are causing the problem, are called media created *pied pipers* in spiritual boot camp. Because the public, are instinctively drawn to follow and worship them, through their media saturation in sycophantic glossy magazines, movies, non-stop talking newsrooms, newspapers and the television. Because unknowingly, it is a natural primordial survival instinct, for human beings to *follow the leader* in the so-called successful top end of town; in spiritual fact, any publicised and 24/7 media saturated leader in any form of expression, not just entertainment.

The spiritual advice from Alf is to be much more selective with what you choose to watch on the television, the internet and at the movies. Simply because much of its adult created news and entertainment, is very confusing, desensitising, often violent, sexually explicit and psychologically damaging to young minds and sends you in the wrong direction in life with its contagious influence whether you see it or not. Downhill, in other words, to the land of unhappiness in adulthood. Because a child's undeveloped mind must pass through defined delicate stages of positive structured growth and emotional development before it can psychologically cope with adult acted out violence, emotional hysteria, foul mouths and sexually explicit behaviour. Immature, delinquent adolescent behaviour that has now become common place and called entertainment in movies, the internet and television, along with its contagious destructive entity/influence invisibly saturating society.

Note: While we are on the important subject of what not to do and copy, also give a big miss to those bash, splat and trash everything computer games and the scary, violent and foul-mouthed *anything-goes* entertainment. Along with brain-numbing techno music and trashy talking lyrics and experimenting in sex and drugs, that are also swamping society. Moreover, for the really hard-one? Your first teenage starry-eyed loves and it's dotty all-consuming lost in my space behaviour for the time being anyway. That is the positive spiritual message from divine Intelligence to you. Moreover, I, for one, have always respected that invisible Intelligence of Nature that created life. I am happy all the time when I do so.

Understand that your parents need your full support after reading Alf's boot camp oratories, for they may well become lost and bewildered at its spiritual content. Understand it is healthy and normal for them to do so. Your parents must find their way back to you, after being lost in superficial commercial product and entertainment space in the mind. A commercial TV indoctrinated space in the mind, of anyone who has been brought up on a saturated diet of commercial TV advertisements, promos, products, reality shows and soap operas. Along with other socially immature and psychologically damaging movies and computer games, saturating the vulnerable and impressionable minds of children.

The other reason parents become lost from their children, is that many parents left home too early themselves. They were not ready for the big world, and the big adult world is a very complex place indeed. We cannot do what we like, when we like, how we like and with whom we like in this world, as children, adults, celebrities, actors or as influential leaders in the public eye. Because what quality of karmic influence we create in this shared world, is what quality of karmic influence we receive back from out of Nature's interactive spiritual and physical workings.

Therefore, positive life-supporting influence in equals positive life-supporting influence back out from primordial Nature. That always supports and furthers our spiritual evolution. However, almighty Nature never supports our spiritual evolution, when it is delusional or destructive influence that we create with our thoughts, actions, creativity and deeds in life. We only create spiritual devolution, that is the opposite of spiritual evolution and always leads to unhappiness and chaos.

Repeat: This lasting created influence from out of our thoughts, actions and deeds, eventually returns to us from interactive primordial Nature and is called karma. So, if we do not give the positive influence of love and kindness to the big world, then we do not receive any back from out of Nature's interactive spiritual working. Good manners, pleasantness and helpfulness to others, is also very important in Nature's, as *we sow, so do we reap,* interactive workings. In simple understanding, as we give, then so do, we invisibly receive back in this shared world and many adults have forgotten this in our commercial television and advertisement saturated consumer world. That has become the chief *pied piper* of superficial lifestyles, commercials, promos, immature reality shows and other self-gratuitous winning programs for big bucks, that fuel greed and false happiness called euphoria. However, unknowingly, it is a contagious delusion creating euphoria, that prevents us from evolving with our spiritual evolution to find lasting spiritual happiness.

Now we must change this spiritless delusional contagious reality and create another life-supportive reality to replace it. We do this, by dissolving its delusion through understanding ourselves and acknowledging and not denying, our wrongdoing to Nature, its Laws and our spiritual evolution … all of us. Including the out-of-control commercial media and anything goes entertainment. Otherwise, we will never get to heaven because we will not have grown up enough ever to reach it.

It is also my spiritual job to explain to you and your parents, that leaving home for good before twenty-one is a spiritually unproductive no, no. Because Nature's invisible intelligence is still structuring your delicate, vulnerable minds and you, cannot cope with the big world and all that is in it, until almighty Nature has done its growing-up job properly in your mind and body. It causes you to be a very unhappy person in later life and creates a lot of problems and unhappiness for your future children. So, spiritually understand that when you reach eighteen, then you can put the invisible adult L plates on and celebrate that's fine. Then, they are to remain on until you reach twenty-one consciously - right? Because, there is still a lot more to learn about life and its invisible pitfalls in-between eighteen and twenty-one and you, still need a happy, secure, loving home environment, to avoid falling in those adolescent hidden pitfalls. That are being promoted and saturated, through the out-of-control media, internet and entertainment.

Thus, twenty-one is the big day, the great day to celebrate your full independence and unrestricted freedom. Because then, Nature will invisibly guide you from that day onwards, to acquire full adulthood with her special blessings. On that special day, you are to paint the town red, which means having a wow of a time 'positively' celebrating your well-earned freedom, from parental restrictions and interference in your adolescent life. On that special INDEPENDENCE DAY, you will then be officially handed the KEYS TO THE CAR and adulthood, not only from your parents but from the invisible Intelligence in the spiritual workings of Nature also. Then you can take those invisible adolescent L plates off and store them in a safe place for your future children. Because then and only then at age twenty-one, can you do your own fully independent thing and know, you are not harming yourself or others, not before.

Q: *Why can you not do your own thing before age twenty-one?*

A: Because within the spiritual workings of Nature, your parents are responsible for all created influence (karma) out of your thoughts, deeds and actions. They have brought you into this physical world and that miracle of creating your life creates a *parental responsibility* to you until you reach twenty-one. Thus, a great responsibility of parenthood, to guide you into adult maturity and a socially responsible, happy, productive life. After age twenty-one, you take full responsibility for all karma (influence) you create out of your thoughts, actions and deeds, not your parents. Therefore, understand this spiritual system and do not rebel against your parent's authority, when you cannot have your way.

Clarification: We must understand that positive family and social rules and sensible regulations, are a very necessary learning process to acquire and adhere too in the family and social structure.

Why?

Because your future adult happiness depends on accepting and respecting those family and social rules. To then enable you to become a mature, responsible adult in society yourself and not, a selfish, inconsiderate, thoughtless, irresponsible, do what you like and when you like delinquent adult in society, on the devolution blink; because we will never collect our spiritual harp with that behaviour only unhappiness.

Therefore, do not be a pain in the butt to society and the spiritual intelligence of Nature, that is structuring our spiritual evolution. A spiritual evolution that happens after you reach twenty-one, not before. Up until that special day of full independence, your mum and dad will talk sensibly between themselves and include you in its discussion. To then guide you maturely, patiently, thoughtfully and give you more and more freedom towards that very special day in your life, twenty-one today, hooray and all that - yes? I will say this again so that the Upstairs spiritual message comes across loud and clear. With no ifs or buts, backchat and tantrums from your end. You are to respect the sensible house rules, especially teenagers. Sensible family and social rules are not made to be broken. They are in place for a very good reason, to protect you from falling into invisible and often irreversible sexual pitfalls that you do not see but mature loving parents do - okay?

By observing and respecting those family house rules, you then become a responsible, caring, mature, very likeable person. That is given more and more freedom and asked less and fewer questions. Because in that magic process of growing up into a responsible likable, happy person, you then create harmony and happiness in the family and social structure and therefore in Nature. When it is your turn to raise a family, then you will understand the sensible reason for the existence of family and social rules. You will then naturally, guide your future children along that same positive path to reach maturity and a happy adult life also. It is that simple.

Soon, we will explore the happy way to love someone properly, respectfully and maturely. Simply by understanding ourselves and learning, how to give and take in life when interacting with others in society. A very important part of the teenage learning curve and its many growing pains. Therefore, being and acting as a responsible, considerate adult when we fall in procreation euphoric love and not, stupid cupid. Therefore, not a thoughtless adolescent delinquent on the blink as well as the brink, when you first fall in love.

Understand that Nature's interactive intelligence must finish structuring your physical, your mental, your emotional and commence your spiritual growth first, before leaving home. That is called gaining full adult maturity. Then, it is easy to find your place in the big world happily. That spiritual acquired maturity is not possible until you have turned twenty-one. Then your physical, mental and spiritual qualities, if you have had a loving, happy childhood environment, are all linked together harmoniously, to enable you to cope with the complexities and responsibilities of adulthood. That family acquired maturity, then enables us to make our way in the adult world on our own two feet and more importantly, not trash Nature, the world and other people with our own creativity and expression, especially in the sexual department. Like a lot of so-called successful human beings in entertainment, the internet and movies and those copying them are doing, without realising it.

Therefore, we must always acknowledge and respect the invisible Intelligence of primordial Nature, that is structuring the biology and growth of our minds and bodies and *order out of chaos* in life. It is that spiritual Intelligence that allows us to feel, to talk, to play, to think, to laugh, to be happy and to procreate. If we observe this very sensible rule of respecting Nature's interactive Intelligence and its laws, then much happiness, much joy comes to us, through a spiritual lasting quiet love contained in the divine Intelligence of Nature.

It is a lasting gift that is available to everyone, through understanding and acquiring spiritual maturity and respecting Nature, this planet and each other. Therefore, if we wish to evolve spiritually, we must understand the meaning of spiritual maturity and not enter sexual relationships, until we are emotionally and sexually mature, in mind and body. Then we are in harmony with Nature and its Laws and all the invisible primordial energies, that structure sexuality and the biology and chemistry of life.

Explanation: The invisible Intelligence that structures our physical and spiritual evolution, is the Creator's active divine Intelligence and its self-referral spiritual Laws creating, *order out of chaos* in life. When we respect those intuitive spiritual Laws and not ignore, abuse and degrade them, then much magic comes to us throughout our lives to enjoy this beautiful living planet; with no returning destructive karma (influence) attached to our mind and body, through *wrongdoing* to Nature and other human beings. In simple understanding, it is our human wrongdoing to Nature and other people on this planet, that creates and fuels all misery and unhappiness in the world. It is called the inescapable Law of Karma. Alternatively, *"as we sow, so do we reap,"* with our thoughts, actions and deeds in life. In other words, we must pay for all wrongdoing to Nature and its laws; we cannot escape it. Its returning destructive influence manifests in many ways, seen and unseen. As is happening now in this shared world and why Alf and Stephen are here. Therefore, to help dissolve its contagious destructive karma (influence) and restore spiritual happiness on this beautiful shared planet.

For example:

When powerful, influential human beings create wars, bloodshed and greed, through their negative, destructive creativity and actions including those nations creating and selling the weapons of destruction, then that *wrongdoing* to Nature with our creativity, eventually returns to us all. The returning influence from that wrongdoing to nature, comes in the form of disease, famine, plagues, wars, chaos, unhappiness and misery. Likewise, when we hurt and damage another human being as an individual, as a family, as a tribe or as a Nation, then disharmony and unhappiness are what those responsible reap, from out of its destructive behaviour and wrongdoing to Nature. It is an accumulative destructive human created influence/entity, that returns to touch all life-intelligence on this shared planet. Karma is Nature's creative spiritual tool, that structures our plus or minus spiritual evolution and destiny, from out of our negative or positive human creativity. Unknowingly, that is how powerful we are as human beings, with our unique creativity and its karma in the invisible spiritual intelligence of Nature.

Why is this, you ask?

Because the creative human being has the master key in physical Creation; that spiritual master key is our conscious free will and an intuitive conscience. A conscious free will to do the right life-supportive thing or the wrong destructive thing to Nature and other human beings. Now perhaps, we begin to understand the reason for family and social rules and learning right behaviour that compliments Nature as we are growing up. That we have also called, learning how to behave with maturity within the family structure and society and the intelligence of Nature. Thus, human beings have free will above all other animals, to choose what they do with their creativity, and this gift is a great responsibility given to the human being by the transcendent silent Creator of everything in Creation that we call God.

The positive spiritual advice from Alf to your parents is for them to learn and practice twice daily correct meditation. That comes as an evolution gift from the divine component of Nature, to help them evolve further with their spiritual evolution underwritten by love. Then your parents will be able to naturally guide you to your full independence, structured in that spiritual acquired love and happiness. So that, in turn, you have love and happiness throughout your busy life. Once the karma/influence from out of that love and happiness is created in all nations, then no more wars, no more bloodshed, no more misery, no more greed, no more human created pollution and natural disasters on this shared planet. This miracle is so simple and easy to accomplish if we all truly desire it. Because then, we will receive the invisible support of divine Nature, to help us in its collective achievement in all nations. However, only if we work together as a global family of nations, to create unity, equality, harmony and peace in the world. The simple universal tool to achieve this miracle is called Correct Meditation.

About Media, Scriptwriter, Television and Entertainment Instructed, One-Night Stands and Casual Sexual Activity with Anyone

The spiritual instruction from Upstairs is simple, never, not ever if you are wise. If you can honour this positive instruction, then you will never be unhappy and lost to know what to do, when the *right time* comes for sexual bonding with the person you truly love, the one for a lifetime. Therefore, the *right person* to share your body and adult life with and not, the wrong person and eventual unhappiness. When the magic time comes to raise your own family, then you will naturally give them a happy childhood structured in a harmonious marriage, mature parental love and firm but kind discipline – that is a priceless gift for a child's future adult happiness. That loving, harmonious family environment is a must-have for children, for their further spiritual evolution ... and the parents.

So, reign in on any movie, television and internet instructed sexual activity and help your parents, throughout this spiritual transition in the family structure. Because your parents need to understand what is being spiritually explained to them by Alf and you, can help achieve that. Then there will be no more unhappiness or shouting arguments in the family and very importantly, you will always feel wanted, loved, supported and guided towards your adult freedom, total independence and a happy life ... that's a promise. But you must do your positive bit in the family and social structure, to create that miracle.

That brings us to the lost subject of manners when interacting with others. A subject matter, we are supposed to learn from our parents as we are growing up. A subject matter the saturated media and entertainment industry have obliterated in society, in the name of, *freedom of expression, acting and entertainment*. So, ask your parents to teach you about social manners and not, those causing the contagious problem in society who will never get to heaven to collect their harp because of it.

As polite Stephen would say, *"Manners, pianos, cartwheels and wheelbarrows,"* is a good way to remember always to be polite to others. Especially to those in charge of your welfare and education. Remember also, that respect is born of respect, as love of born of love in the invisible workings of Nature. Therefore, treat others as you would have others treat you, a very simple, intuitive spiritual rule to remember throughout your precious life.

Now according to Alf, Stephen is going back to school after his annual archaeological holiday. Because he must brush up on his diction and writing. Because Upstairs has said, they cannot have you all writing like Stephen in his archaeological stories, when you create and reach heaven. That is, of course, this beautiful planet that we are on and that no-one knows about yet.

Why?

Because heaven is where you create it, as Jesus and Mohammed knew long ago, and not many people wanted to listen to them either at first. They were far too busy doing their trashing and winning thing on the planet and calling it progress, especially in Greek and Roman times. Just like Hollywood and commercial TV having their annual human worshipping time at Oscar's place and in the commercial television studio. With all its silly, *I love-me* and look how *successful I am,* celebrity razzamatazz, and its contagious media saturated progress but spiritually speaking, eventually to no-where land the land of unhappiness. Plus, there were some very mean, nasty and destructive people about in those creating progress long ago. Who could never understand the word love and its progress? However, of course, Upstairs learns by past mistakes. Unlike some powerful human beings' in the top end of town, that are creating and in charge of our progress downstairs. Along with creating the dead-end destiny of those following and worshipping them. Who also, have never heard of spiritual progress, only all-consuming economic progress, winning at everything progress, entertainment progress, internet progress, technology progress and big greedy business progress?

So according to Upstairs, it is time to create the miracle of, *spiritual progress* for a change that does not contain those age-old human ego problems of worshipping other human beings, self-aggrandisement, self-gratuitous behaviour, megalomania, conquering everything, consuming everything, winning at everything, owning everything and of course, hate, nastiness and violence. That is also permeating and growing, in our much talked about and admired technological, science, entertainment, commercial television and consumer driven progress. Moreover, as children innocently know, miracles can be everywhere. But not, when we do the *wrong thing* to Nature and its Laws on this beautiful planet and hurt other people with our immature thoughts, behaviour, creativity, actions and deeds.

Q: *What are the spiritual self-referral Laws of Nature?*
A: They are God's manifested personal active Intelligence in spiritual Creation. That is the unseen Universe that underwrites our physical seen universe and where everything physical is born from. Within that spiritual universe, also reside the spiritual deities of EARTH - AIR - FIRE - WATER and SPACE. That are the divine elements within all things physical in our universe. They are pure eternal spiritual Intelligence, not human intelligence. However, that also, is a hidden secret that we find out when we reach our full spiritual development. That spiritual accomplishment is something we must earn during our lifetime; by doing the right life-supporting positive thing and not, the negative wrong to Nature thing with our human creativity and expression.

Also, it is the non-judgemental love within the spiritual heart of a human being, that creates that miracle of spiritual accomplishment and its progress and links, to the simple short practice of transcendent meditation using a correct mantra. So, we cannot buy spiritual accomplishment with money, fame and power. We cannot acquire its miracle by thinking about it or pretending to be in its spiritual domain. Thus, that spiritual accomplishment and its evolution is a gift from the silent Creator to the human being. A miracle that develops, through love and respect for this beautiful Creation and all that is in it. It is a miracle to acquire in adulthood fully.

Coming back to Stephen and his peculiar writing and diction in his stories:

God loves Stephen very much, but one Stephen is enough in his office talking and writing as he does. For it aggravates Upstair's painful gout, as Stephen knows well. So, do not copy the peculiar writing and spelling in his stories and translations of B.C. tablets. The way your mum and dad talk are just fine and that goes for the conventional writing that you learn at school. Because Stephen's peculiar writing and spelling is caused through dyslexia and missing out on all-important school when he was a boy; because he never had a mum and dad to look after him and make sure he went to school. But he is learning fast how to overcome this education hic-cup, thanks to the computer and its spell checker and much hard work at the keyboard. Because they never had those tools when he was growing up, only pen and ink and blots and blotting paper and doodles and detentions.

Repeat: If you do not understand some of the words and their meaning in this special letter to you, then ask your parents and teachers politely, to explain what you do not understand. This is how we learn by asking sensible questions from our teachers. Stephen is a little clumsy in his writing, and his spelling is not what it should be, but he does not mind if you laugh at him. He is very good natured, as well as being a spiritually learned man and the divine Intelligence that underwrites Nature has touched his pen, to help us all understand spiritual love and how to acquire it. To then be able to create lasting happiness within ourselves that invisibly/spiritually touches everything in Creation. A spiritual love that is also locked up within everything on this shared planet. The secret we are going to learn and share, is also the key to unlock the door to its invisible spiritual kingdom. Love to you all and love one another – and that is the magic key.

Kind regards from the author and the pen of Stephen, adopted son of Alf.

Important postscript:

You will find one of Stephen's introductory history stories in SECTION FOUR called, 'The Missing Manuscripts'. He has also translated some ancient history tablets into stories, that he dug up on his last archaeological dig overseas, you will find them at the end of this section. This coming year, he is going to examine a few more ancient historical sites around the world, to fathom out the perpetuating ancestral karma problems, that their civilisations created long ago and are plaguing this civilisation. Those ancient people have long since gone, but not the negative, destructive influence (karma) they created, through terrible wrongdoings of greed, violence, bloodshed and wars upon each other. We should all understand, that the created karma (influence) from out of wrong-to-Nature destructive deeds remains in the spiritual atmosphere to return to future generations. So that we, in turn, practice the same destructive to Nature deeds in this present world as our ancestors. It is called, perpetuated ancestral karma created destructive influence.

So, we must break this cycle of ancestral returning destructive influence if we are to reach heaven our created heaven that is. Therefore, the physical heaven we all must help create on this shared planet. Along with the spiritual help of Nature and its divine Intelligence, of course. That is another invisible secret we have yet to uncover in Nature. Because for all the science acquired physical knowledge taught in schools and universities, existing science and education, know nothing about the invisible spiritual workings of Life and Nature. That means our existing education acquired knowledge is incomplete and not the full story, but only half the story of Life and Nature.

B.C. Stories from the Pen of Stephen

Gleek archaeologist and tablet translator extraordinaire.

Plus, a pay-back dig to the education system of my youth (long ago), for all my classroom detentions at school. It was not my fault that they could not read my classical writing in-between all the ink blots and doodles or understand the new words I invented for the Oxford Dictionary in my essays. So now, they must re-read my Gleek translations of history, because St Peter is going to test them on their content at the Pearly Gates. He did not mind my rotten writing and spelling and missing punctuation and give me real hard time. He gave me 8 out of 10 and a harp, Lol.

Signed - Stephen. School Dissident.

Introduction:
   Stephen solves the strange archaeological mystery, of prolific dismembered statues and sculptured reliefs from the Greek civilisation. Also found for some strange reason, in other nation's museums, private collections and gardens, without the Greek nation's permission.

Note: Because if something does not belong to you, then a law of human harmony inscribed on the pearly gates states that you should not take it. It is a great wrong to do so in Nature's Laws with lasting negative karma repercussions. So those nations concerned, should officially give them back to the Greek nation and then politely, ask if they can borrow them back on loan to display in their museums. That is called good manners, thoughtfulness and respect for the spiritual dignity of another nation's heritage, culture and historical artefacts. Objects that belong to that nation's heritage, unique culture and people, not to another nation. Nor to any other nation's misguided wealthy individuals, collecting historical artifacts on the antique black market that do not belong to them. Is it very bad karma.
   Also, with the help of the Delphi Oracle, Stephen foils a big business marketing genius plot, to dismantle the Parthenon from right under the Greek nose and install it in the product and porn-saturated internet. Where it will disappear forever in its current murky depths. Just like some of Stephen's computer files recently. That had been hijacked by computer trashing delinquents, in their destructive

quest to stuff up everything positive on the internet and impress Darth with their computer trashing skills, but not St Peter, with the Upstairs heavenly computer keys. And no! it wasn't Micro Soft either. Bill is in the clear on this one and doing a good job with his acquired wealth for the world's born misfortunate. Unlike some in big money-making corporate business and its wealthy shareholders, he has a conscience that communicates with his thoughts and hip-pocket simultaneously. Those very wealthy people hoarding all the money in this world, have forgotten they cannot take it with them in the inevitable departure lounge. Where the karma Law of, *'as we sow, so we reap,'* is inescapable.

A Greek Tragedy

A new translation by Stephen.

About the Greek Parthenon or the parliament of the human gods, as it was known in those hectic days of the sculpturing of anything that walked, talked, sat down or moved. The whole population were at it, sculpturing that is, However, first a short recap of ancient Greek history and don't forget, to verify it for yourself in the Greek Section of the British Museum.

The Greeks were determined to make up for all the past constant dismemberment and trashing of each other during the internal wars of the early Greek city-states, which according to Stephen's good friend Plato, was mostly due to a big ego-driven conquering and winning problem. This, in the never-ending human ego quest for acquiring self-esteem and adulation from other human beings for winning at everything. You know, who's the biggest and best at trashing and winning and being a worshipped god or celebrity, as they are now called, along with another unresolved adolescent argument as to who had the biggest ego and loudest oracle in the land. This is still a very popular argument in A.D. political circles and commercial television and radio stations.

Anyway, the long and short and loud of it all was that it never got resolved. You know, that conquering, trashing and worshipping the winners to acquire self-esteem, which merely escalated into trashing other nations down to this present day to acquire that all-consuming human self-esteem or power, as it is called in the delusional top end of town. Anyway, the Greeks under the kingship of Alexander the-great-at-trashing, (as he was known by the primordial Gods of Nature), took off for a world record on global hacking and whacking in other Nations and called conquering, winning and creating progress to acquire self-esteem for the delusional ego ... in Nature's dictionary that is.

Alexander was under instruction from Aristotle, his education teacher and mentor, to create as much very important Greek educating progress in other nations as possible. On Alexander's way to see the Persian law firm, Darius, Xerxes, Darius, Associates at law ... their law that is ... who had paid an earlier self-esteem Persian funded trashing visit to Greece and had left much rubbish, trashed buildings, overturned Greek statues and smashed boats behind for the Greek citizens to clear up afterwards who, upon returning to Athens after their gold bar funded holidays in the Aegean islands, were not very impressed at having to stand all their temple columns and statue's upright. This, after the Persians had rearranged them in the horizontal position, but without official authorisation from the Greek political big wigs in the Parthenon ... very bad B.C. manners again.

Anyways, the Greeks had been advised by the Delphi oracle to take out a summons for reparation and compensation for all the hernia's they suffered from having to manually raise all the columns and statue's in the vertical position once more. So, after yet another never-ending argumentative debate and political point scoring in the parliamentary tea rooms of the Parthenon, the Greek political big wigs finally elected Alex-the-great-at-trashing, to go and serve the compensation summons on the Persian nation and start trashing proceedings on the culprits responsible for all the vandalism. Plus, along the way, Alex was determined once and for all, to settle the age-old unresolved problem of who was King of the world, that evidently, no king or politician had been able to resolve since the last great Biblical flood, because there were quite a few catastrophic floods back in those B.C. days, that always came after much hacking and whacking called wars, to wash away all the human-created mess afterwards. As the archetypal primordial Gods of Nature are very tidy and do not like human self-esteem trashing progress on their downstairs Earth turf ... so to speak.

The above retribution from Nature is another story of epic proportions that we humans call natural disasters, along with the never-ending dismemberment of the human torso by other human beings; because it was also a self-esteem custom to re-arrange the body parts of the Kings in charge of other nations, especially when they stated that they were King of Kings and a winner of winners. Evidently, whenever you made that ego authorised self-esteem proclamation in your own nation, all sorts of Genghis Khan type fruit-loops suddenly appeared at that nation's door to contest its legality. What is more, they did not knock first before entering either ... like the non-stop talking news media. More bad manners again.

Anyway, with all its B.C. nation trashing through very bad manners and the self-esteem ego quest to be crowned King of the world and a worshipped winner, it caused perpetual trashing conflict in all nations, right down to this present day, because we are still at it hammer and tongs, even as I write this tall story to you. This never-ending human winning and trashing problem comes from perpetuating destructive karma inherited from our ancestors and that, evidently, our civilisation keeps adding to in Nature's primordial workings and created out of conquering and winning to acquire self-esteem and a mention in our history books and the media as a winner. Anyway, Upstairs has said, that we must all help dissolve its perpetuated bad news ancestral karma and restore harmony into the primordial spiritual workings of Nature that underwrites, orchestrates and propels all life on this planet, otherwise, we will never get to heaven to collect our harp, but the other place. You know, stoking the boilers in Beelzebub land when we kick the downstairs bucket so to speak.

As I was saying before I got interrupted by the media and commercial television. Heaven is another story of epic proportions too. Unfortunately, everyone is far too busy doing their commercial product and image creating thingo, popping pills and worshipping winners, artists, pop stars and celebrities and watching dead-brain commercial television programs, promos and, ads along with reading glossy magazines and visiting Fred's casino in the desert, and Oscar's place in Hollywood to acquire their self-esteem. So, they are not really interested in collecting their spiritual harp Upstairs, only in making money, buying products and worshiping human idols and other media created celebrities to acquire that elusive ego self-esteem.

Note: Therefore, you will have to tell your media misinformed parents about it - you know, the heaven Upstairs. Plus, we are not supposed to sycophantically worship and idolise other human beings, not for any reason. This creates bad karma for everyone. However, according to Upstairs, we can respect and congratulate the achievement and success of others, but only if they deserve our respect and congratulations for helping others born less fortunate, not for winning at everything to collect gongs, big bucks and saturated adulation from the media and the public. It becomes a contagious euphoric delusion (entity) that impedes our individual and social, spiritual evolution.

Note: Along with sending those being worshipped and idolised backwards with their spiritual evolution as an unknown fact, because universities, science and academia have yet to uncover this spiritual fact with their acquired incomplete physical knowledge. Therefore, its spiritual knowledge and wisdom does not exist in our existing education systems and classrooms.

Anyways, coming back to the missing bits and pieces from lots of Greek statues and the reason why.

Now, in those ancient Greek days, some people could sculpture heads good, but not the rest of the body, while other people could sculpture arms and legs good, but were hopeless at making heads and bodies. So, to sort the Greek dilemma out, half the Greek population did the heads and the other half did the arms and legs. However, here is the Greek crux of the problem because only one bloke in the nation could do the body and all the muscles properly.

This man was PHIDIAS of Olympia, honoured citizen and artisan of Athens, who, was a very talented man with the hammer and chisel. However, being a temperamental artist, he had a very short Greek fuse on his temper as his students knew well. Anyways, one day they decided to play an Athenian prank on him for all his motor mouth shouting, ranting and raving whenever they accidentally made a boo boo on one of his works of art made of marble, which they were all chipping away at and manufacturing, under licence, for the Greek big wigs at the top end of town. The big wigs lived just up the street on top of the hill next door to the Parthenon.

Evidently, what his disgruntled students did was to hide his personally inscribed tea mug that even the tea-lady was not allowed to touch or wash up. It was this student prank which caused the whole problem of the missing bits and pieces and whatnots, missing off all the Greek statues found around the world today...and why they never got reassembled on the Greek assembly line at Athens anymore. All because Phidias blew his top at finding his mug missing at tea break time and refused to do any more torsos with muscles until it was returned. Also, as we know from glossy magazines and advertisements, muscles and especially abs and pectorals are very important for our self-esteem and ego; according to commercial television and marketing agency's selling consumer products to delusional no-where land. The land of spiritually lost human beings that is.

Phidias was so indignant about the loss of his tea mug that he marched into Athens and placed his grievance in front of all the big political wigs at the Parthenon, where Zeus was boss. Demanding that they sort it out there and then and send the Greek constabulary to his workshop post-haste and find his missing tea mug. Otherwise, it was down tools as far as he was concerned. Thus, no more fully assembled works of marble art and muscles, would come out of his statue and artisan workshop anymore - full stop.

Evidently, that explosive red-faced declaration from Phidias caused pandemonium amongst the big political wigs in the Parthenon, as well as the Greek economists, who, according to Alf, normally spent most of the day lounging around the Parthenon drinking cups of tea or mugs of café latte and scoffing biscuits, and in-between mouthfuls, talking to the money-making big business gods. As well as discussing where they were going on holidays next Greek semester and how much money and gold bars they had accumulated in the Greek piggy bank; they also discussed who they were going to trash next overseas to obtain some more gold bars to keep the Greek economy wheels turning and the people happy and gainfully employed.

Evidently, if Phidias the sculptor was to down tools and go on strike, that ultimatum would mean that the whole Greek nation would come to a grinding economic standstill. Riots would erupt from the citizens of Greece for not having enough sculptured torsos to stick all the arms, legs, heads and whatnots on. Moreover, believe it or not, that's exactly what did happen and why we have so many Greeks statues, with bits and pieces missing, in all the museums. All because they never did find the missing tea mug.

The missing mug was only discovered in the 1950's in Phidias's rediscovered overgrown workshop premises at Olympia. The missing mug had been swept under the workshop carpet in a million pieces, where it had been hidden by the student perpetrators. Evidently, the students had accidentally dropped the mug when trying to place it back on the hook in Phidias's locker, before the Greek constabulary turned up from Athens to sort them all out and give them Egyptian curry or something hotter for causing so much trouble with the Greek economy.

Anyways, the moral of this tall Greek story is, do not take what is not yours because it causes big problems for everyone, even a whole nation and its people. As in our Greek tragedy.

Stephen Translates the B.C. Doings of the Phrygian's, the Lydian's and King Midas and his Blocked Ear Problem

All that glitters is not gold, so stated Goldfinger to 007 with his feet up slurping on a gold martini with a bent straw and an olive stuck on the end of it, after studying his pay check for A.D. discrepancies on Friday afternoon, after the day's film shoot on the banks of the river Pactolus in Turkey. This river once flowed with gold and where King Midas first contracted his blocked ear problem back in 800 B.C. As a result, King Midas had to travel to the Dadonnat Epirus oracle to sort out his ear blockage problem with the entrepreneurial wife of Philip, the King of Macedonia, who operated the mystical Oracle for extra pocket money to help out with her household budget.

Evidently, King Philip was right stingy and tight with money, except when he was celebrating his trashing and bashing victories and publishing his books on the art of trashing other nations. This was a very popular pastime in those B.C. days and prescribed free reading for everyone in Macedonia whenever King Philip was away on overseas self-esteem trashing business, collecting other nation's gold bars to put in his treasury, so that he could rightly claim the title of Goldfinger and not King Midas or that other private enterprise upstart King Croesus of Lydia, who was placing a hex, via the ear of King Salinas, on King Midas who had been tied up by the Greeks for being inebriated and over vocal.

Evidently, King Midas had one too many in the Greek pub after the loss of the return game from Spartacus United the day before at Athens Olympia stadium, which had recently been refurbished to accommodate more anticipated overseas visitors for a never-ending global economy debate. This debate was about who was running the global trashing show, and to sort out the discrepancy of the missing gold bars.

As it turned out, the gold bars had been stolen from downtown Thebes by King Philip's son Alexander, who was learning the art of rearranging cities at the battle of Chaeronea down the road from

Athens, and at this point in his trashing education, had not written any important trashing books like his dad who, being stingy, wouldn't give him any pocket money to start his gold bar collection. Therefore, he had to get his own stock of gold bars out of King Midas who was King of the gold bar All-ordinaries Exchange. This Exchange was nothing like the Greenwich meantime Exchange, but more like Black and Blue Exchange for the trashed citizens in the town of Chaeronea who were taking a stock market pasting, because they had run out of marathon runners who had always run on time at the stock exchange, but were now on a go-slow that the Worker's Union had organised the previous day.

Evidently, they were not getting paid enough gold bars and paid annual holidays which also meant bad gold bar news for those waiting in the Olympia Stadium to do a hand wave and worship the winners for their dose of important self-esteem, which also meant the spectators would not receive any gold bars, along with the Greek timekeeper who had run out of time to correct the time that no one took any notice of anyway.

By this time, King Midas was going deaf with all the political and economic racket going on and suffering elongated ear syndrome from all the ear pulling by his instructor, a gold bar specialist from a bank in Switzerland. He finally threw in the sponge and coined that very famous phrase, 'All that glitters is not gold,' especially in Hollywood, commercial television and in glossy product magazines.

King Midas, then returned home much happier than when he had set off on his travels with his original earache the year before. Evidently, his earache had come from all the gold dust stuck in his ear from the gold contaminated Pactolus river that he did his morning ablutions in. Anyway, a much wiser King was he after he got rid of the gold dust in his ear, stopped collecting gold bars and went home to his wife according to the Greek historian Herodotus, who wrote all the historical tablets in those days, so that we would have a scholarly account of the hectic B.C. gold rush days to acquire self-esteem. This was very complex indeed with lots of question marks - full stop.

The Unknown B.C. Tablet about Helen of Troy

Stephen translates the Hittites and the Hurrians from B.C. tablets found in a disused loo in the North Wing of the British Museum. The loo had somehow become blocked up with a lot more too hard to translate tablets. Evidently, the tablets had originally cluttered up the help desk on the ground floor back in 1902 and the paperwork lost. The tablets had somehow ended up in the North Wing loo, through a 1902 clerical error in the catalogue dept; at least that's the line they spun to Fred the Plumber called in to fix it a hundred years later. This, after a letter of complaint about the unusable loo from Stephen and the Tea Lady who is a very knowledgeable and important person, pushing her tea trolley and biscuits around the B.M. corridors to all departments twice a day.

Firstly, the disappearance of The Hittites of Bogazkoy who, evidently, were plastered by Paris into the walls of ancient Troy back in 1305 B.C. This after objecting to the marriage of Helen who, incidentally, had been married umpteen times before but kept forgetting to inform each of her new husbands of that fact. In fact, just like in Hollydude and Days of Our Life on commercial television that has been running with endless repeats since B.C. times and is also to be found on a tablet in the Smithsonian Museum donated by the British Museum. Evidently, the B.M. couldn't decipher that one either back in 1902, so they sent it back to the 'good ole U.S. of A.' who were very good at making thousands of movies, reality shows, advertisements, promos and commercial television stations, but were hopeless at deciphering tablets.

Anyway, according to the translated tablets, quite a fracas had ensued from all the irate husbands of Helen. When at the marriage ceremony in Troy, it was asked if there were any objections from those attending its marriage ceremony; some of whom had travelled far and wide in big motorised power boats from all the Greek island holiday resorts in the Aegean Sea. Evidently, the Greeks had been accumulating gold bars in-between their trashing conflagrations to acquire self-esteem and having never-ending debates on who had the biggest Oracle and who was the best at re-arranging other cities on the mainland in the off-season. This out of season trashing progress, to keep Helen of Troy in the luxury she was accustomed to in-between marriages that were arranged politically but not always politely in those days. This trashing progress was to consolidate the global gold bar all ordinaries index that anyone and everyone who could trash professionally dealt in, including the Anatolian opposition that lived in Anatolia, just across the Bay of figs or dates or somefing.

Now, this is where B.C. history and A.D. history becomes a little confusing, because the Bay of Figs or somefing, is where the Greeks rowed to from the mainland, in order to hold their annual picnic trashing day and leave all their pottery, fast food wrappers and plastic bottles behind. This was to confuse the archaeologists who came later in the A.D. of history, to pick up all the pieces and glue them all back together again, so that they could then be re-buried and dug-up once more after our A.D. techno civilisation had kicked the bucket and the new post A.D. civilisation, could carry on with the job of digging and sieving. This was also a secure job to have during the long years of high unemployment in-between civilisations which, as we all know comes and goes in the human trashing business to acquire our self-esteem. Evidently, this takes up a lot of the time of human beings and stops them from becoming bored and lazy.

Note: At least, that's what the Romans were to say when they visited Greece a few centuries later looking for a wooden horse full of Spartans and Martians to sort out. Evidently Helen of Troy had told them about this Trojan Horse in a letter to the Romans, via the Corinthians, after she had run out of husbands and gold bars in Greece. Anyway, Helen's marital activity of having many ex-husbands, had coined that famous expression, *A little gold digger,'* which until recently was thought to have been a twentieth century A.D. phrase, from either out of a Hollywood movie script or The Days of our Dysfunctional Lives on commercial television. However, in fact, this phrase was found inscribed on a gold bracelet in a burial mound in southern Anatolia.

Also found in the burial mound was a lot of decorated pottery pieces in the very popular red Athenian style of 1898. It was cleverly deduced by those A.D. archaeologists that they must have been on loan from the Olympia museum in Athens for the burial service in Anatolia, but obviously not returned in time to be found in the archaeological dig of 1925, which meant that not only was this B.C. tablet very confusing but that Helen, must have escaped from all her irate husbands in Greece and founded a new dynasty of, *little gold diggers* in Anatolia, that eventually went to America and became corporate lawyers and marketing geniuses.

Anyway, this tablet translation is still very much an ongoing hot debate in archaeological circles, therefore it will not be found in next month's journal of new archaeological discoveries. However, further information on this blockbuster discovery will change forever the way modern archaeologists stick all their bits and pieces back together.

This information will be found at the fictitious clerical section of the British Museum, providing they are not out on one of their fast food extended tea breaks or sitting on the repaired loo in the North Wing scratching their heads reading this tablet manuscript.

Translation of Another Time Elongated B.C. Tablet. No 20071600 B.M. Post Circ 1200 B.C. Approx

The following is a re-investigation into the chariot spoke wheel phenomena that was to revolutionise the speed of self-esteem trashing throughout the Middle East. This information contained in an unearthed B.C. tablet found at the Yazilikaya excavation site and attributed to the personal scribe of Ramses the 2nd. Evidently, this scribe always accompanied Ramses when paying unannounced trashing visits to other nations to enquire after their self-esteem. The scribe also doubled as the rock face translator in the graffiti business that went hand in hand with the tablet scribbling business in B.C. times.

About the Hittites and the spoke wheel, the hieroglyphic wheel and the noisy wheel. The interpretation of which, led to an academic row between other archaeologists and professor Henry Fonze-for-short Winkler at the B.M. in 1902, when much confusion arose between interpreting the cuneiform spoke wheels of King Tiglath-Pileser the 1st that spun faster, and the hieroglyphic embedded Egyptian silent wheels of Ramses the 2nd, that suffered from constant bogging in the sand through a lack of punctuation in the embedded hieroglyphics.

Anyway, according to Ramses' scribe, it was at the self-esteem chariot trashing battle at Kadash that Pharaoh Ramses first learnt to speak the Hittite language when he lost both of his solid hieroglyphic chariot wheels on the battlefield, after they had overheated and developed noise problems at the height of the chariot trashing. Evidently, Pharaoh Ramses had to call a halt to the chariot battle and politely ask the Hittite opposition if he could borrow a couple of their spare chariot wheels, because someone in the Egyptian spare parts department, (who later got a hieroglyphic earful), forgot to pack the spare wheels in the over-sized spare parts chariot. This extra-large chariot always accompanied the army when visiting neighbouring nations to exchange spears, marketing strategies, products and other self-esteem acquiring pleasantries.

It was through this friendly wheel exchange that Pharaoh Ramses got chatting to King Tiglath-Palliser's daughter while they were changing his wheels. The King's daughter had come out onto the battlefield during the drink's interval with some much-needed liquid refreshments for the over-heated participants, and immediately became infatuated with Pharaoh Ramses hieroglyphic decorated chariot wheels. This resulted in a complicated bi-lingual conversation between them on the merits of un-decorated spoke wheels versus hieroglyphic artistic wheels in desert warfare. A conversation that went on and on and on just like the *Days of Our Life* serial on commercial television. Anyway, just like the script in that TV series, one conjugal thing led to another and a proposal of marriage had to be made, that eventually led to a famous peace treaty being signed between the warring nations. It came to be that after the extended drink's interval they all moved off the battlefield to more pleasant surroundings without spears, promos, products and the media. However, as always, when something is done in conjugal haste, then other things start to go wrong. Correspondingly, the *Days of our Life* lawyers are sent in to clear up the marital mess and subsequently send the opposing parties bankrupt.

Such was the bankruptcy result of the billing hours from the B.C. lawyers. This, after the Hittite princess brought along her nation's thousand gods in an extra-large chariot to the wedding breakfast and honeymoon nuptials in Cairo. Evidently, these gods had greatly outnumbered Pharaoh Ramses' Egyptian gods, so that the wedding table conversation was very one-sided indeed. Evidently, many of the Hittite gods were female gods and highly vocal, whereas most of the Egyptian gods were male gods and rather inclined to excess inebriation. This meant big verbal trouble at the wedding breakfast table from coarse toasting and rude gestures with fingers.

As a result, the temple atmosphere became very black through Egyptian and Hittite spoke trashing. This led to a big self-esteem punch-up at the breakfast table from differences of opinion on whose gods were the biggest and the best at trashing. Finally, after many months of expensive negotiations through their respective lawyers, a divorce settlement was finally reached, and they both signed an addendum never to watch commercial television, soap operas and reality shows ever again.

According to the Greek historian Herodotus who backpacked through the Middle East on B.C. tablet business, things were never the same in Upper or Lower Egypt after that verbal altercation. Also, Herodotus was not above creating big mischief with tall Gleek stories in the history tablet recording business either, which was all the rage in early Greek academic circles that traipsed around the Middle East circuit, keeping a tablet record of all the self-esteem trashing conflagrations and punch-ups between nations.

Anyways, the B.C. moral of this historical tale to the A.D. male population is two-fold. Firstly, beware of commercial television and soap operas, reality shows and lawyers. Secondly, don't forget to pack your spare wheels when visiting other nations, because look what happened to Pharaoh Ramses. Even Cleopatra's needles couldn't sort out the on-going self-esteem trashing and marriage problems, after Cleopatra went to Rome to stitch up Julius Caesar and Marc Anthony a few centuries later. Evidently, the world has never been the same since, and according to the tea lady where I work, we are still at it hammer and tongs in our civilisation, which can be sourced to all that ancestral B.C. spoke wheel verbal trashing to acquire the most self-esteem and be crowned the winner.

Regards -Stephen. On-site in a tent at Yazlikaya.

The Gates of Darius and his Famous Rock Inscriptions at Behistun in Persia, Now Called Iran

This is an historical time warped translation by an indignant Persian citizen over the B.C. improper use of his family surname on a rock face in Persia. It is interspersed with an A.D. colloquial translation of our techno trashing civilisation and its progress, which would not fit on the rock face at Darius's Gate or in the repaired loo in North Wing of the British Museum. Following in the footsteps of Professor Stanley Unwin and a past recognised expert on strange words and languages, this translation comes in the new-age commercial media babbleitus script that has swamped our consumer world in the 21st century. This script has been used to prevent confusion in the mind of the Commercial T.V., Radio and Glossy Magazine educated reader.

Now, this is a very complicated long-winded posterity story, especially for those who come after us, but not because it had been A.D. punctuated by Stephen. Evidently, they didn't have punctuation in those B.C. days. Punctuation was only used on tablets in the A.D. of human tablet progress, in order to make it harder to decipher and translate when the next lot of archaeologists come along, post A.D., to work out what had happened to our science, techno and commercial television educated civilisation.

Evidently our deceased techno civilisation had been commercially product saturated and brainwashed with computer tablets, plastic pottery, plastic bags and plastic everything else, along with rusty techno robots, DVD movies, musical dud-pods and selfie cell phones, babbleitus commercial television, marketing geniuses, glossy magazines and celebrities selling products. Anyway, according to the Delphi Oracle when recently asked, this terminal commercial product and binary calamity to our civilisation, was due to our techno and science civilisation complicating and marketing everything we could fiddle with and re-arrange and make money on. Plus, at the techno micro level, making our commercial product progress go faster and faster so that our techno civilisation could conquer the planets and outer space first, before the Klingnong microbes ... and of course, be declared the worshipped winner by the non-stop talking media for our very important human self-esteem.

Evidently, the Klingnong microbes are related to the techno Martian PR microbes that, according to the tea lady in the British Museum, don't live on 'the face' of Mars anymore, but a face on a gigantic rocket hanger at Cape Canaveral with N.A.S.T.A plastered on it. This Klingnong takeover happened after our techno civilisation consumed too much techno pizza, electronic hamburgers, chicken bits and pieces, binary fries and drinking café latte and fizzy techno coke, along with consuming synthetic science created chemical pills and gallons of techno plasticated spring water to wash them down. As a result, our civilisation became zonked-out on decibel deafening Klingnong dancing pole disco music and the ear-shattering electric guitar playing Klingnongs. This commercial media created babbleitus catastrophe, was to blast our techno civilisation into a super-amplified product noise hole that was contained in a commercial media created 24/7 celebrity worm hole, which was already congested with heaps of other human micro-universes.

Evidently, just like our consumer product civilisation, the occupants had also forgotten to brush their hair and teeth and say their prayers before hopping into bed at night, on top of watching too much commercial television and developing bad product habits and manners, popping synthetic pills and scoffing takeaway food. Anyway, they too had disappeared down the astrological astro-fizzics created intergalactic cosmic plughole, after being commercially barcoded and product stamped by the image creating commercial marketing Klingnongs who, evidently, started all the product advertising, promo and babbleitus training on commercial television. In addition to promoting product brain frequency jam sessions every day for media medicated human beings.

As a scientific techno result, our civilisation had become stoned-out on TV commercials, soap operas, promos, reality shows, glossy magazines, dancing with the stars, yuppy cooking programs and macho cops and robbers. Not forgetting to mention, saturated sex in the metropolis and science fiction movies, bling galore, tattoos, boobs, abs, pectorals, gladiatorial motor mouth sport commentators and media-saturated winners and celebrities on the big buck product blink.

Anyway, according to Alf, who had received an invite from Dr Who at the BBC to help with the global distribution of anti-Klingnong techno product badges, Dr Who told Alf in confidence that our electronic techno civilisation has been awarded the downstairs Alex-the-Great-at-trashing medal from Upstairs, because we keep polluting Nature and changing everything into something else on this life-sustaining planet, to fuel the global economy and make money. This could then be politically called creating economic progress for the benefit of everyone's bank balance, health, longevity and self-esteem, e.g. as in making techno cloned human beings to client's specifications, from science harvested female eggs and catalogued frozen male sperm and no love. We could then choose genetic preferences for our techno-age offspring from catalogues and glossy magazines which, according to science, is a much better way to do it than Nature's time-tested natural way of doing it. All thanks to brainy technoscience, entrepreneurial free enterprise, big bucks and following the laboratory marketed life re-arranging scientific way to have children.

Note: We can then rightly scientifically pat ourselves on the back and receive a self-esteem gong and remuneration from Mr. Nobel, this to preen our ego and help-out with the bank balance and have our name registered in the media for future closet information, because we are super clever and highly techno, science and product educated in the 21st century. This means we can now do anything we like with life on the planet in the name of creating progress, innovation, the economy and collecting gongs, providing that some enterprising billionaire or corporation coughs up the finance to start the product ball rolling and contacts their favourite marketing babbleitus agency to arrange a multi-million-dollar publicity promo on land, sea and air and have their picture in glossy magazines, newspapers and television newsrooms and a mention in the Upstair's book of downstairs, trashing.

Note: Just like Francis Weirdo Bacon the painter, and his older brother Francis Baron Bacon the animal enthusiast of Baconsville who, evidently, was on the fiddle in the House of Lords in England and had a big row with James the1st of Hollywood over huge stipendiary entitlements that we call bribes. As a result, Baron Bacon was consequently kicked out of the Houses of Parliament and not allowed through the Pearly Gates. Evidently, Baron Bacon had reasoned in his clever scientific mind that we humans can do what we like with animals, especially chickens and dogs and mice and rats and wiggly's of all shapes and sizes in experimental science laborotoriums, because they are mechanical and not technological, so obviously they don't go to heaven when they pop-off, because they didn't go to University, read science fiction books and glossy product magazines and can't talk the scientific techno talk or watch commercial television, munch hamburgers, fly to the moon and dance with the stars, like we humans can.

Anyway, Alf says if that scientist bloke said that about animals, then he must have suffered a Freudian inferiority product complex in the school playground when he was growing up, because his surname was Bacon and he was called piggy by all the other children. Evidently, he had to take his name-calling frustration out on animals, as human beings are entitled to do, because humans have two legs and not four and can chuck things up in the air with their hands. Alf reckons this human dexterity probably started the techno polluting space race to conquer the planets and dance with stars for our A.D. scientific acquired self-esteem, after our B.C. non-techno hairy cave ancestors got hit on the head by a whirling obelisk techno thingo in that weirdo space movie 2001; which was made ... by weirdo talking Hal of Hollywood in the 1960's for all the science fiction and spaced-out techno Moonies, who had taken one giant leap into a Klingnong techno crater with a warped hole full of tax spending government microbes. Evidently, this multi-billion-dollar tax spending on conquering outer space happened after astronauts had conquered the moon, to scientifically examine its rocks and verify that the moon wasn't made of green cheese, and there was no cats or fiddles or cows jumping around either. You know, like what's been written in children's fairy story books and nursery rhymes.

Anyway, childhood has never been the same since that scientific statement and now the clever lawyer microbes logically reckon, by using that other new A.D. science called Klingnong litigation, we ought to lawfully be able to collect a few million bucks as disappointed adults at the courthouse, from those telling big porkies in fairy tale story books.

We can then stick the big payout in the piggy bank to tide us over for when we are too old to trash anymore, and stuff everything up on our planet in the name of techno-progress, the economy, making money and winning at everyfing, along with realising our childhood top end of town indoctrinated dream of conquering the universe, collecting gongs, having our picture in the paper and being a worshipped winner in newsrooms and dancing with the stars for our important self-esteem.

Pause for a Commercial Break and go to the Loo

Anyway, coming back to the rock face graffiti message that Darius left us for posterity. There has been a right A.D. muck-up in the post-Gleek geometric translation by some wooden-spoon stirring commercial media Klingnongs, who have a bad habit of telling drama elongated porkies in Mogul owned glossy magazines, newspapers and commercial newsrooms to grab our attention. Evidently, one of their highly paid celebrity product experts with lots of commercial awarded gongs, stated that Stephen ... that's me, had got it wrong with his scientific facts. This, after I had traced the translation problem to a tempremolacleatured pufferentional in the wind currents affecting the original translator. Evidently, the wind pufferentional had suddenly scientifically materialised as the translator swung back and forth at the rock face, suspended on a bit of rope, while trying to copy three different languages without punctuation at the same time.

Anyway, the long and the scientific dangling of it all ... that is not a commercial newsroom porky ... was that the original translator must have encountered a tempremolacleatured wind current and contracted the non-stop talking media affliction of commercial product babbleitus. This affliction had caused the translator to mix up the Cuneiform with the Akkadian and the Gleek language and what Alexander-the-Great-at-trashing had to say about the King of Persia on the rock face, because unbeknown to archaeologists, Alex the-Great-at-trashing did not pass by the gates on his self-esteem conquering trip around the world, to realise his childhood ego dream, without chiselling his two drachmae and one pennyworth of graffiti on the rock face. Unbeknown to anyone, Alex had also done the dangling rope trick on the rock face and added his version of historical events, which was not very nice to read at all.

The worst of that ancient Gleek graffiti from Alex has now been chiselled out of the rock face, this to save any embarrassment to those who also read the classic B.C. protalirat Gleek. Unfortunately, this obsolete classic version has now acquired a new A.D. commercial version to be found in tabloid newspapers and glossy product magazines, scriptwriting, movies, commercial radio and television and called closet news, entertainment and gripping bleep bleep drama; all having its origins in the hacking and whacking B.C. days of the mighty Greek empire, and like A.D. commercial television and its babbleitus, had run amok and conquered the world with its protalirat products. However, unlike commercial television, the Greeks were stopped in India after Alex and his Army couldn't handle the Indian curry. Nevertheless, they had brought much trashing progress, Olympic sports, the body beautiful, democracy and olives to all the other Greek conquered nations who, like commercial television, had not known about Indian full-strength curry and its counter-trashing properties. *Note: The Stephen translation of the ancient B.C. word protalirat is, you guessed it, to trash. The extensions of that word are of course, trashed, trasher and trashing.*

Anyway, as is the way of human progress, modern nations are not only very grateful to Alex and the Greek nation but also the ancient Romans and now, new-age commercial television for its continuing contribution to protalirat progress, as in saturating commercial owned gladiatorial (win or else) sport and other money-making human products in nations. This commercial television babbleitus education allowed human beings to continue worshipping human gods called winners, stars and celebrities ... and once a year, democratically vote for their favourite one ... which, evidently, is all down to absorbing B.C. protalirat Gleek in their languages long ago.

Consequently, when travelling overseas as new-age commercial television conquered tourists, they know how to read all the advertisements for coke, soft drinks, pizza, colonel chicken, Ron the hamburger clown and flashing neon signs for old Nicks sports footwear. These illuminated signs are now everywhere in nations, along with other famous celebrity-marketed products, promos and advertisements on commercial television, mostly based on the body beautiful and its procreation whatnots. Along with additional free corporate and piggy bank takeover instructions in newsrooms, on how to get rich quick and buy up the world at the local Stock Exchange and acquire a corporate box at the newly renamed, A.D. big business commercial games.

Note: This was once called the Olympic Games and is not managed by the Greeks anymore, because it is now owned by big corporate global business, entrepreneurial marketing geniuses, commercial television, global piggy banks and I'm all right Jack, got-it-in-the-bag affluent shareholders. Evidently, they are watching endless repeats of Days of Our Dysfunctional Life, The Old and the Restless and Sex in the Metropolis as well as commercial sponsored gladiatorial sport, where losing is not an option, only winning and big buck are. Otherwise, no media and public adulation and gongs of course, because losing at anyfing downstairs is the ultimate disaster to acquiring our all-important self-esteem, especially when *joined with* that other adolescent self-esteem disaster, of missing out on protalirat written and acted out commercial television entertainment programs.

These babbleitus educating programs included, Nude Watch, Bachelors Paradise and Housewives on the Prowl in boardrooms and on private jets with sunken baths and gold taps that you can stick your big toe in, along with free complimentary product soap to get it out again. Then afterwards, watching the latest exciting Sky and Fox News on same-sex toilets and product vending machines, plastered with posters of skinny models in flimsy undress costumes. Evidently, these models are always tripping up on catwalks and showing off what they shouldn't to paparazzi Klingnongs, newsrooms and fashion fops studying the latest glossy genome model catalogue. This was to make sure that their parents hadn't been diddled at the scientific gene factory where their offspring had been genetically re-engineered, and product cloned to the media, newsrooms and commercial TV on a big buck playing field full of marketing whizz kids, super salespeople and spin doctors, with a severe dose of commercial product acquired babbleitus.

Note: The above, like clever politicians, all know how to talk the hind leg off not only donkeys but rabbits, sheep, mice, dogs, cats and Star Trek fans. This to convince them that big corporate business and techno science can change, modify and clone anything providing someone else pays for it. Consequently, this enabled them to finance their expensive holiday homes in the new-age climate re-arranged North Pole and weekly skiing trips to the iced capped Sahara Desert. Financed of course, from out of the profits of animal resource factories and sales of magic synthetic chemical product pills.

These super pills, having been created out of scientifically approved test tubes, syringes, freezers and Bunsen burners in laborotoriums. Evidently, this science innovation was to revolutionise the techno product progress of humankind and create a scientific magic cure-all for our commercial product and TV entertainment created psychological problems, financed by the corporate piggy bank Klingnongs of course. Who, according to Alf, are experts at wheeling and dealing with other people's money and organising the money markets, so that the global economy does not come to a grinding product halt and throw everyone into an economic heap. This global economic disaster, having been aggravated by having no commercial education and product clone training on the television, at schools and Universities and called Marketing by the rich, and product brainwashing by Alf.

Anyway, according to a secret White Paper from a Government think tank, this calamity of no commercial television product education ... or brainwashing, would mean the next generation would become lost and unhappy from having no disposable income to buy techno products and synthetic chemical pills at rock concerts and techno nightclubs. Therefore, as unemployed product-illiterate teenagers on the electronic and chemical blink, they would go on a texting rampage with their techno cell phones and verbally take it out on the politicians. This after becoming hooked on smash and trash computer games and going deaf with their musical dud-pods and fiddling with their pocket calculators, to calculate how much their bankrupt parents had lost on the collapsed global stock exchanges.

As a calamitous bankrupt result, their parents had gone bungy jumping off Wall Street without an elastic band, because they couldn't afford to take their kids to see Disneyland and the White House, buy products, watch commercial television, go dancing with the stars and worship celebrities and winners anymore.

Well, I had better bring this very complex posterity time-warped tablet on our techno civilisation to a product conclusion, before I get into more trouble from the Guverment for blowing the whistle on Darth's Commercial Media Empire, which according to the tea lady where I work, are brainwashing and controlling everyone downstairs from the time they are born. Evidently, this commercial Pied Piper alchemy was achieved by knowing exactly what money-making, entertainment, sport, quiz programs for big bucks, advertisements, reality shows, promos, celebrity worship and other entertainment product knobs to fiddle with in their commercial television and radio stations and glossy product magazines. Thereby, keeping the mega advertising bucks rolling in from their big business corporate sponsors and preventing celebrity and techno product withdrawal symptoms in the public. Otherwise, according to another reliable big business Guverment source, those product and celebrity withdrawal symptoms would result in stretched chariot jams in cities and public punch-ups and celebrity closet altercations because everyone on the planet had gone potty, through getting stuck into the fizzy buzz drink, fast food and science techno pills to drown their product sorrows and withdrawal symptoms. This would then cause everyone on the planet to become very agitated and bleep bleep vocal, just like King Midas had done many centuries earlier when the Greeks had established their trashing and conquering progress to acquire their self-esteem and gold bars. Evidently, this perpetual trashing in nations, has also proved very useful over the millenniums as an economic means of natural birth control and the genetic restructuring of the human species into trashing products.

Anyway, as the wise Greek philosopher Socrates said to the advertisement, promo and commercial product pickled Athenians, before downing his Hemlock potion and departing earthly matters, *"If you do not want to become a cloned product or a product clone, then keep the Market Place in the Market Place and the Commercial Television out of the family home."* Otherwise, according to an addendum from Alf, we will never earn our spiritual harp and receive the thumbs-up from St Peter at the Pearly Gates.

Now the Correct Translation on the Rock Face should read as Follows with A.D. Punctuation

Part One

I Darius, King on the rock face, King of the Graffiti Kings, whose father's surname name was King, and whose father's fathers' surname was King, as his father's father was called King in the sands of time. Be it known that my name is Darius King, and not King Darius, over all those who say they are a blank-blank (untranslatable) King. I chisel my graffiti three hundred feet up in the air on the rock face, so that everyone that passes by knows for posterity that, I was here first with the chisel. So, I'm the real Darius King and not the other bloke in the picture examining my boots and doing up my shoe-laces. Therefore, in case you haven't got your specs on or a bit of rope on you, I am the real Darius King of the Graffiti King family.

Part Two

Anyway, as I was saying in part one, this bloke under my foot in the rock picture, stole my name and turned it back to front, and was not related to the Graffiti King family. He has put the King bit in front of the Darius bit and told everyone in Persia that he was to be called King Darius and worshipped. So, I'm just letting him know that it is wrong to take that which does not belong to you or worship other human beings called celebrities and winners if we ever want to get to heaven.

Also, all who pass by the Gates of Darius can recognise the rest of the dudes tied together in the picture on the rock face. These dudes had helped King Darius with his commercial marketing promo and told everyone in Persia that they were also members of the Graffiti King family. They are also telling big porkies and are not related to my family in the sands of time. Anyway, as there is not enough room on the rock face to show the family shoelace de-Kinging boot ceremony performed on them, don't worry about it. I definitely sorted them out for telling big porkies in promos, advertisements and commercial television newsrooms, and pinching my name and credit cards on the internet.

Translation by Stephen, on behalf of the ghost of Darius King. B.C. graffiti expert and citizen of Persia.

Postscript:

The repeated positive spiritual advice from Alf to your parents is for them to learn and practice twice daily correct meditation, also called *transcendent meditation*. This comes as an evolution gift from the divine spiritual component of Nature, to help them evolve further with their spiritual evolution, underwritten by spiritual sourced lasting love. Then your parents will be able to naturally guide you to your full independence, structured in that spiritual acquired love and its happiness.

In turn, you will have spiritual acquired love and happiness throughout your busy life. Once the karma/influence from out of that love and happiness is created in all nations, then no more wars, no more bloodshed, no more misery, no more greed, no more human created techno and science pollution and natural disasters on this shared planet. This spiritual miracle is so simple and easy to accomplish if we all truly desire it, because then we will receive the invisible support of divine Nature to help us in its collective achievement in all nations. However, this can only be achieved if we work together as a global family of Nations to create unity, equality, harmony and peace in the world, and not through conquering and winning at everything and acquiring dissolvable adulation, big bucks and fame.

Kind regards from the author.

The End

www.ingramcontent.com/pod-product-compliance
Lightning Source LLC
Chambersburg PA
CBHW071555080526
44588CB00010B/916